OVERCOMING BAD HABITS

A Self-Help Book
to Breaking
Chronic Addictions

LOY B. SWEEZY, JR.

Why so many different Bible translations? The many different translations are design to give you a better understanding of the scriptures to grasps the full meaning of what is attempting to be conveyed. I have observed that many people are aware of certain scriptures and have become very familiarized with where to find them; however, they do not really know what certain words truly mean in its original context.

One word in the Greek or Hebrew can mean up to several different meanings, when researching words in the Bible, it is important to know what certain words mean in the particular text it is located. The reason is that this same word can mean something very different in another text. Therefore, the different translations give you a better view of what the Word is saying and how the Word can be applied, today.

Dedication

I would like to dedicate this book to two women, specifically, who have greatly influenced my life by their godly lifestyles. Your lives as Christians have had a tremendous positive effect upon who I am today. The greatest thing I have learned and have seen in you both is the love of God. I have learned to keep the love of God in my heart no matter what is done to me and who does it to me.

First is my wife, Nyouka D, who has loved me and supported me unconditionally. Your life as a virtuous wife and sister in the Lord has greatly affected my life. (Proverbs 31:10-31) You are my partner, encourager, friend and my greatest inspiration. Thank you for all that you do.

Second, my mother, Jeannie Sweezy, who has taught me to love all people, to stay humble, respectful and always treat people kindly. You taught me to be non-judgmental and always use a common-sense approach when dealing with things. You have been to me a true friend, mother and a strong advocate for righteousness; you are to me the best mother in the world. I thank you for your unconditional love and patience with me. Thank you for all you have done. Your son, Junior.

Acknowledgements

The Lord gave the word: great was the company of those that published it." (Psalms 68:11)

This book reflects on many different individuals and higher schools of learning that have contributed enormously upon both my personal and educational maturity in Jesus Christ. Therefore, because of your God-given revelations, impartations and exhortations, now I am able to publish what I have heard, seen and learned from you.

To start with, I would like to express my sincere appreciation to Pastor Creflo A. Dollar, Jr. and Pastor James Robinson, who have spoken the word of faith in my life and challenged me to live a life of honesty, integrity and excellence, first at home and then in the community.

In addition, I would like to express my sincere appreciation to Erlanger Medical Center located in Chattanooga, Tennessee, Carolina Medical Center located in Charlotte, North Carolina, and Princeton/Montclair Hospital located in Birmingham, Alabama.

Thank you, for the experience of CPE, (Clinical Pastoral Education). These programs have made a tremendous difference in my life. I will use many techniques and approaches in this book to share some of the principles that I have learned as a pastoral counselor for the hospitals.

On a collegiate level, I would like to thank East Coast Bible College located in Charlotte, North Carolina and School of Theology located in Cleveland, Tennessee for the opportunity to receive impartation and revelation from many fine academic scholars. In addition, I would like to thank Oral Roberts University (ORU) located in Tulsa, Oklahoma, who has fueled my commitment to godliness, education and ministerial excellence.

Thank you all for making a difference in my life, and now I am writing this book to make a difference in other people's lives all because of you. You have truly made a difference in my life and inspired me to stretch beyond the norm and to be committed to entering into God's greatness for my life. Therefore, I acknowledge you for this book. Again, thank you.

Table of Contents

Introduction

This book is designed to be both a clinical research book and a self-help book. It is a clinical research book in that there is an extensive study of steps, approaches and techniques that a person can implement into his/her daily life to overcome difficult situations. In this book you will find medical data, biblical and theological research, case studies, health specialist insights, political and personal testimonies and experiences.

This is a self-help book in that you will not need to go and consult with a counselor or spiritual advisor because I am bringing them to you. The summation of what you will be advised to do from a therapist or Christian counselor you will find in the very pages of this book. In fact, this book will give you additional information that you will not find with some professional clinicians because this book is written from a biblical perspective with an enormous amount of scriptural references.

One of my objectives in writing this book is to be an advocate for God, as a preacher of righteousness; I will attempt to help you to understand with God Almighty on your side, there is nothing that you cannot overcome. My desire is to paint a picture to where God is bigger and better than anything you will face.

There are too many people who are putting their trust in the world system; although, the United States of America's dollar bills are sealed with the imprint that *in God we trust,* many people, including Christians, are running everywhere for answers but to God to help them. They are relying on everything but God to make them better.

My desire is to get you to look to God in everything, to see God as **El Elyon,** which is the *most high God,* the Bible says, *"For thou, Lord, art high above all the earth: thou art exalted far above all gods." (Psalms 97:9)* God's desire for your life is to bring you up and out of all bondages, sickness, diseases and sin.

In this book, you will find also both an enormous amount of scripture quotes from the Bible and quotes from renowned authors who are trained experts, specialists and scholars in their field of study. These quotes are designed to help support and validate the approaches and the techniques of different principles that are laid out to help you overcome your bad habits. In addition, some chapters may repeat certain points; this repetition is intentionally designed to reinforce certain pivotal points and to strongly emphasize the importance of certain principles.

This book is written as a self-help guide to those who struggle to obtain and maintain their victory over self-destructive behaviors and chronic addictions. This book is written as an aid to help you discover your God-given freedom, to help you understand why you keep falling into the same old temptations and traps, over and over again. This book will give you the solutions for how to change and how to get out of tough spots. This book will help you explore why you do what you do and what you can do to stop doing what you don't what to do.

This book will set your course for maximum living. As you read the pages of this book, you will gain insight, revelation, inspiration, restoration and deliverance. You will be determined to walk in total life success. This book is written especially for those who are seeking clear answers as to why their lives have been unsuccessful and what they can do to change it. This book will undoubtedly make the readers' lives better.

Personal Experiences

I do have the personal experience of overcoming some addictions, bad habits and compulsive behaviors. I will share some of my personal experiences, not for you to feel sorry for me (God has healed me.) Therefore, I will only share to help others who may be experiencing similar situations, to understand that if God can deliver, heal, forgive and set me free, then He can help anyone be free.

Many people in the church are struggling with addictions and bad habits. Many Christians are bound to overeating, smoking, thinking negative, losing their tempter, alcohol, drugs, internet pornography, homosexuality, lesbianism, gambling, embezzlement, lying, cheating, stealing, and other addictions or bad habits.

These people are preachers, teachers, church leaders, and members faithful to the church; they are good people and have a desire to want to do right but are unable to because their addictions or bad habits have them on lock-down. This book will shed some light on what you can do to overcome bad habits and break chronic addictions.

As a young boy I was picked on a lot by other boys in the community. I would never fight back, which resulted in me developing a spirit of fear. This fear followed me into adulthood, which resulted in me having skepticism about getting too close to people for fear of them hurting me.

I learned that I feared because I did not know who I was in Jesus Christ. In Jesus Christ there is no fear but perfect love, which cast out all fear. (I John 4:17-21) I also learned that I had very low self-esteem, not only within myself but also with God. I did not put my trust totally in God and I did not allow God to fight my battles because I tried to fight them, or better yet, run from them.

In addition, as an adolescent I was sexually abused by one of the neighbors in my community. She gave me money to have sexual relations with her and I was only about 10 years old. In my adult years I then found myself doing to other women what this person did to me as a child; I would find myself having sexual relations with different women and would even spend money for pleasure.

As a teenager, I experienced a tremendous amount of discrimination and racism. One of my high school teachers said in front of the whole class that I was too dumb to go to college. In addition, speech therapists told me that I would always have a speaking impediment. I was so mentally abused by those words until I purposed in my heart to become educated.

The interesting thing about receiving a master's degree is that I still felt incompetent and uneducated. I had developed as a child a root of low self-esteem and an inferiority complex. All the education in the world could not make me feel adequate about myself because I did not know who I was in Christ Jesus.

When I began to learn who I was in Christ Jesus, then I understood the importance of attending a church that preaches the full gospel. When I say full gospel, I am speaking of a church that believes in salvation, healing, deliverance, prosperity, living in good health, walking in integrity and honesty, preaching against sin and calling every person to a lifestyle of holiness.

The full gospel is teaching the whole Bible, the inerrant, infallible, inspired and irrefutable word of God. God used Dr. Creflo A. Dollar, Pastor of World Changers Church International (WCCI) to uproot and gut out corrupt thinking and wrong behaviors. It was the teaching and the preaching at WCCI that educated me on how to become competent and efficient in God and in what God has called me to do.

What I learned in church was far better than what Bible College and seminary taught me. Actually, there were some things in Bible College and seminary that were very difficult to comprehend. It was the church that clarified the confusion of biblical interpretations.

Again, it would be the church that straightened out and gave clear insight to certain doctrines and scriptural interpretations learned from higher learning institutions. In church there was practical teaching of the word of God with simplicity and understanding so that I could apply what I learned in my everyday living.

Preaching to the Klu Klux Klan

I remember one racist event that occurred in my hometown Shelby, North Carolina. I was out of Bible College for the summer and had just returned home from missionary work in India. I was at the Cleveland County Library, minding my own business when an older woman, who I would see occasionally in the library, came up to me. She was shaking considerably and said," *Young man, have you heard, have you heard, the Klu Klux Klan is up town, the Klu Klux Klan is up town.*" Then the woman just took off.

As I was reading my book, I began to think about the Klu Klux Klan being up town, and how I had never visibly seen a Klu Klux Klan rally. So, I closed my book and headed up town to observe what was going on.

When I arrived up town with my car windows rolled down, I noticed that the grand dragon or the captain was saying things like, the nigger this and the nigger that. He was speaking through a microphone publicly in the town square in front of many police officers and citizens of Shelby. He was saying that niggers are to be hated, and Jews were not people. The sad thing was no one was doing anything about it.

This event was very demoralizing to me as a young adult. I was torn. I became bitter at whites, especially officers, because here were law officials permitting hate advocates to speak derogatorily and racially against other races of people because of color and nationality, and the law officers were allowing it to happen. I thought to myself, how in the world this could be justifiable.

It is also important to note that up until this time I had no education on black history. In my days of elementary and high school, I never heard any of my teachers talk about Afro-American history. Although I am fully aware that they have black history classes in high school now, at that time, my high school had no black history classes.

I remember one of my high school history teachers saying that although Abraham Lincoln initiated the Emancipation Proclamation, he was not for the freeing of black slaves. I find it to be very interesting how some recent reports, political leaders, teachers and even preachers are extremely quick to educate people on the history of World War I and II, Pearl Harbor, Adolf Hitler, Saddam Hussein, and other massive killings.

Very seldom, if at all, do these same people talk about all the blacks who were killed right here in America from slavery. I believe one of the reasons is because people do not like to deal with themselves; people are more prone to look at others' issues than to face one's own.

In the book, *The Words of Martin Luther King, Jr,* says,

> "It is pretty difficult to like some people. Like is sentimental and it is pretty difficult to like someone bombing your home; it is pretty difficult to like somebody threatening your children; it is difficult to like congressmen who spend all of their time trying to defeat civil rights. But Jesus says love them, and love is greater than like." (P.23)

I knew that God was not a racist; my mother did not raise my family to be racist; she taught us to love all people regardless of color or nationality. It was at this point that I really began to grow up spiritually and come to the realization that the world needed Jesus. Scripture says, *"God so loved the world, that he gave his only begotten Son, that whosoever believeth in him should not perish, but have everlasting life." (John 3:16)* God loves every human being; God's love is demonstrated by how we deal with other people.

Love never hates, discriminates, or even isolates because of a person's skin color. Therefore, I just could not understand why these white men would hide behind white sheets and tell the American citizens of Shelby, North Carolina that they were better than other people.

What they said sparked a righteous indignation in me toward hatred and racism. It really did not matter to me who the Klu Klux Klan was talking about, to preach hatred in public was wrong. Better yet, to teach and preach hatred period is wrong and should be considered a crime regardless of who you are. It does not matter if you are white, black or in between, if you are teaching or preaching hatred, it is wrong.

In his book, *Race, Religion and Racism*, Dr Fredrick, K.C. Price, says,

> "We get upset, righteously indignant – and correctly so – when we think about Adolf Hitler and the annihilation of six million Jews during World War II. But who gets righteously indignant and upset about the fifty million black Africans who were abducted or killed by the forefathers of this nation?" (P.164)

When I arrived up town, I heard the Klu Klux Klan preaching hate and no one doing anything about it. Again, I had a righteous indignation. When my feet hit the ground after getting out of my car, immediately I began to shout aloud, *"Jesus Christ is Lord, Jesus Christ is Lord, Jesus Christ is Lord!"* I walked up and down about a block saying Jesus Christ is Lord. Everyone became quiet, including the Klu Klux Klan. You could hear a pin drop on the town square.

Immediately, three officers came running over to me. Yelling and saying as they approached me, "Hey! Hey! Hey! You can not do that, you can not do that, you are going to start a riot," of course that was definitely not my intention to start a riot. One of the officers was a white female and the others were white males. They told me that if I did not stop saying that, they were going to put me in jail.

I walked about another ten feet or so, communicating nothing but Jesus Christ is Lord, Jesus Christ is Lord. It was as though I could not stop. My adrenaline was flowing. I felt that

I was experiencing a glimpse of what the prophet Ezekiel experienced when saying that the spirit of the Lord came on him and took him away. (Ezekiel 8:3, 37:1) I believe that this taking away was literally in the spirit to where they had no control over what was being done unto them, until the spirit had completed the mission through them.

As I was walking back to my car, a very elderly woman came up to me and said, *"Young man, young man, I want you to know that what you did was of God."* This elderly woman continued to say, *"When you were speaking a holy hush came over the whole place and the only thing you could hear was Jesus Christ is Lord."*

I indicated to this elderly woman that I was walking to my car and I would like to talk with her more, but when I returned from my car with a pen, this woman was gone. She had not stood that far away from me. I estimated she had stood maybe 20 or 25 yards away. Therefore, I proceeded to walk down the block, but the elderly woman was nowhere around.

There was a small alley. I thought maybe this elderly woman could have possibly walked down the alley, but as I walked down the alley, no one was there. I knew that this elderly woman could not have run all the way down the alley without me seeing her. Therefore, I considered this elderly woman to be an angel of the Lord who was protecting me from any danger that could have occurred.

That night at home, I began to reflect upon my day. I asked the Lord why He used me to do something like that. This is what God revealed to me about the situation: First, everyone who was at the town square that day who did not accept Jesus as Lord and personal Savior, would be without excuse when they stand before God on Judgment Day, including the Klu Klux Klan.

The Lord continued to say, all who heard that Jesus Christ is

Lord that day, will not be able to say that they did not hear and know the truth on judgment day. God continued to say to me to set that particular day aside as a memorial before heaven, the preaching of an unlearned, young black man from Shelby, North Carolina making a mark in history that would be remembered before all eternity.

God continued to reveal to me that what the Klu Klux Klan had thought was going to be a motivational hate rally. God set it up to be a <u>day of remembrance,</u> which all who heard would be without excuse. In addition, it was clearly obvious to me that some people heard, because about no more than five minutes after I had spoken, the Klu Klux Klan began tearing down their set and everyone started to leave.

In Luke 16:19-31, the Bible talks about a beggar who went to Heaven and a rich man who went to Hell. The rich man went to Hell, and in Hell this rich man was able to remember all the times he had an opportunity to get it right with God. Although, this rich man was in Hell, he remembered those times. Therefore, he could not use the excuse that he did not know.

Interestingly, when this rich man saw that he could not get out of Hell, he immediately remembered that he had five brothers alive at home who were living just as he had been living. The rich man begged for special treatments, signs and enlightenments to come to his brothers, in hope that these events will cause them to change, to prevent them from coming to the same place of torment.

The answer to the rich man's request was, "*They have Moses and the prophets: let them hear them.*" Moses signified the pastor and the prophet symbolizes the spokesperson for God. The rich man learned that if your brothers do not listen and take heed to the pastors of the local church or the evangelist, preacher or teacher of the Gospel of Jesus Christ, then surely, they would not be convinced nor have cause, to hear anyone else—even if God raised a prophet from the dead to speak to them.

It is important to understand that you cannot let other people's hatred become your hatred. Throughout my young adulthood, I allowed this to happen to me. The more I would try to get away from white people, the more God would put me in their setting.

I attended a predominately white church in Shelby, North Carolina. I attended a predominately white bible college in Charlotte, North Carolina. I attended a predominately white seminary in Cleveland, Tennessee, and I attended one year of CPE (clinical pastoral education) in a predominately white setting. So the question in all of that is this, what was God trying to teach me? God was teaching me that I had to let go of my past hurt. Just because some white people did me wrong growing up does not mean that all white people are evil.

God taught me that no one owes me anything. When you forgive a person you forgive them of all things. I also learned that it is sin to hold someone responsible for something that the person had no control over. It is also sin to hold a white person responsible for slavery when he/she was not even born during the period of slavery or had any association with that time period.

I learned that where I was in life was actually where I chose to be. I could not blame the white man, slavery, a lack of education or any unjust act for where I was in life. God began to teach me that He set me around white people because I had the ability to forgive, love, heal, restore and build a bridge to where whites and blacks could work together to achieve more, than to work against each other and receive less.

As, I continued to work in a multicultural setting, I learned that not all white people were bad and that white people learned from me that not all blacks are evil. I learned to understand the true meaning of the word team. The word team means *together everyone achieves much.*

Joyce Meyer in her book, *Reduce me to Love*, says, "*When we forgive an injustice, we are actually doing ourselves a favor; we are giving ourselves a gift of freedom.*" (P.122) God expects us to love everybody regardless of what they do to us. In order to love others you must first love God. He will enable you to love yourself, so that you can love others. If you do not love yourself, you cannot love others. You cannot give away something that you do not have.

One of the things about hate is that when you hold on to it you are troubling yourself. The only way to have true peace in your life is to have the love of God in your heart. In addition, you should not expect any scriptures whatsoever to work for you, when you are not walking in love. Every promise of God hangs on love and without love; you can do nothing for God. Love is the first and greatest commandment.

Notice this scripture:

> *Jesus said unto him, Thou shalt love the Lord thy God with all thy heart, and with all thy soul, and with all thy mind. This is the first and great commandment. And the second is like unto it, Thou shalt love thy neighbor as thyself. On these two commandments hang all the law and the prophets. (Matthew 22:37-40)*

Dr. Creflo Dollar, in his book, *The Color of Love*, says,

> *"As Christian people, when Jesus said,* Love your enemies, *He meant all of them – our black enemies and our white enemies, too. When he said,* Do good to them that hate you, *He didn't say you were to do good to everybody – except for that white man or that black man. You are walking in strong deception if you think you can call yourself a Christian, whether white or black, and still feel hatred toward that brother or sister whom you see every day." (P. 8)*

The last thing that God shared with me about preaching to the KKK is that I was preaching from a wounded spirit. God indicated to me that my message was one that was crying out for help. It hurt me when I was hearing those hate words and it moved me to action in a non-judgmental response by saying that Jesus Christ is Lord.

God indicated to me that He really appreciated my zeal; however, my zeal would have to move to a place to where I could sit down with people of various races and nationalities to work out racial differences. We were to explore past history, and to work through misconceptions about different races so that we could work together to reach the world for Jesus Christ.

One of the tools that the devil uses against society today is to keep the different races of people separated. When people choose not to explore their differences, we limit ourselves. There is a lot that whites can learn from blacks and blacks can learn from whites, but we must put our racial prejudices down and embrace multicultural togetherness.

During the early 20th century, evangelist **Aimee Semple McPherson** was a pioneer for women in ministry. She was the first woman to preach the word of God over the radio, to possess a radio license and to operate a radio station.

One of her most outstanding achievement was January 1, 1923, when Angelus Temple was dedicated, a project that took several years to construct. The church held 5,300 people and it overflowed to the full, three times a day, seven days a week.

Her ministry was built on the love and compassion of God. Her messages were simple. They conveyed Heaven as a place that every human being needed to be, and that the only way to find true peace and happiness is to come to Jesus Christ who loves, forgives, heals and restores all people.

The Four Square church Website says,

> *With Aimee, all were called and all were welcomed. God was no respecter of persons and neither was Aimee. She evangelized when segregation was rampant in the South. Although she invited all to come to her meetings, many times she would go to the "black" part of town and hold meetings after the main meeting was over. She broke down racial barriers such that one time at Angelus Temple, some Klu Klux Klan members were in attendance, but after the service, many of their hoods and robes were found thrown on the ground in nearby Echo Park. She is also credited with helping many of the Hispanic ministries in Los Angeles get started, and there was even a great Gypsy following, after the wife of a Gypsy chief and the chief himself had been healed in a Denver revival meeting. With Aimee Semple McPherson there was no color, ethnic, or status separation line. (P.8)*

That is what we need in the body of Christ today; we need men and women of God who are willing to look beyond color and reach out to the needy, no matter who they are. If there is a need, as Christians we are to meet the need.

It does not matter what people's past hang-ups, setbacks, or addictions are, God is calling every born-again Christian to love, and to reach out to a dying and lost world for Jesus Christ. To take it a step further, it does not matter what people's present hang-ups, setbacks or addictions are, God has still called every born-again Christian to love the hell (Gehenna) out of people.

My Sister Isaac

When I was about seven years old, I was playing in the front yard of our home and my younger sister Isaac was playing with me. Some neighbors called her to come across the road to talk with them and then it happened. As my younger sister Isaac was crossing the road, a school bus ran over her head, instantly killing her.

I ran in the house to tell my mother but she had been looking out the window and saw everything that happened. I think that was the first time I actually experienced intense pain; when I observed my mother crying and I could do nothing about it. This intense pain started the process for me to sit with people in pain, comfort the hurting and encourage those who were down. I continue to do that to this very day.

The transition of my sister going home to be with the Lord did two things for me: 1) It made me draw closer to my mother and to become very protective, if not overly protective for my loved one. 2) I was angry with my biological father, because he was not present when my family was in need of comfort. I felt abandonment, isolation and fear during that time period. I could only find trust and comfort in God, as I understood him as a child.

The reason I say isolation is because I went through the experience alone. I was a child and did not want to put any more stress on my mother than what she was already experiencing. I had no one to talk with; therefore, I began to talk to God because when I was a child I heard in church (Macedonia Baptist Church and Antioch Baptist Church) that God was good.

This is why it is so important to attend church. You will hear words that will comfort and support you for what you are going through. However, I had some confused thinking. I was mad at God and myself for what had happened to my sister.

The reason I was mad at myself is because my sister and I were in the front yard sitting down on the grass playing and some neighbors called to her from across the road. I really did not want my sister to go because I was enjoying being with her.

After persistent calling by my neighbors, my sister jumped up and ran across the road. Her death happened within a twinkling of an eye. My sister was run over by a bus; I will never see my sister again until we met in Heaven.

One of the things that I learned from that situation is that it is important for you to let people know how you feel about something. When people come to you for answers or when you feel that someone needs guidance, do not sit there and withhold valuable information.

If you are close to a person and if you sense that person needs to consider his/her actions, then it is perfectly ok to share what you feel, especially when you feel something happening in your spirit. The information that you withhold can be a matter of life and death for the individual.

In addition, my sister's experience helped me see the importance of not moving too quickly because people are asking you to do something. Again, what you do could be literally a matter of life and death. I learned not to quickly jump or move on things just because people ask you to do something.

I learned to listen and observe a person's behavior to determine whether or not what they are saying is right. I attempted to make sure that nothing like what happened to my sister would ever happen to my family or me again. I became extremely protective of my family.

I was able to forgive my father and we became very close before he went home to be with the Lord on December 14, 1994. I was able to forgive my biological father for not supporting me as a child.

I remember sharing with my father on one occasion how I knew he had not supported me like my mother, but I told him that I loved him just as much as I loved my mother. He did not say anything, but he did buy me a car my junior year of bible college. He began to give considerably to my life before he went home to be with God.

There were **four significant things** which aided in my recovery. **First,** my wife. She demonstrated unconditional love, and because of her godly life and being a virtuous woman, it spilled over on me and changed me into a different man.

Second, my pastor, Dr. Crelfo A. Dollar, Jr. His teaching and preaching imparted within me an ability to walk in integrity and holiness, to understand my identity in Christ, to love my wife and to understand that my family comes before my ministry.

Third, Oral Roberts University (ORU). The school fueled

my commitment to excellence, godliness and education, to live a life of uprightness, first at home and then in the community.

Fourth, my mother. She would take the time to listen to me about anything; she did not tolerate a bunch of foolishness. I learned to be honest, respectful, mind my own business, work diligently and keep God always before me in everything that I do, although, I did stray away from some of these principles at times. Nevertheless, it was these same principles that would bring me back to God and keep me in times of trouble.

Why have I chosen to write this book? I have chosen to write this book so that the real you can come out and play. I have experienced that many people's joy, happiness and greatness is shut up within them. These people want to have fun; they want to enjoy life to the fullest but are unable to because of certain bad habits that keep pulling them down.

When I was a child, some of my neighborhood friends would come over to my house and ask my mother if Junior could come out and play. The key thing to me being able to come out and play was contingent upon me having all of my chores done. If I had completed all of my homework and duties around the house, I was always allowed to go out and play.

Today, from a mental perspective, the reason why many people cannot come out and play is that they have not dealt with certain inner deficiencies and inadequacies. Only until you overcome certain inadequate, corrupt thinking and habitually wrong behaviors, will you be able to come out and play, maximizing your potential fully, living a life of peace, joy and abundant success.

From approaches and techniques that I have both learned and experienced, I have decided to share some of these approaches and techniques to help others who might be going though similar situations. First, to let them know that if I can overcome bad habits, then anyone can overcome bad habits because God is no respecter of person but a respecter of faith. (Hebrew 11:6)

Second, if I can encourage, inspire or motivate change in one person, then the purpose of this book will be accomplished. My desire is to help others get out and stay out of traps, and live the abundant life in Christ.

Scripture says, *"All things are possible to them that believe."* There is nothing negative that you will ever encounter that God cannot get you out of. Oh yes, God can get you out of it, the question is, do you really want to be out of it.

The question is not can God do it? God can do anything and everything but fail. *"Then Job answered the LORD and said, I know that You can do all things, And that no purpose of Yours can be thwarted." (Job 42:1-2, NAS)*

The word **thwart** means *to stop, hinder, prevent or to set up roadblocks*, which means that God cannot be road blocked. There is nothing that can restrict, sabotage or hinder God from doing anything that He needs to do for you.

The question is will you allow God to work through you to accomplish what needs to be done for you or in you. If your answer is yes, then congratulations, because you are ready for God to do great things in your life.

Whatever you are trapped in, God can get you out. Whatever you are struggling with, God can release you and cause what is working against you to be a blessing to you. How is that possible? God can do it, and not only can God do it, but He will do it. God will do whatever is necessary for you to love and honor Him. God will show himself strong on your behalf.

Note this scripture:

> *"The Lord says, I will rescue those who love me. I will protect those who trust in my name. When they call on me, I will answer; I will be with them in trouble. I will rescue them and honor them. I will satisfy them with a long life and give them my salvation." (Psalms 91:14-16, NLT)*

God said that he would rescue you and deliver you from whatever has you in a position that you do not like. That is awesome. I pray with you right now that whatever you are going through, with the help of God you will come out of it. I declare that whatever you are facing right now that is not working on your behalf, God is presently turning things around to work in your favor. (II Chronicles 16:9)

God is going to do a shifting and cause what was working against you to work for you. Scripture says, *"And we know that all things work together for good to them that love God, to them who are called according to his purpose." (Romans 8:28)* I come into agreement that you will walk in the perfect will of God for your life, nothing short of greatness. I speak it, believe it and seal it right now in the name of Jesus. Amen

CHAPTER 1

||||||||||||||||||||||||||

How Badly Do You Want It?

"Neither have I gone back from the commandments of his lips; I have esteemed the words of his mouth more than my necessary food." (Job 23:12)

Job said his desire for the word of God was more precious than anything else, which includes the food that he ate. Job had come to a point to where he held the word of God in high esteem above everything. You have to hold in high esteem the word of God above any and everything that you encounter in order to overcome a bad habit. When you can get to a point to where you are not willing to allow anyone or anything to prevent you from going after your greatest desire, then nothing will stop you.

In his book, *The Power to Change Anything*, Pastor Gregory Dickow, says,

"To change anything, you have to, first, desire it more than you desire just about anything. That's when things will begin to change for you. Jesus even said in one of the

most famous passages of Scripture, **"whatsoever things you DESIRE, when you pray, believe you received them and they shall be granted you"** *(Mark 11:24) A young man was walking down a dock one day and he noticed a man fishing who he read about and followed for many years. The young man desired to be a great salesman and the older man had been one of the best in the world. When he approached him, he asked the man what he needed in order to be great. The old man grabbed his admirer and stuck his head under the water. The young man kicked and pushed and did everything he could to get up until he couldn't hold his breath any longer. When the young man finally fought his way out of the water, gasping for air with a furious attitude, he declared, "Are you crazy? I couldn't breathe!" The man responded, "Son, when you want to succeed as much as you wanted to breathe, that's when you will become a great salesman and a great success." So you have to desire to change. You need to admit you have a need and desire it as much as your breath." (P. 25-27)*

KEY THOUGHT: Whatever you desire; if you stay with it, you can accomplish it.

One evening at home I was watching a baseball game. There were two outs and the team batting had a man on third and second base. They only needed one run to win the game. The batter hit the ball and, I mean, he hit the ball! The fans stood up and began to scream *Yea! Yea! Yea!* as though they had won the game.

All of a sudden, the outfielder came in view of the ball and the outfielder kept running and running, he dove for the ball, and caught it. Everyone became quiet and was amazed at how the outfielder ran so far, fast and hard to catch the ball. The outfielder, upon catching the ball, took the ball out of his glove and held it up in his hand for everyone to see, as though to say I got it, I got it, I got it and he did have it.

The point of the story is that whatever you desire; if you stay with it, you can accomplish it. If you want it bad enough, you can do it. If you work hard, do not give up, and stay with it until you can get it. Many times, people are not willing to endure long enough and work hard enough to sustain the necessary victory.

Evangelist, teacher and author, Kate McVeigh in her book *Seven Habits of Uncommon Achievers*, says,

> *"The bottom line is this: discipline yourself to do the right thing long enough, and eventually the right thing will happen to you. Often people get tired of doing the right thing and they give up. The Bible says that* **you will reap if you faint not** *(Gal. 6:9) ... Remember, discipline often is doing something you don't like to do in order to create something you love. If you want something you've never had, you have to do something you've never done. For instance, you might not like working out, but you love the results it produces." (P. X, 24)*

In looking back at the outfielder, he had to work through many distractions; such as dealing with the sun in his eyes; hearing the fans yelling and screaming; not running up against the wall and potentially injuring himself; and keeping his eyes on the ball.

Although he had to deal with all of those elements working against him, he caught the ball. He caught the ball because he stayed with trying to catch it. He wanted to win, and he did not allow the opposition of the struggle to make him lose concentrated focus.

Do not give up on what you believe. You can change; everything is subject to change, except for the word of God. Take the word of God and apply it into your everyday life, because you can get what you desire. You can have what you desire, you can do what you desire, and you can accomplish what you desire.

One of the major keys to overcoming bad habits is that you will have to set your will to win no matter what is going on in you and around you. Your mind-set must be one of a winner.

In his Book, *Free at Last from Old Habits*, Dr. Jerry Savelle says,

> *"This process of being free begins with your decision to be free. Your will has everything to do with how much God can do in your life. If you're still saying, 'I'll quit Monday. Give me one more day of this,' then you don't desire freedom badly enough." (P. 27)*

If you do not want to be addicted to substance abuse, losing your temper, being a pushover or smoking cigarettes, then you don't have to go another day doing that, if you don't want to overeat, then you don't have to go another day pigging out. If you do not want to steal, lie and cheat, then you do not have to go another day doing that. Scripture says,

> *"No, despite all these things, overwhelming victory is ours through Christ, who loved us. And I am convinced that nothing can ever separate us from his love. Death can't, and life can't. The angels can't and the demons can't. Our fears of today, our worries*

*about tomorrow, and even the powers of Hell can't
keep God's love away. Whether we are high above
the sky or in the deepest ocean, nothing in all creation
will ever be able to separate us from the love of God
that is revealed in Christ Jesus our Lord." (Romans
8:37-39, NLT)*

You overcoming a bad habit is going to be very much
dependent upon how badly you want to do what it takes to get
rid of the bad habit. The writer of Romans said that nothing
would separate him from his desire to love God. (Romans 8:39)
Therefore, I say unto you that there is nothing that can stop you
from achieving your best in God, You can kick the bad habit,
you can break the addiction, you can arrest impulsive craving,
you can take control of negative desires, you can, you can, you
can, you can do all things through Christ who strengthens you
(Philippians 4:13.)

Joyce Meyer in her book, *Managing your Emotions*, says,

*"Do you know there are people who really don't want
to get well? They just want to talk about their problem.
Are you one of those people? Do you really want to get
well or do you just want to talk about your problem?
Sometimes people get addicted to having a problem. It
becomes their identity, their life. It defines everything
they think and say and do. All their being is centered
around it. If you have a "deep-seated and lingering dis-
order," the Lord wants you to know that it does not have
to be the central focal point of your entire existence.
He wants you to trust Him and cooperate with Him
as He leads you to victory over that problem one step
at a time." (P.55-56)*

Over the years, one of the advantages of working as a mental health/substance abuse counselor for recovery institution(s) is that I really get to see how badly people really want to change. I have seen patients come into the programs with all types of addictions and successfully recover.

I have experienced patients desiring to recover so badly that they were willing to go through; detoxification, regurgitation, shaking unbearably, crying, restraining, and some assisted to isolation or seclusion. Others are put on behavior contracts. These patients successfully recovered because they were willing to endure the negative associations with their addiction, to regain and reclaim the peace and sobriety back into their life.

Alexander Graham Bell

A good example of a person demonstrating that if you want something badly enough you can get it, is Alexander Graham Bell. He refused to allow those who would not support his telephone invention financially stop him from carrying out his passion to be a blessing to the world.

There were many who did not believe in him. Many people felt that what he really wanted to do was a waste of time and that the telephone was not necessary to have during that time period. The people who felt that way were unwilling to think outside the box. They were not open-minded to the process of change, nor did they use the common-sense approach.

In order to experience the benefits of change, you must be open- minded and willing to make the necessary adjustment(s) to produce the necessary result that you desire. In the book *Boiling Point,* it conveys a good example of Alexander Graham Bell attitude on winning.

"The invention of the telephone suffered from the same myopic deployment. Alexander Graham Bell told an investor that his device would eventually enable a businessman in New York to talk to another business-man in Boston. The incredulous investor asked why any businessman in New York would want or need to talk to someone in Boston when all of his associates were in New York. Since it had never been possible to talk to someone in Boston, the investor was confident that he and everyone like him would get along fine without the new device. Discouraged but not devas-tated by the rejections, Bell then raised money for his invention based on the idea that the "killer app" for the telephone would be enabling live concerts to be played in one city and listened to in another. Bell pre-dicted that people would call in to listen to concerts, speeches or religious revivals. People were unable to think "outside the box" long enough to envision the true value of the invention." (P. 173)

Alexander Bell refused to give up on his heart's desire; I believe one reason that he refused to cave in, give up and quit is because he had a strong passion to see his telephone invention come into the making. It will be your strong passion and your strong desire that will take you over and not under whatever you are going through. Alexander Bell's invention demonstrates to us today that if you want something badly enough, then you can do it. The question is, how badly do you want it?

Again, Alexander Bell had the attitude of a winner. He enacted the saying *winners never quit and quitters never win.* Your attitude must not only be one of strong passion and desire but your attitude must be one of a winning attitude. I speak into your life right now that you are a winner; you are more than a conqueror. (Romans 8:37)

Kenneth Copeland, in his book, *The Winning Attitude*, says,

> *You've probably heard it said, "it's not whether you win or lose, it's how you play the game." Do you believe that? I don't! Man was created to be a winner. The Bible tells us so! We read in Genesis, for example, that man was originally put on this earth as dominating lord. God gave him dominion over the earth and everything that crept, flew, crawled and breathed there. In fact, man didn't even know what losing was until he separated himself from God through disobedience in the Garden of Eden. When that happened, man ran headlong into defeat. He was forced to accept failure as his lot in life, lowering himself to a subordinate position—a position he was never meant to occupy." (P. 3-4)*

God Heals in the Hospital

While working as a hospital Chaplain (pastoral counselor) at Carolina Medical Center in Charlotte, North Carolina, I received a call from a unit secretary to pray with a family member whose son was hit by a car. Upon arriving on the unit, I was briefed by the mother that her son had broken about a hundred bones in his body. The mother told me that the doctors said that her son might possibly never walk again; that he would be in a wheelchair for years, if not for life.

The boy's mother refused to believe the doctors' report; she had what Jesus called in Matthew 8:10, **great faith**. I noticed that this woman kept saying to me, "We have to trust God, we have to trust God, we have to trust God, God can do it, God can do it, Chaplain, I know God can heal my son."

In accordance to Matthew 18:19 *"again I say unto you, That if two of you shall agree on earth as touching anything that they shall ask, it shall be done for them of my Father which is in heaven."* The mother and I came into agreement in prayer that God would heal her son. We spoke to every tissue, muscle, bone and cell and we commanded them to function to the perfection to which God created the body to function. We spoke life, declaring that her son would live, and not die. (Psalms 118:17)

We prayed for every doctor, nurse, and any other person who would come into contact with her son's body, that they would operate with excellence, wisdom, direction and guidance. We prayed for every equipment and instrument, and medication to work to the proper cause and intent to which they were designed.

We finished the prayer in the name of Jesus (John 14:13-14), believing that we received everything we had prayed for; we declared that we had the answer to our prayer right then.

About five months later, I was in the cafeteria of the hospital and a woman came up to me; she was the same woman who I prayed with concerning her son. This woman indicated that her son was healed; she said that he was back in school. She went on to say that her son was trying out for the football team.

The key to this miraculous healing in the hospital is that the family wanted it; they refused to believe anything that did not agree to their son's healing. This family received exactly what they believed; believing that God would heal the boy because they really wanted the healing. Again, the question is, how badly do you want it?

The Man at the Pool

> *Afterward Jesus returned to Jerusalem for one of the Jewish holy days. Inside the city, near the Sheep Gate, was the pool of Bethesda, with five covered porches. Crowds of sick people – blind, lame, or paralyzed- lay on the porches. One of the men lying there had been sick for thirty-eight years. When Jesus saw him and knew low long he had been ill, he asked him, "Would you like to get well?" "I can't sir," the sick man said, "for I have no one to help me into the pool when the water is stirred up. While I am trying to get there, someone else always gets in ahead of me" Jesus told him, "Stand up, pick up your sleeping mat, and walk!" Instantly, the man was healed! He rolled up the mat and began to walk..."* (John 5:1-9, NLT)

Several things can be learned from the man who Jesus healed at the pool. The man at the pool had come to develop what I call addictive pool behaviors; let us explore some of these pool behaviors. **First,** *we see that the man had a wrong concept about his condition.* The man at the pool thought it was perfectly okay for him to be in that condition for that long.

The man's concept about his condition was so distorted until he thought it was perfectly normal to be abnormal. When you do something for so long, it is possible for you to think that you are doing right, when actually you are doing wrong.

This type of behavior is not denial but is a reprobated mind. To be in denial is to refuse to recognize or acknowledge what is right, although you have a sense for what is right. **Denial** occurs *when you know what to do, but for whatever reason you* *turn down, reject or simply do not allow to happen what you know should happen.*

A **reprobated mind** occurs *when you do wrong for so long until you do not even know that it is wrong when you are doing wrong.* The wrong has been so implanted in the mind, until there is no idea, clue or inkling that you are all messed up in the head. The interesting thing to note about a reprobated mind is that this kind of person knew before they started doing wrong that it was wrong, but they refused to put the brakes on doing wrong. Now the wrong appears right and they do not even have a clue that they are doing wrong.

Notice these scriptures:

> *And they did not like to retain God in their knowledge, God gave them over to a reprobated mind, to do those things which are not convenient. (Romans 1:28)*

> *When they refused to acknowledge God, he abandoned them to their evil minds and let them do things that should never be done. (Romans 1:28, NLT)*

> *And because they did not think it worthwhile to have God in their knowledge, God delivered them over to a worthless mind to do what is morally wrong." (Romans 1:28, HCSB)*

Another thing to note about a underline reprobated mind, is when you keep turning down what is right, you will be turned over to what is wrong. In addition, when you do what is wrong for so long, you will become an expert at doing wrong. You will become so skilled at what you are doing until you can be classified as a professional addict, liar, overeater, con artist and so on. In order for you to overcome bad habits and chronic addictions, you must know that it is not all right for you to be in a negative condition.

Second, *we see that Jesus did not enable the man;* Jesus did not assist or aid in the man's problem. Jesus instructed the man on what he needed to do and asked him to do it. Many times, people cannot overcome bad habits because a family member or a friend is contributing to the problem. Instead of helping someone overcome his/her problem, the family member or friend contributes to the bad habit, which only makes the bad habit worse.

On Friday, May 11th, 2007 the *Atlanta Journal-Constitution* reports,

> *The manufacturer of the potent painkiller OxyContin and three current and former executives at the company pleaded guilty Thursday to falsely marketing the drug in a way that played down its addictive properties and caused scores of people to become addicted, prosecutors said. The Purdue Fredrick Co. and its chief executive, top lawyer and former medical chief agreed to pay a total of $635 million to resolve charges filed by the attorney in the Western District of Virginia, who called OxyContin "one of our nation's greatest prescription-drug failures." (P. A1)*

The *Atlanta Journal-Constitution* went on to report,

> *From 1996 to 2001, Purdue claimed that the "miracle drug" was safer than rival medications despite repeated studies that suggested patients had developed a risk of abuse and had serious trouble withdrawing from OxyContin. Purdue collected $2.8 billion*

through sales of OxyContin during that time, court papers said." (P. A6)

Many physicians contribute to patients' addictions and bad habits when they prescribe medications that a patient really does not need. When the patient takes things that he or she does not need, the patient overdoses, which means that abuse and addiction is inevitable.

When the man at the pool responded to the word of Jesus, the man recovered. Jesus asked the man to get up and when <u>the man put forth action</u>, he became well. The man at the pool could have been healed many years before he actually was healed if he only would have taken some action about what he was going through.

Third, *we see that Jesus did not listen to the man's excuses.* Rather than the man taking the responsibility for being in his condition for so long, he began to make excuses, *"I have no man to help me," "I can't sir," "another gets in front of me."* You have to get to a point that you stop making excuses about your problem and do something about it. Jesus' response to the man was somewhat like this: I hear what you are saying, but are you going to do something about it. Jesus was looking for results, not excuses.

Fourth, *the man believed in the wrong system to help him.* The man had his total confidence in people, when all he needed to do was to put his confidence in the Lord. This man spent years waiting for someone to help him and did not know that his help was already there. Scripture says, *God is our refuge and strength, A very present help in trouble. (Psalms 46:1)* Whatever conditions you are in, just ask God to help and He will be right there. Your help is in the name of the Lord (Psalms 121:1-2).

Fifth, *the man was in this condition for thirty-eight years.* This demonstrates two things: one, if you do not deal with your issues, they will not get better, but worse. Two, you cannot live a life so bad to where God cannot restore you. You cannot get too low to where God cannot pull you up.

Notice this scripture:

> *"I waited patiently for the LORD; And He inclined to me and heard my cry. He brought me up out of the pit of destruction, out of the miry clay." (Psalms 40:1-2, NASB)*

Sixth, Jesus asked the man this million-dollar question: *Do you want to be well?* Jesus put everything on the man. Basically, what Jesus was saying to the man is how badly do you want it. If you want to stop whatever you are doing that is displeasing to God, yourself and to others, you can stop it. If you do not want to do another day of addictive, chronic, psychotic or buzzard behavior, you do not have to.

"Who am I? I am the guide to your success, I will be the motivating force that will drive you to win or I will be the motivating force that will drive you to lose. I can be your worst nightmare or I can be the reality to all of your dreams coming true. I am your greatest supporter or I can be your worst critic. I can take you to the top or I can make you hit rock bottom. Who am I? I am your habit."

What is a Habit? A habit is defined by **the American Heritage Dictionary** as *a recurrent, often unconscious pattern of behavior that is acquired through frequent repetition.* A habit is a thing you do repeatedly without control. It is doing the same thing over and over again until it becomes so ingrained that you do not even think about doing it, because it becomes automatic.

A habit is another form of an addiction. An **addiction** is that *thing you do without control or restraint.* An addiction is a strong, intensive, overwhelming or overpowering desire for something until it becomes chronic.

There are good habits and there are bad habits. Bad habits are those things that you do on a consistent basis that have no positive effect on your life. Bad habits can be easily formed, but very difficult to break once they are developed. However, with strong determination and concentrated focus, you can successfully overcome a bad habit.

A good biblical example of a list of bad habits is located in (Galatians 5:19-21) of the Amplified Version of the Bible:

> *"Now the* **doings (practices)** *of the flesh are clear (obvious): they are immorality, impurity, indecency, Idolatry, sorcery, enmity, strife, jealousy, anger (ill temper), selfishness, divisions (dissensions), party spirit (factions, sects with peculiar opinions, heresies), Envy, drunkenness, carousing, and the like, I warn you beforehand, just as I did previously, that those who do such things shall not inherit the kingdom of God."*

The word **doing** that is located in verse 21 is translated *Prasso.* It is pronounced as *prus'-so*, which means, *"practice" to perform repeatedly or habitually.* Anything you practice a long time will become an obsession to where you have to do it. However, in this particular text, the people who obsessively practice the wrong thing, that practice of the wrong thing will eventually destroy the people, unless they change their behavior.

A bad habit will always be inconsistent with the word. A good habit will produce life, health, and productivity; a good habit is designed to produce abundant living that creates a consistent flow of total life prosperity (body, mind, and spirit). Good habits will always line up with the word of God.

KEY THOUGHT: Anything you repeatedly do will become a habit

How is a habit developed? A habit is developed when you consistently repeat a thing. It is important to note that habits are habit-forming, the more you do them the more you become adapted to them. For example, when I was a child my mother taught me to say a blessing of thanks to God over every meal that I would eat. Now that I am an adult, I still say a blessing of thanks to God over my food before I eat; this was a learned behavior, which became automatic over a process of time.

There is an old saying: *"Practice makes perfect."* In other words, the more you work hard at doing something over and over again; you will eventually get to the point to where you are proficient and effective in what you are doing.

Note this scripture:

> *"And He came out and went, as was* **His Habit,** *to the Mount of Olives, and the disciples also followed Him. And when He came to the place, He said to them, Pray that you may not [at all] enter into temptation. And He withdrew from them about a*

stone's throw and knelt down and prayed." (Luke
22:37-41, Amplified)

The Amplified Bible translated the King James word **wont**
as *habit*, which means that Jesus made it a habit of praying,
therefore if praying was good for Jesus then praying would be
good for us today. Praying is a good habit that will definitely
need to be implemented in your life to overcome a bad habit.

> *"Also [Jesus] told them a parable to the effect that they*
> *ought always to pray and not to turn coward (faint,*
> *lose heart, and give up)." (Luke 18:1, AMP)*

When you do not have a good habit of prayer, in accordance
to this passage, you will faint, lose heart and give up. That is
what a bad habit will do to you, it will cause you to cave in,
give up and quit. However, I have good news for you: You do
not have to cave in, give up and quit because you can and will
overcome!

When you do not have consistency with a good habit, then
you will become weak and susceptible to a bad habit. Again, bad
habits are developed when you repeatedly do negative behaviors. I believe, deep down, that within every person, he or she
knows exactly what is his or her struggle.

The things that you constantly do that result in displeasing
God or things that you do that pull you away from the things
of God are not of God; they are bad habits. A bad habit will
always bring you down and ultimately destroy your life. All
bad habits are designed to destroy you, regardless of how good
things may appear at the beginning. The ultimate state of a bad
habit is total destruction.

Notice what the Apostle Paul says, *"All things are lawful unto*
me, but all things are not expedient: all things are lawful for me, but

I will not be brought under the power of any." (I Corinthians 6:12)
What the Apostle Paul was communicating to the Corinthians
Church is that if you do not want to be brought under the powers
of any (addictions and bad habits) then you will need to have
some type of self control in your life.

Some people do not mind telling you *this is my life and I will
do whatever I want to do with it.* A song was written: *"It's your
thang, do what you want to do, I can't tell you who to sock it to."* The
problem with this type of thinking is when God instructs you
to do something you cannot do whatever you want to do.

**If you are going to be blessed by God, you will have to do
the God thing.** If you do whatever you want to do, you are not
doing what God wants you to do. Only what you do for Christ
is going to last.

Notice this scripture:

> *What? Know ye not that your body is the temple of the
> Holy Ghost which is in you, which you have of God,
> and ye are not your own. For ye are brought with a
> price: therefore glorify God in your body, and in your
> spirit, which are God's. (I Corinthians 6:19-20)*

A person doing anything he or she wants to do totally wipes
out God. In order to have godly success, God has to lead you, *"for
all who are led by the Spirit of God are children of God." (Romans 8:14,
NLT)* This scripture indicates that God will lead you. As a result
of God leading you, you learn that your life is not your own.

Although you are free to do whatever you want to do, if you
are trying to live right (for Christ), there are certain things that
you just will not do. Even if there is nothing that can prevent
or prohibit you from doing what you want to do, you will not
do it, because it is wrong.

How will you know when something is wrong? Simple... **when it contradicts the word of God**. Whatever is in opposition to the Word of God, it is wrong no matter where the wrong thing is coming from. *"For the word of the LORD is right; And all His works are done in truth." (Psalms 33:4)*

One of the major phrases in I Corinthians 6:12 that must not be overlooked is that some things are not expedient, the word **expedient** in this specific passage of scripture is *sumphero*. It is pronounced as *soo-fer'-o* which means *advantageous, beneficial or profitable*. This meaning of sumphero is pivotal. Just because things are permissible for you to do, does not mean that it is beneficial for you to do them.

Again, sumphero is pivotal. Just because you can do whatever you want to do at times, does not mean that they are the right or beneficial things to do. People get caught up in bad habits because they do the wrong things and those wrong things become negative consequences. These negative consequences become the bad habits that pull people down.

Bad habits can be anything from talking too much, lying, cheating, stealing, being addicted to alcohol or drugs, overeating, gambling, adultery, anger, smoking cigarettes, blaming others, negative thinking, being a "yes" person and so on.

A bad habit is consistent excessive negative behavior that an individual does and is unwilling or is unable to stop, although he or she is very much aware of the harmful and potential damaging consequences. Again, the thing to remember about a bad habit is that the road ends in destruction.

God has created within every individual the ability to be successful. The key to a successful life in God is developing good habits. *"Study this Book of the Law continually, Meditate on it day and night so you may be sure to obey all that is written in it. Only then will you succeed." (Joshua 1:8, NLT)*

The word *continually* denotes *habits*; it is a consistent practice of reading the word of God that Joshua developed that made him and his ministry very successful.

One of the reasons people do not have true success in God is that they do not obey the *all* part, they do the *some* part, and it is the *all* that is going to make a dramatic change in your life. The true result of change is that you do not do what you used to do.

Pastor Greg Powe, in his book, *Soaring Above Average,* says,

> *"If you are genuinely called to leadership, you will experience a great deal of change in your life. In fact, the degree of change you undergo determines the degree of your development. Little change equates to little development, but great change indicates great development. You have not developed an excellent spirit if you are still thinking the same way you thought before you were saved. If you are still acting the same way, making the same decisions that you were two years ago, then you have not changed."*
> *(P. 161)*

CHAPTER 2

|||||||||||||||||||||||||||

It all Begins with God

"In the beginning God created the heavens and the earth." (Genesis 1:1)

It is only in God that you will find your identity and existence for living. Everything that you do must have its starting point with God. It is God who will give you the creative ability to produce great results; it is God who will give you the knowledge and ability to overcome a bad habit.

> *"Wherefore, seeing we also are compassed about with so great a cloud of witnesses, let us lay aside every weight, and the sin which doth so easily beset us, and let us run with patience the race that is set before us. Looking unto Jesus the author and finisher of our faith; who for the joy that was set before him endured the cross, despising the shame, and is set down at the right hand of the throne of God." (Hebrews 12:1-2.)*

Kenneth Copeland, in his book, *How to Discipline Your Flesh*, says,

> *"There are many, many believers today who are struggling with all their might to lay aside the sins that defeat them. However, most of them are failing miserably. Why? These are not bad people. Quite the contrary. They are sincere people who love God but – because they've missed an important part of the message that passage conveys-they are still in bondage. Ye see, it doesn't say, "Lay aside the sin." It doesn't just say, "You shape up and be holy!" It says, "Look at Jesus!" Get rid of the sin by looking at Jesus!" (P.51-52)*

There are two things that need to be noted about the word **look**. 1) the word **look** means *to take a deep fearless searching inventory inside of oneself* and to be honest with what you see and to be determined to change by working on what needs to be better. 2) the word **look** is used to refer to *literally taking a hold of the word of God, opening it and reading it* to understand who God is and what He (God) has said concerning you and your situation. Exploring through the pages of the Bible with this thought in mind, whatever is wrong in my life God is going to make it right.

Also, in his book *How to Discipline your Flesh*, Kenneth Copeland indicates how you can get to know Jesus Christ better:

> *"...During my first five years as a Christian, I wanted to see Him so badly I could hardly stand it. I wanted Him to appear to me in a vision or something...I*

finally saw Him all right, but not like I'd expected.
I saw Him in the Word. I've been seeing Him in the
Word now for well over thirty-six years, and I'm tell-
ing you, I know what He is like. I know His nature. I
know Him better than I know anybody. I don't know
Him as well as I want to, but thanks to the Word I
continually know Him better." (P. 52-53)

KEY THOUGHT: Looking unto Jesus is
where you will find all the answers and
solutions to your problems.

**There are certain things in life that can only be achieved by
you turning to Jesus.** Looking unto Jesus is where you will find
all the answers and solutions to your problems. When you look
unto Jesus, you focus on what He says and what He is going to
do for you. You understand and know where all of your help
comes from, which is God.

The word **looking** is defined as several different meanings in
the Greek or New Testament of the Bible, however, in Hebrews
12:2, the word **looking** literally means *to turn (look) away from
one thing to see another.* It comes from the Greek word *aphorao,*
which means *to lock into.*

"And Peter answered him and said, Lord, if it be
thou, bid me come unto thee on the water. And he
said, Come. And when Peter was come down out of
the ship, he walked on the water, to go to Jesus. But
when he saw the wind boisterous, he was afraid; and
beginning to sink, he cried, saying, Lord, save me.
And immediately Jesus stretched forth his hand, and

caught him, and said unto him, O thou of little faith,
wherefore didst thou doubt?" (Matthew 14:28-31)

This looking (locking into) is what allowed the apostle Peter to walk on water, when all natural laws stated that it is impossible for a human to walk on water. Peter turned his mental attention away from the boisterous waves and roaring sea and set his regards on or locked into what Jesus said to him, which was to come.

Dr. Fredrick, K.C. Price says,

> *"The fact that Jesus said "Come" implies two things. First, Peter had permission to come. This means it must have been the will of God for Peter to walk on the water. Second, it implies that Peter had the ability to walk on the water. If he did not have that ability, Jesus would have known that as soon as Peter stepped out of the boat, he would sink, and He would not have told Peter to come." (46)*

As long as Peter stayed locked into what Jesus said and kept his mind, which is Peter's will and emotions on Christ, Peter overcame his unbelief by walking on water. However, when he turned his attention off Jesus (the word) and began to pay more attention to what he saw (waves rising) and heard (wind roaring), Peter immediately began to sink.

Every time we turn our attention from God, we will fail. However, as long as we set our will to believe in God, no matter what, God will always allow us to succeed. **There is no failure in God.** His spirit will guide you; therefore, there is no failure in you. Failure only occurs when we get away from God and the things of God.

Dr. Jerry Savelle says,

*"When you lose focus, you become disillusioned. It causes you to lose sight of your goal....lay aside every weight, and the sin which doeth so easily beset us... Hebrew 12:1. To win you have to get rid of the "weights" that are pulling you down. You have to look **to** the Word and look **away** from everything else that is contrary. Focused people are not easily distracted. Focused people refuse to compromise what they believe. They make no provision for failure. Focused people do not easily change what they believe just because of negative circumstances. Focused people finish what they start. They will not give up." (P. 100, 101)*

Looking unto Jesus means that you are gazing, you are setting your attention and focus on what He (Christ Jesus) can do through you. You will stop looking at the past failure, hurts, and disappointments and you will zero in on what God's word has to say about you. Your success in life will only come through Jesus.

You can do what you set your mind to do with the help of God. That is right... you can do it! You can break the bad habit, kick the addiction, and be free of the hurt, bondage and sickness. However, for you to overcome these issues, you will need to not let anyone or anything stop you from receiving your blessing.

In her book, *How to Dream Beyond Your Means*, Dr. Bridget, E. Hilliard says,

The key to getting out of your present situation is the dream that you have on the inside of your heart. You

*must hold onto your dream and do not let anybody
abort it. It does not matter that everyone around you is
saying the Word does not work. It worked for me and
if it worked for me, it has to work for you. (P. 25)*

The words **focus** and **concentration** is synonymous, in that
you will have to zero in on your challenges. You will have to get a
clear image of what it is that you need to do and work at getting
it done. When a person becomes focused, he or she has his/
her mindset on a particular thing. This person focuses on that
thing until the desired result is completed.

Dr. Creflo A. Dollar, in his book, *Walking in the Confidence
of God in Troubled Times,* says,

*"I absolutely believe with all my heart that the answer
to all of our problems is to make sure our hearts are
fixed on the Word on a daily basis. The Bible says,
"set your mind and keep it set" (Col.3:2 AMP) This
requires consistency. I believe this works in my life!
I believe that when I set my mind and keep my mind
set, I am keeping myself set toward a successful and
victorious outcome..." (P.100)*

The word focus is similar to a jet fighter plane; which,
when fixed (locked) on the enemies' aircraft, it patiently waits
until all indicators are a go to launch the rock missiles. When
all indicators are a go and the rock missiles are launched, the
missiles will hit exactly wherever they are programmed to
destroy.

**When you fix your mind set on Jesus, bad habits are
destroyed.** If you are going to overcome weaknesses, failures
and shortcomings, you will need to commit first to Jesus, literally

locking into the word of God, fixing your undivided attention on Him to direct and guide your life.

Notice this scripture, *"I will lift up mine eyes unto the hills, from whence **cometh** my help. My help cometh from the LORD."* *(Psalms 121:1-2)* What the psalmist says is that his eyes were fixed on God and what He can do for the psalmist. This fixing allowed the psalmist to focus on the positive side of things and not the negative. If things are going to get better, you must believe that they can get better and with the help of God, they will get better.

> *"A certain woman, which had an issue of blood twelve years, And had suffered many things of many physicians, and had spent all that she had, and was nothing bettered, but rather grew worse, When she had heard Jesus, came in the press behind, and touched his garment. For she said, If I may touch but his clothes, I shall be whole. And straightway the fountain of her blood was dried up; and she felt in her body that she was healed of that plague."* *(Mark 5:25-29.)*

The woman with the issue of blood stayed focused. She worked through the crowds and did not allow what she went through to stop her from obtaining her promise. With a concentrated focus and an intense effort that was so strong until it could not be denied, she received what she believed.

This woman could have saved herself time, energy and money if she would have looked (turned) her attention to Jesus first. Some people can mean well but never do you any good. This is what the doctors did to this woman, they did her no good, and she went financially broke, seeking medical attention. Not to discredit doctors, because we need them.

Kevin Trudeau, in his book, *More Natural "Cures" Revealed*, says,

> *"The fact is there are ways to prevent disease, and there are ways to cure disease with natural means. The most important thing for you to consider is the pharmaceutical cartel wants more people to get cancer. Cancer is the most profitable industry in the entire field of medicine and health. There are major financial incentives to increase the percentage of people getting cancer. In my opinion, this cartel is knowingly producing products that give us cancer, therefore increasing their profits."* (P. 79)

The woman with the issue of blood looked to God to understand what He (God) had to say about her situation. God can do what natural law and medical science cannot do. He can heal, deliver and restore at any moment. This woman believed in God's healing power. She fixed her attention on Jesus (the Word of God) and she received healing.

To God be the Glory! I boast not within myself but in God. I am currently 39 years old and I have never had any surgeries on my body. I am in perfect health. I take no medications of any type. I only visit the doctor's office once a year for an annual examination.

I believe that God can empower his people with good health, especially, when you choose to both read the word of God and pray constantly. *"Dear friend, I pray that you may enjoy good health and that all may go well with you, even as your soul is getting along well."* (3 John 2, NIV) When you choose to physically exercise your body and eat healthy, you will prolong your life, and your mind will prosper.

God will create an environment to where no germs, sickness or disease can be exposed to your body. If any life-threatening illness comes into direct contact with your body, it will die instantly because of the protection that God has placed upon your life.

People who God protected
1. **Job's family**, they were protected from any form of danger. (Job 1:5, 9-10)

2. **Cain, God placed a mark on him, so that no one would harm him. (Genesis 4:14-15)**

3. **Joseph,** God protected Joseph in the pit, prison, and elevated him to the second highest position in Egypt. (Genesis 50:19-20)

4. **Nation of Israel,** God promised to remove all sickness and disease from among the people. (Exodus 23:25)

5. **Elijah,** God provided food and water for Elijah, when others were dying of starvation. (I King 17:2-3, 8-16)

All of theses people who received healing, protection, and deliverance had two things in common; they both prayed to God and read His word on a constant basis. The word will work for you, if you will work it. Gloria Copeland, in her book, *God's Will for Healing,* says,

> *To fill God's prescription for life and health, you must be diligent in attending to His Word. You must give the Word the place of authority and spend time in it daily. The forces of life and power coming out of your heart will be in direct proportion to the amount of the Word going in you. There is no limit to the amount of God's medicine that you can take. You*

cannot get an overdose. The more you take, the more powerful you will become. (P. 61-62)

Prayer works! Speak the word of God over your life. Calling on the name of Jesus Christ works, pleading the blood of Jesus over your life works and going to church works. Although it may not make sense to some people, as a believer it will make plenty of sense to you, especially, when God keeps you healed, protected, happy, and blessed when everyone else around you or in your circle of influence is struggling.

Demonic Decoys

I remember going to work on a particular day, and this day was a very challenging day; things were not working as well as they should. Therefore, I began to pray and meditate on the word of God to myself as I worked. That evening I received a phone call from a co-worker who was very upset. His words were very unpleasant; it was obvious to me that this person was having some issues.

I felt disrespected, and began to share some of my concerns with this person. That was a big mistake! Instead of the situation getting better, it became worse. Later that evening, I called this person and tried to resolve what was wrong.

I experienced the same thing, nothing different than when we had spoken the first time. This person was even more disrespectful and refused to help resolve what was wrong. After I finished talking with the person, I just continued to pray, listening to inspirational Christian music.

The next day at home, I woke up still praying in the Holy Spirit, listening to inspirational Christian music and reading the word of God. I prepared for the home-going that would take place at church later that afternoon.

I arrived at the church an hour before the event, praying in the Holy Spirit and full of the word of God. We gathered together all of the volunteers to pray for the service. After the volunteers had prayed for the service, we continued setting up for the home-going service. As we were arranging things for the service, we continued to pray softly to ourselves in the Holy Spirit.

As a result of our praying in the Spirit, people began to come through the door, the Spirit of God began to move, people were being healed, comforted, strengthened and encouraged by the volunteers. We received so many compliments that day on how good a job we were doing.

After the eulogy, the minister gave an altar call or an invitation for those who would like to accept Jesus Christ as Lord and Savior to come forth. That day we had 115 young people come down and accept Jesus Christ as Lord and personal Savior of their lives!

God revealed to me that the confusion on the job was just a demonic decoy. A demonic decoy is evil spirits creating confusion in the spirit, mind and body of a person. A demonic decoy is designed to strictly distract; it causes you to lose focus of your spiritual assignment, with the intention of you never fulfilling God-intended purpose for your life.

I learned that keeping some things to yourself is much better when negative thoughts occur in your mind. In most cases, if you observe certain negative things that are going on around you, God has revealed it to you so that you can pray about it, not talk about it to others.

When there is no apparent reason for things to be chaotic or discombobulated, do not get frustrated because God is about to do something great in your life. When there appears to be intense struggle and extreme agitation in your life, go deeper in the word of God and prayer.

Jesus instructs Peter: *"...Now go out where it is deeper and let down your nets, and you will catch many fish." (Luke 5:4, NLT)* When Peter obeyed the instructions of Jesus and entered into the deep, he came up with some great results. He caught more fish than he could even imagine. As Christians, we are to walk in this same mentality. It makes no difference what is going on with you; God is going to do something great, awesome, and very significant in your life.

Things are going to happen to you that you do not like. Just stay focused and keep moving in the direction that God is leading you. Stay in a Spirit of love and forgiveness, and do not be stuck in the defensive mode. Stay humble, be kind and keep heading toward what your God-given spiritual assignment is to be.

This co-worker of mine was not in a position to receive anything I had to say. This person was so self-absorbed; nothing that I said mattered to him. It is important that you recognize this type of behavior and stay away from it. The Bible says, *"Make no friendship with an angry man; And with a furious man thou shalt not go: Lest thou learn his way, And get snare to thy soul."* (Proverbs 22:24-25)

Walking in the love of God is one of the best ways to calm an angry spirit, although, it is up to the individual to change. Love will have a profound effect on the angry person to where he/she will sense a need to change. There is a song that says, *"Love lifted me, love lifted me, when nothing else could help love lifted me."*

When you love a person who is unloving, it is the love of

God that the unloving person will see and it is the love of God that will lift the unloving person up out of anger. One of the best ways to deal with an angry man is to love him. Love can climb the highest mountain and penetrate the toughest heart. It is love that will lift you up when you are feeling down. Love will never fail. (I Corinthians 13:8)

It is important to pray and walk in the love of God because some things can catch you off guard. My co-worker's negative behavior initially felt like a bomb exploding; however, because I understood the strategies of a demonic decoy, I quickly got myself in the love of God to keep both the peace of God and the blessing of God upon my life. Now, I am here to say that it was love that lifted me.

Moreover, God showed me how we, the volunteers, played a great role in the 115 young people coming to the Lord. God revealed that because the volunteers arrived an hour early, we were able to set the atmosphere for the Holy Spirit to do great things at the home-going celebration. Because of the volunteers praying in the Holy Spirit, we were tearing down strong holds, taking authority over the spirit of grief and depression, and creating an atmosphere for the people to be delivered, healed, set free, made whole, and to become born-again.

Church Makes a Difference

I remember attending a particular Church in Charlotte, North Carolina and at the end of the message the pastor gave an altar call. The pastor asked if anyone needed to accept Jesus Christ as Lord and personal Savior to come forward, or if anyone needed to rededicate his/her life back to Jesus, join the church or if anyone just needed prayer. A Christian, who was knowledgeable in praying for people, would pray for those who came down front.

There were many people who came forth for the altar call, so the pastor asked me to help. A young, black male came down who appeared to be in his mid 30's. I asked the young man what he would like prayer for. The young man said, "You do not want to know what I am thinking about doing." I shared with the young man, "Sure, I do, and there is nothing too hard for God." (Job 42:1-2)

This young man informed me that he was getting ready to leave the church to kill a man. I did not get into the whys and wherefores with this particular young man because I was a visiting minister; I prayed and referred him to the pastor and certain administrative personnel of the church which was trained to handle this kind of situation.

To make a long story short, this young man, after a Spirit led directed prayer, accepted Jesus Christ as Lord and his personal Savior. Not only did this young man become born-again, but he was filled with the Holy Ghost with the evidence of speaking in tongues. This man left the altar with a changed mind. The yoke of homicidal ideation was broken. This young man left saved, healed, delivered and set free.

How can someone tell me that the church does not work! How can someone tell me that prayer does not work! How can someone tell me that the Word of God does not work! Oh yes, they work! You might not be doing your part right. If you have not tried church, prayer or the Word, then stay silent. You don't know how church, prayer and the word of God works.

As I look back over my life experiences, God gave me the strength, knowledge and desire to overcome everything negative that I had to endure. God brought me out. God rescued, delivered and set me free. I learned that God would use the church to help me overcome bad habits and break chronic addictions.

God would use the praise and worship leaders to sing the right songs; God would use the assistant ministers to teach and preach messages that would reach me exactly where I was in life; and God would use greeters to smile, give hugs when appropriate and to say words of kindness. God will do the same for you if you go to church.

How to Get Out of a Tough Spot

KEY THOUGHT: Every change starts with a decision to want to change.

A further examination of the woman with the issue of blood in Mark 5:25-29 is that this woman made a decision to turn to God. That is one of the main principles to getting out of a tough spot. Jesus said that I am the way (John 14:6); **we must make a decision to follow Christ if things are going to get better.**

The woman with the issue of blood made the decision, not someone else. When someone else makes the decision for you to change, the result for you is not as lasting and effective, as it could be when you, alone, make the decision to change.

This concept is big. If you are going to overcome a bad habit, you must turn to God when you are in a tough spot. Notice this scripture, *"God is our refuge and strength, a very present help in trouble." (Psalms 46:1)* During tough times you must not turn to your negativity or addictive behaviors, you must turn to God and He will be the source that will get you out of the tough spot.

The desire for change must come from within, although you can be greatly influenced by others to do the right thing. Again, ultimately **you must make the decision to change** by turning your will over to Jesus Christ.

In his book, *So You Call Yourself a Man*, Bishop T.D. Jakes says,

> *"Your attitude today is something that is totally under your control. You Choose. You choose whether you will be prejudiced, angry, hateful, bitter, and resentful. It is in your power to make a decision about what you will think and how you will act."*

The Bible says,

> *"And Isaac prayed much to the Lord for his wife because she was unable to bear children, and the Lord granted his prayer, and Rebekah his wife became pregnant. [Two] children struggled together within her; and she said, if it is so [that the Lord has heard our prayer], why am I like this? And she went to inquire of the Lord. And the Lord said unto her, Two nations are in thy womb..." (Genesis 25:21-23 NLT)*

There was one thing that Isaac did that was very significant in this passage of scripture, he prayed. It was Isaac's prayer that enabled the hand of God to get involved with his situation. Prayer has always been one of the main channels that God has provided for people to come into direct contact with Him.

There are five reasons that most people do not overcome during tough times.

1) **They don't pray.** In Luke 18:1 *"And he spake a parable unto them to this end, that men ought always to pray, and not to faint."* People often give up and quit when they are not consistent in prayer. Every failure in life is because of a lack of prayer.

   Kenneth, Copeland, in his book, *Prayer Your Foundation for Success*, says,

In order to expel doubt and unbelief, you must make God's Word final authority in every matter. Do not allow what religious tradition says, or what you think about it, to be the deciding factor. Pray according to the will of God and believe you receive when you pray. God's Word is His Will. He does not will one thing and say something else. God cannot lie. Refuse to be moved by anything except what God's Word tells you. When you pray, expect things to change. God's Word will not fail. (P. 82)

Prayer will keep you from doing the wrong thing. *"And said unto them, Why sleep ye? Rise and pray, lest ye enter into temptation." (Luke 22:46)* People who do not pray consistently and effectively often get into trouble; they are more vulnerable to the attacks of demonic activity, and they are more susceptible to experiencing life-threatening addictive, chronic behaviors, because they are not praying.

2) **Most people don't believe God.** *"...and all things, whatsoever ye shall ask in prayer, believing, ye shall receive." (Matthew 21:22)* Prayer not believed is prayer not received. Do you believe? Many people when experiencing tough times will, after a period of time, begin to doubt and become weary about overcoming what they are going through. Many people give up, let go or even compromise their positions during tough times.

One of the keys to overcoming tough times is that you must believe God; you must put your confidence in God and not in the doctor, lawyer, medicine or your own intellectualism. It is God who will help you and deliver you, it is God who will break the addiction and destroy the bad habit, and it is God who will give you the strength to overcome.

The question, is do you believe it?

3) **Most people don't ask in the name of Jesus.** "*...that whatsoever ye shall ask of the father in my name, he may give it you.*" *(John 15:16)* God will give to those who ask in the name of his son Jesus Christ, every prayer should be: "Father, in the name of Jesus" before you pray and after you pray. Everything must be done in the name of Jesus.

While in Jamaica doing missionary work, we went to one particular house. The woman asked for prayer for her son. She said that her son had been in 10 fights at school. The year had just started and he had been suspended for the whole year. She said that her son was very, very angry (rage episodes) and began cutting himself. He constantly refused to listen to anyone, and he was always getting in trouble. She said that she could not seem to do anything with him. We asked the woman to bring her son into the room.

This was the first time I ever saw anything like this. When the woman's son came into the room, I noticed that he took long jumps. When I looked down, I saw that he had a rope around his ankles about two inches thick. I noticed that his hands were tied together. This boy looked bad. You could see clearly that there was some demonic activity going on.

I remember laying hands on the young boy and speaking the Word of God over him. The young boy began to smile; his mother said that he had not smiled in a very, very long time. The mother removed the rope from around his ankles. The boy began to cry and hugged his mother saying he was sorry. God allowed me to witness at an early age that whatever had an individual bound can be broken. It is only the name of Jesus which is going to set him or her free. If you ask in the name of Jesus, God has promised to rescue you from whatever need you have. (John 16:23)

One of the things about asking in the name of Jesus is that you must have certain things in order. You cannot be in sin, anger, unforgiveness, or disobedience and expect God to break the cycle of your negative or addictive behaviors. The Bible says,

> Listen! The LORD is not too weak to save you, and he is not becoming deaf. He can hear you when you call. But there is a problem – your sins have cut you off from God. Because of your sin, he has turned away and will not listen anymore. (Isaiah 59:1-2, NLT)

4) **Most people are not active listeners.** *"A wise man will hear, and will increase learning; and a man of understanding shall attain unto wise counsels."* *(Proverbs 1:5)* One of the reasons most people are not active listeners is because they are self-absorbed in their own stuff (problems) that handicap them from hearing (listening and obeying) positive directions. We are instructed to be *"swift to hear, slow to speak."* *(James 1:9)*

5) **Most people do not obey their positive intuition.** Many times when making a decision, people can sense what is right or what is wrong. People can sense when they should not go to a certain place, do a certain thing, or hang around a certain person. Nevertheless, many people do what they know is wrong. The reason for doing wrong is that they do not obey their intuition.

The word **intuition** is derived from the Latin word *"intueri"* which means, *"to see within"*. Your intuition is more of an inner gut feeling, a perception of knowing something without the facts or credibility to explain it. Intuition is a an ability to sense that something is right or wrong, even though there is no clear understanding.

Every person has a human intuition. Whether or not you are a Christian, every person has the ability to perceive, discern, sense, or get a feeling for how things are going on around him or her. Some people use their intuition for good and others use it for bad. Nevertheless, the more you develop in obeying those things that are right, loving, uplifting and promoting life, your intuition will pick that up, and it will eventually become a habit of you doing what is right, uplifting and promoting life.

When things occur that are negative, destructive, or just not good for you, your intuition will also pick that up and indicate to you that something is not right. The reason your intuition can pick up negativity or something that is not beneficial, is that your intuition is trained and developed to do right. So, when something that is not good for you comes to you in your life, your intuition will sound an alarm on the inside of you.

When you get in a habit of doing right there will be some sort of check in your mind that will go off. When something is not right, it is like your car; when a service light comes on, that is an indicator that something is not right. When your intuition starts going off inside you, that alarm signal is the indication that you need to examine what is going on around you.

When I started college, it was suggested the best way to study for a test was to memorize the correct answers from the study notes, and not to spend any time knowing the wrong answers. When taking the test, I learned that the answers would be very easy to identify, because I had spent hours knowing the correct answer. Therefore, when I saw anything other than the answer, I knew that it was the wrong answer.

It has also been said that one of the ways bankers can immediately identify counterfeit money is by getting to know how the genuine money looks. Once the bankers familiarize themselves with the real thing, they recognize fake bills. In his book, *The Believer's Guide to Spiritual Warfare*, Thomas B. White says,

> *A friend of mine has an uncanny ability to "read" the character traits of individuals and the social dynamics likely to develop among groups of people. She is not a Christian and does not presume to have any spiritual ability in this regard. But she has reliable perceptive insights that help her know how to avoid involvement with unethical or selfishly motivated people. This capacity to see quickly and keenly behind the outer appearance to capture the quality of a particular person or event is a natural but usually latent human ability...such perception is a part of the package of human excellence built in by the Creator. When such persons become Christian and receive the Holy Spirit, their natural perceptive ability seems to sharpen significantly. (P. 90)*

I have some dictation software on my computer that allows me to talk to my computer instead of typing. The only thing I have to do is just speak the words through a headset and my dictation software will type every single word that I say. However, Initially I had to spend several minutes speaking into the headset so it could recognize my speech. The speech recognition had to get accustomed to recognizing my voice. Once my voice was consistently recognized, the dictation software just took over, and automatically began to type every word that I spoke, because it was familiar with my voice.

Your intuition is somewhat like the dictation software: First, you must get to a point to where you can recognize what your intuition is saying to you. Second, you need to do exactly what your intuition is indicating for you to do. I think it is extremely, extra important to say this idea. Your intuition will never tell you to do something that will physically harm or mentally abuse an individual. Your intuition is a safety guide for you; your intuition is only concerned with your safety. Third, the more you obey your intuition, the easier it will become to hear and do what is being instructed to you by your intuition.

Your intuition is your conscience guiding you. If you are a born-again believer (Christian) who has trained your Spirit in the word of God and prayer, your intuition is your spirit witness. Notice this scripture, *"I say the truth in Christ, I lie not, my conscience also bearing me witness in the Holy Ghost."* (Romans 9:1) Your Spirit has an inward voice. This voice will prompt, stir, confirm and direct you to make proper decisions.

Kenneth, E. Hagin, in his book, *How You Can Be Led by the Spirit of God* says,

> *The number one way the Spirit guides us is through the inward witness. Number two is by the inward voice. The inward man, who is a spirit man, has a voice – just as the outward man has a voice. We call this voice of the inward man* **conscience***. We call this voice the still small voice. Your spirit has a voice. Your spirit will speak to you. (P. 39)*

The more Christians yield to the Holy Spirit, the keener their intuition to perceive things from God's perspective will develop. Disobeying your intuition is unhealthy behavior; it is unhealthy because when you disregard your positive intuition you will become involved in things that are hard, difficult, and demanding. The way you stay or get out of a tough spot is by simply obeying your intuition; your intuition is a safe guard to keep you in the peace and the rest of God

Let me give you an example of not obeying your intuition. When I was working for a particular company, I decided to work in another department while working in my current department. During the interviewing process with the department heads, I felt extremely uncomfortable and I communicated this uncomfortable feeling to them. It was passed off as maybe not knowing each other well. As I looked back over the situation, I realized that that was not the case at all; that uncomfortable feeling was my intuition (Spirit) indicating to me not to get involved.

Feeling uncomfortable about taking the job was not my fear but more of a maybe you should not do this. The whole time the interviewers were talking to me, I was sure they were sizing me up to assure the fact that I met the minimum requirement for the position. However, I was also observing them to determine whether or not I would fit in this particular department.

The people extended the opportunity for me to work for them as well as gave me a pay raise. The interesting thing about that is that I was not at all excited about taking the position, but the money sounded great. Later I learn that when you do things for God you do it because you love the Lord. It should not be based on how much money you will receive.

God will supply all of your needs for doing His service. (Philippians 4:19,) In regards to money, you must first be right or get in a right relationship with God for your money to have kingdom-of-God effectiveness, for you.

Jesus said,

> *If you take your gift to the altar and remember your brother has something against you, leave your gift on the altar. Go and make right what is wrong between you and him. Then come back and give your gift. (Matthew 5:23-24, NLV)*

Jesus is indicating that money does not matter when your relationship with God and man is dysfunctional. When your relationship with God and man is wrong, your main focus should not be on how much money you can make or give; your greatest desire should be to correct, mend or restore your broken relationship with God and man.

If you want your money to have kingdom-of-God effectiveness for you, then you will need to have the heart of God in your giving. When you have the heart of God, your money will have great sufficiency toward kingdom-of-God effectiveness, Again, God is not concerned about how much you can make or give, He is concerned about you getting your heart right toward Him.

The Bible talks about a man who had a lot of money. In Luke 12:1-21, this man allowed his money (*possessions*) to govern his decisions and not God. When this man died, he went to Hell because he allowed his money to control his life and not God. When God is leading you, He will never lead you wrong.

Many people make decisions based on money. They will take jobs, careers, kiss up and do all sorts of things for fear of going broke, or for a desire to make it to the top. However, if you listen to God and do what He says, God will never allow you to go broke.

In his book, *I'll Never Be Broke Another Day In My Life*, Dr. Leroy Thompson says, "Receive "I'll never be broke another day *in my life! As your Word from God. As you do, God will see to it that those revelations manifest in a physical sense, not just the spiritual." (P.168)*

King David said it this way, *"I have been young and now am old, yet have I not seen the* [uncompromisingly] *righteous forsaken or their seed begging bread." (Psalms 37:25, AMP)* God will make sure that money comes to you and that you have more than enough to give some away.

God knows that we need money in the body of Christ. God just does not want your money to control your decisions. God knows how to get money to the uncompromisingly righteous person. However, if your money controls you, then when God speaks to you about a decision, you will be unable to hear Him because your mind is on your money and not on God.

Returning to my job interview, I agreed to accept the new position at work. On the first day of work in that particular department, when I walked through the door, I knew that I did not need to be there. I could sense it in the air. I sensed that I needed to stay within my present department.

People asked me how I liked the job. I would say things like, *"Oh, its fine,"* as an attempt to not say anything negative about the department. Nevertheless, the more I worked on that job it became an uphill struggle; I was moving too slowly, making a lot of mistakes and rushing to do more. I was trained by a minimum of 13 different people within a three-week period and all of them were saying something different which complicated the whole process.

The whole time I was working, I was thinking to myself, why am I here? I do not really like this job. There were several days where I worked eight hours and did not even take a break, and when I would leave for the day, there was still a lot of work to be done. In addition, there was confusion, cliques and competitive jealousy. I really did not want to be a part of that.

I talked with one of the department heads about the struggle I was experiencing and I was encouraged to stay with it; things would get better. Things did not get better; in fact, they got worse. I wanted to walk out the door several times. Finally, after so much training, I was exhausted.

Then one of the department heads suggested that I was not going to work out in that particular department. I thought to myself, *boy, what a relief!* I had been contemplating letting the job go for weeks, and when the department head told me that, I felt a heavy burden lift off my shoulder.

I should have gone with my intuition at the first; when I had feelings or perceived that this job was not good for me at the initial interviewing stage, I should have said right there that I did not want the job.

My intuition was trying to keep me from weeks of frustration, staying up later at night, spending little time with my family, and regretting that I ever became involved in the whole situation.

In Acts 27:10-11, the Bible says,

> *"And said unto them, Sir, I perceive that this voyage will be with hurt and much damage, not only of the lading and ship, but also of our lives. Nevertheless the centurion believed the master and the owner of the ship more than those things which were spoken by Paul."*

Your intuition can indicate to you how certain things are going to turn out even before those things occur. When the Apostle Paul was on a ship sailing for Rome, he had a perception; an intuition that the voyage was not going to be good. I think it is interesting to note that Paul did not say, *"The Lord spoke to me communicating that the voyage will be with hurt and much damage."* Paul just perceived. He had an inner prompting or sensibility that something was not going to be right, up ahead of them.

Notice what happened when the men on the ship did not obey the Apostle Paul's intuition. These men kept sailing and ran directly into danger. The storm became so bad that it started tearing up the ship. These men began to fear, throwing things overboard, and felt for certain, that they were going to die.

The Bible says,

> *No one had eaten for a long time, finally, Paul called the crew together and said, "Men, you should have listened to me in the first place and not left Fair havens. You would have avoided all this injury and loss. But take courage! None of you will lose your lives, even though the ship will go down. (Acts 27:21-22, NLT)*

It did not have to be that bad for the folks on the ship. If they would have listened, they could have avoided all the injury and losses of the ship. In addition, when you do not listen to your intuition, whatever you are involved in will only take you down further. These men's ship sank all because they refused to be sensitive to what was going on around them.

In II Chronicles 18:1-34, which I strongly recommend you read in the New Living Translation of the Bible, King Ahab of Israel wanted to go to war against his enemy (Ramoth-gilead) but before he went to war, King Ahab asked Jehoshaphat, King of Judah to join him against Ramoth-gilead.

King Jehoshaphat agreed to go to war with Ahab. However, before King Jehoshaphat would join in war, he wanted to know first what the Lord had to say about it:

> *"Will you join me in fighting against Ramoth-gilead?"*
> *Ahab asked. And Jehoshaphat replied, "Why, of course!*
> *You and I are brothers, and my troops are yours to*
> *command. We will certainly join you in battle." Then*
> *Jehoshaphat added, "But first let's find out what the*
> *LORD says." (II Chronicles 18:3-4, NLT)*

Seeking the Lord first and finding out in the beginning what God wants you to do is extremely important to overcoming bad habits. You need to know what the Lord says about what you are going through. Whatever God has to say is always with the intent of you coming out on top or coming out the winner.

After, King Jehoshaphat enquired to seek the Lord first, King Ahab summoned his prophets to him, and they prophesied lies. His prophets said that it is all right to go into war. However, King Jehoshaphat began to use his intuition; he did not feel comfortable about the prophets' words. Therefore, King Jehoshaphat asked a prophet to come, only this time one that was not a part of the king's prophets.

King Jehoshaphat was concerned about his life; he needed spiritual guidance. He did not want to go into a war and die prematurely. He wanted to know his outcome or at least gain a sense of whether or not this was the proper time for him to go to war. He also wanted to know whether or not this was good judgment to support King Ahab in war. Notice this scripture:

> *Howbeit when he, the Spirit of Truth, is come, he*
> *will guide you into all truth; for he shall not speak of*
> *himself; but whatsoever he shall hear, that shall he*

speak: and he will shew you things to come. (John 16:13)

When both King Ahab and King Jehoshaphat went to war against their enemies, it is interesting to note that King Ahab died, but King Jehoshaphat lived all because he was sensitive to his intuition. King Jehoshaphat felt that it was safe for him to go into battle, and as a result, he was not hurt. (II Chronicles 18:33-19:1)

Sometimes when overcoming bad habits you have to look beyond what you hear, you have to look beyond what sounds good or what sounds bad, and you have to look beyond what is being done or what is not being done. You need to listen to what is going on inside of you. What is your intuition or your gut feeling saying to you?

In most cases whatever your intuition is saying to you, that is what you need to do, especially when your intuition is full of the word of God and the Spirit of God. A Christian Spirit (intuition) will always lead you in the right direction. The reason you can be certain that the Spirit of God will lead you in the right direction is because you have the Spirit of truth within you. Therefore, when you are walking in the Spirit of truth you cannot be living a lie. (John 16:13)

World-renowned healing evangelist Kathryn Kuhlman, attributes the Holy Spirit, the inward witness, for thousands of people who received healing. Kathryn Kuhlman acknowledges that she could do nothing without the Holy Spirit (intuition) leading her on what to do and how to do it.

Robert Liardon, in his book, *Kathryn Kuhlman: A Spiritual Biography of God's Miracle Worker,* indicates how Kathryn Kuhlman relies on the direction of the Holy Spirit to heal during meetings:

I see the Holy Spirit in this area of the auditorium, she exclaims and points to the wheelchair area. Tears begin to trickle down her cheeks as she looks at the upper balcony and says, "Up there, someone is being healed of sugar diabetes." Suddenly, it's happening all over the building! People are rising from wheelchairs and from seats, amazed and inexpressibly happy. Braces are discarded. Wheelchairs are abandoned. Hearing aids are removed – forever! They are healed on the stage they go, to stand in front of the woman who has summoned them, the woman who believes in miracles. (P. 14)

The dependency upon the Holy Spirit was the main source to Kathryn Kuhlman's healing ministry. She would wait to discern or sense what she felt her intuition (Spirit Guidance) indicated for her to do. Only until she would feel the spirit empowerment, would she begin her healing service, placing special emphasis on the role of the Holy Spirit in healing.

Morton Kelsey, in his book, *Healing and Christianity*, says,

...As people came forward, Kathryn Kuhlman reached out to touch them and they fell semi-conscious into the arms of those who assisted her. Many people claimed to be healed at the service. She seemed able to discern the condition of people far from her in the highest balcony. Her book, I Believe in Miracles, was enormously popular for many years. (P. 191-192)

KEY THOUGHT: The key to successfully overcoming a bad habit is that you must get God involved.

Getting God involved in your tough spot will be the determining factor to whether or not you will go over or under. *"Call on me, and I will answer thee, and shew thee great and mighty things, which thou knowest not." (Jeremiah 33:3)* It is perfectly okay to call on God when you are in trouble. Many people think that they are misusing God or that they are unworthy of God's help during tough times, especially when they know they are not living right.

Let me say this to you: **First**, God cannot be played; you cannot use, manipulate, or fool God. **Second,** God's desire is that you ask Him for help, and when He answers you, His desire is that you will continue to follow Jesus Christ as Lord and Savior of your life. Let us look at some biblical examples of people who called on God during tough times and how God answered them and provided victory for them.

People who God helped during Tough Times

1. **Jehoshaphat and all of Judah** called on the name of God and He helped them to victory over their enemies, who had come down to destroy them. (II Chronicles 20:1-30)

2. A great fish swallowed up **Jonah the prophet**, and God heard his cry and delivered him out of his affliction. (Jonah 2:1-10)

3. **The Children of Israel** cried because of their bondage to the Egyptians. God heard them and delivered them out of trouble. (Exodus 2:23-25)

4. The Psalmist **(David)** called on the name of the Lord and God heard him and lifted him up out of the pit of despair and destruction. (Psalm 40:1-3)

5. The **demon possessed boy**'s father asked Jesus to help his

51

son and Jesus healed the boy of his demonic possession. (Mark 9:14-29)

6. A **blind beggar** received his sight when he asked Jesus to have mercy on him. Jesus showed mercy and healed him. (Luke 18:35-43)

When you call on God during tough times, God is able to heal, deliver, and set you free from fear, hurt, wrong, disappointments, buzzard behavior or repeated offenses. God can get you out of a tight place or a tough spot. The thing to remember is that there is nothing too hard for God. All you need to do is humble yourself and get God involved in your situation. God knows how to get you out. God will talk to you about what you need to do and how you need to do it in order to accomplish your need.

In her book, *Approval Addictions*, Joyce Meyer says;

> *"Determination and discipline are important in breaking the cycle of addictions, but receiving supernatural strength from God is the real key to success. Learn to run to Him instead of running to the substance or wrong behavior to which you are addicted." (P. 117)*

Many people often make commitments and vows but break them as soon as they make them. I believe one reason is they do not run to God asking Him to get involved. God will not do anything without your permission. The word **permit** means *to give one's consent or authorization to do something.* The important thing about permitting is that you allow access to be granted in your life.

Note this scripture: *"Thus saith the LORD, the Holy One*

of Israel, and his Maker, Ask me of things to come concerning my sons, and concerning the work of my hands command ye me." Isaiah 45:11) In defining the Hebrew word for **command**, it means to *give legal right to by appointing or assigning.* This concept means that God cannot get involved in your situation without you appointing Him.

For God to get involved in your situation without your approval would be in violation of the word of God. *"Behold, I stand at the door and knock; if any man hear my voice, and open the door, I will come in to him, and will sup with him, and he with me." (Revelations 3:20)*

This scripture indicates that Jesus cannot enter your life without you opening the door of your heart for Jesus. If you do not open the door of your heart, giving Jesus authority, and appointing Him to work on your behalf, Jesus will be in violation of entering your life because He was not permitted to do so. You have to give God permission to help you.

In Genesis 25:21-26, Isaac's wife, Rebekah, contrary to the woman with the issue of blood, sought God first about the complications she was having in her stomach. God immediately told Rebekah that she was birthing twins and these twins would be two rival nations that would be against one another, explaining the reason for her stomach complications.

Now think about this for a moment. If Rebekah would have sought a relative, friend or a doctor about her complications before she consulted God, she could have heard some bad news or incorrect advice. She could have been improperly diagnosed as having experienced a miscarriage, or needing to take medication for pain relief.

Rebekah did not need any advice from others at that time; what she needed was a word from God, so that she could know the truth concerning her struggling. This truth caused her not to lose unnecessary time, money and energy on things she should not be doing.

Dr. Reginald Cherry says,

> *"Don't misunderstand me. God can and does use doctors. But thank God there is a growing group of spirit-filled doctors who believe in prayer and are not confined to just one way of healing. There are too many surgeries being performed. There is too much medication being prescribed. There are pathways that God has for His people that may deviate from standard, traditional medicine and treatment as we are taught in medical school. God's ways, though, are better than our ways." (P. 51)*

In looking back at the woman with the issue of blood (Mark 5:25-29), the Bible indicates, *"She said within herself."* This statement signifies that she kept repeating this thought until she achieved what she believed.

This is very important to overcoming bad habits. **First, you need to know that you can achieve what you believe.** *"All things are possible to him that believeth"* and this woman no doubt said this belief by attempting to get to Jesus.

She knew that there lay within Jesus a supernatural ability to set her free. It is the same thing in your situation today, my brother and sister. If you can just make a point of contact with Jesus, He will make whatever is wrong right; He will fix it for you.

Second, we see that this lady stayed with it. She did not quit even though she had to put forth a lot of effort and work around crowded conditions. To get what she wanted, scripture says that she pressed. The word **press** denotes *to bear down upon, push steadily against.* Press is similar to squeezing out all the juice of a lemon.

Pressing is one of the keys to overcoming addictive or negative behaviors and mental cravings. You have to bear down, squeezing tightly and not letting go; you have to stay with it, you have to desire to recover, turn, and change so strongly that you are willing to soak up as much knowledge and input that is necessary to make you better.

Paul (Bear) Bryant

The all-great college football coach Paul (Bear) Bryant won six national championships (1961, 1964-65, 1973, 1978-79) and 13 Southeastern Conference titles during his coaching career at the University of Alabama Crimson Tide team. He did something that no other coach had done during his coaching career.

Coach Bryant strongly believed in two things: 1) *Always think of you as a winner.* His way of thinking was always to get the winners into the game. They won because of this mentality. 2) *Never quit.* When you fail or come up short, the failure should only make you want to try that much harder to win. There is an old saying, *"winners never quit and quitters never win."*

According to Barry Krauss, a key player for the University of Alabama 1978 National Championship Football Team and author of the book, *Ain't Nothin' But A Winner* says:

> *Coach Bryant did have some universal lessons that were taught to everyone—sometimes in very different ways. His biggest lesson in life and football was simple: Never quit. Yes, there were other commandments, like*

"always call your momma," and "always show your class," on which other lessons were built. But the big lesson was "never quit." (P. 22)

KEY THOUGHT: You only fail when you give up and stop trying.

If you are going to overcome bad habits you have to stay with what you know is right to do. Do not quit, you only fail when you stop trying. Although it may get tough, you have to be anchored and committed enough not to let anything distract, damage or deter you from what you are trying to accomplish. You can do it. The woman who had the issue of blood (Mark 5:25-29) stayed focused on what she believed.

A good example of a person not quitting under intense duress is our former 42nd President of the United States of America, **William J. Clinton.** During his impeachment period President Clinton stayed with his presidency; he did not step down, he did not step aside, nor did he quit. He was committed to doing what he set out to do and that was to successfully complete his second term as President of the United States of America.

Although, on a local and national level, people ridiculed, degraded, verbally abused, and invaded the former President's privacy and the privacy of his family, President Clinton did what the woman with the issue of blood did; he stayed with it. If you can hold on to what you believe, God will see you through.

Former President Bill Clinton contributes his success to the people who was around him. It is important to note that you need to surround yourself with people who will lift you up when you don't seem to have your balance in life. Former President Clinton in his book, *My Life Bill Clinton*, says:

After the impeachment ordeal, people often asked me how I got through it without losing my mind, or at least the ability to keep doing the job. I couldn't have done it if the White House staff and cabinet, including those who were angry and disappointed over my conduct, hadn't stayed with me. It would have been much harder if the American people hadn't made an early judgment that I should remain President and stuck with it. (P. 848)

It does not matter what you go through. You do not have to lose your mind; you do not have to accept defeat, or failure as your final answer. You can win, you can come out on top, and you can overcome, although it may appear that all of the surrounding evidence is pointing against you, you can win.

Senator Hillary Clinton affirms, like her husband, former President Bill Clinton, that it was her friends such as Diane Blair, Betsy Ebeling, most successful and well known artist in the world, Stevie Wonder, and many others whose support and comfort was significant in her staying focused, helped her overcome those difficult times. Senator Hillary Clinton in her book, *Living History Hillary Rodham Clinton,* says:

...As he played, I kept moving my chair closer to the piano until I was sitting right next to him. When Stevie finished, tears filled my eyes and, when I looked around, tears were running down Betsy's face and Diane's. This was one of the kindest gestures anyone made during this incredibly difficult period. (P. 478)

Another key factor is that the Clintons **continued to move on;** they did not get stuck. Anything that becomes still long enough will become stagnate; you have to keep moving. The very fact that you keep moving forward is the indicator that you have not been conquered. There is an old saying *"tough times do not last, but tough people do."*

It is also important to note that if you are going to overcome a bad habit you will need to **put forth a strong effort** to change or accomplish what you desire. You are going to have to put forth your best effort. This is what the woman with the issue of blood did; she was willing to work through any struggles to get her healing. Putting forth a strong effort caused her not to cave in, give up or quit under pressure.

Samkon Gado

A good example of a person putting forth a strong effort is the pro football player named Samkon Gado. He was the starting running back for the Green Bay Packers in 2005. He overcame great odds and refused to give up on his dream of becoming a professional football player.

The Green Bay packer website says,

> *An unlikely candidate to become the Packers? Featured back, ascended from the practice squad to lead the team in rushing, the first Green Bay rookie to hold that distinction since Kenneth Davis in 1986. (P.2)*

What was some of the things that he had to endure? He only started a few games in his college career at Liberty University, playing behind fellow backs Dre Barnes and Eugene Goodman. Gado was the third string running back. That means that two other players would start or go in to the ball game before him.

The point that I want to make is just because people are ahead of you or appear to be above you does not mean that they are better than you. **God created you to be the best.** Therefore, it is important for you not to become frustrated about what is going on in your life right now because where you are presently is not where you are going to be permanently.

Samkon Gado tried out for the Kansas City Chiefs in 2005 and was unable to make the practice squad, but running back coach James Saxon and head coach Dick Vermeil of the Chiefs encouraged Gado to continue to play football. That brings me to the next point I would like to make: try to surround yourself with people who have your best interest in mind, because when things don't look so promising in your life, people who have your best interest in mind will encourage you not to give up and support you to do what is right.

In other words, **try to find friends who will celebrate you and not tolerate you.** Through the encouragement of Coaches James Saxon and Dick Vermeil, Samkon Gado tried out for the Green Bay Packers in 2005. He started out on the Green Bay Packers practice squad but due to nagging injuries to star running back Ahman Green and backup Najeh Davenport the Packers were forced to promote Gado to sign to the Packers active roster.

> *On November 13, 2005, (which was ironically on his 23rd birthday), Gado started his first NFL game against the Atlanta Falcons. He responded to the challenge with an outstanding performance that instantly turned him into a household name for Packer faithful. Gado rushed 23 times for 103 yards and two touchdowns, and also caught a one-yard touchdown pass from Brett Faver, as the Packers won 33-25. Gado received the NFL Rookie of Week 10 award for the game. (P.3)*

This leads me to the next point I would like to make. **God can locate you right where you are;** the key to God locating you is that you remain faithful, dedicated and committed to doing what you are called to do. If you do not stop trying and if you stay committed to being faithful and walk in integrity right where you are, opportunities will become available for you to make a difference.

People that God Located

1. God located **David** out in the field: The prophet Samuel was sent by God to go to Jesse of Bethlehem to anoint a king from among his sons. Jesse presented seven sons to Samuel and the Lord chose none of them. Samuel the prophet asked if there were any more sons, so Jesse sent for his youngest son David who was out in the field. When David came in the house the prophet Samuel anointed David to be King over Israel. Although David was the last one to be called to stand before the prophet, God worked through (bypassed) all of David's brothers and located David in the field tending to the sheep. (I Samuel 16:1-13)

2. God located **Rebekah** at the well: Abraham prayed and sent his servant to find a wife for his son Isaac. When the servant arrived at the well in Abraham's home town, he prayed again for a wife for Isaac, and immediately Rebekah arrived. She was the answer to Abraham's prayer. Rebekah stayed faithful right where she was, and God located her at the well. (Genesis 24:1-26)

3. God located **Moses** on the backside of the desert: Moses was leading his father-in-law's (Jethro) sheep in so-called,

no-man's-land and God located Moses right where he was. God appeared to Moses through a burning bush. The bush was on fire, but the bush was not being burnt. This was strange to Moses, so he walked over to observe this phenomenon. It was here that Moses received his call into the ministry, to be the Pastor over the children of Israel. (Exodus 3:1-22)

4. God located the **Ethiopian eunuch** in the desert of Gaza: The Ethiopian eunuch needed guidance to understand the scriptures so that he could accept Jesus Christ as Lord and Savior of his life. God sent the Evangelist Phillip unto him. Phillip, by the direction of the Holy Spirit was able to leave a massive revival in Samaria and locate this eunuch in the desert. Phillip helped the eunuch with both becoming born-again (Christian) as well as to be baptized. (Acts 8:26-40)

Many times, breakthroughs, recoveries, or blessings come by way of you just staying with it; you have to keep chipping away at the problem, challenge, struggle, or whatever you are trying to overcome.

Just like George Washington who chopped down the cherry tree, if you maintain steadfastness or perseverance, whatever you are challenged with will break; it will come down and you will overcome. All problems can be solved. Every challenge has a solution.

The thing to remember about a problem or a challenge is that you might not receive the answer or the solution to your challenges immediately. While you are waiting is when you have to keep training to make yourself better.

Samkon Gado, although he was on the Green Bay Packers practice squad, stayed accountable and committed. He kept lifting weights, running drills and studying plays to stay active so that when his name was called, he would be ready to step in and step up and do better than what the team was accustomed.

Dr. Fredrick K.C. Price, in his book, *Integrity,* says:

> *It is easy to spout off and say you are committed to something when there is no pressure. But the true test is when the challenges start. This is when reality is revealed. You can never know whether you are acting from a deep and steadfast principle until that principle is challenged, and if you are never challenged, you never really know how deeply you believe it. Not really. (P. 102)*

An Arabian proverb quotes that perseverance is *"the greatest of all teachers." (P.433)* This proverb is important when things do not look good, feel good or sound good. You have to stay faithfully committed to doing what you do. Your time will come. Many times, people want to experience the results of instant satisfaction or success, but they fail to realize that opportunity comes with integrity, perseverance, hard work, and accountability.

> *Then the Lord said to me, "Write my answer in large, clear letters on a tablet, so that a runner can read it and tell everyone else. But these things I plan won't happen right away. Slowly, steadily, surely, the time approaches when the vision will be fulfilled. If it seems slow, wait patiently, for it will surely take place. It will not be delayed." (Habakkuk 2:2-3, NLT)*

Again, God can locate you right where you are; you just need to be faithfully committed where you are. The Bible says,

"And all these blessings shall come on thee, and overtake thee, if thou shalt hearken unto the voice of the LORD thy God." (Deuteronomy 28:2) God knows how to locate you and be a blessing to you right where you are. You just need to be consistently optimistic in doing all you know you can do and then God will help you do what you cannot do.

Although there may be delays, set backs, or even hindrances to what you are trying to accomplish, you have to keep a right attitude and be respectful to all people. Your time will come. God will bless you and increase you. Let us look at some biblical people who were faithful and committed, thus opportunity came knocking.

Opportunity came knocking to these people:

1. **Queen Esther**–She became the queen in place of Queen Vashti. This replacement allowed Queen Esther to be in a position to be a lifesaver and restorer when a commandment came forth to kill her people, the Jews. A nation was saved from death because of Queen Esther making a difference. (Esther 2:17, 4:14)

2. **The Apostle Peter** – He was on the rooftop of his house praying when God came to him in a trance and told Peter that three men would come looking for him. He was not to hesitate in going with them or to doubt anything. (Acts 10:9-23)

3. **The First Disciples** – Jesus came to each disciple specifically, calling them by name to follow him and to be his disciples, and they (Simon surname Peter and his brother Andrew, James and his brother John) followed him. (Mark 1:16-20)

Samkon Gado knew that he could be a professional football player. You have to know that you can get through whatever you are going through. With strong determination and commitment; you can bounce back, overcoming the adversities from a great struggle in your life.

In addition, Samkon Gado went on to have a remarkable year, winning Rookie of the Week awards and NFL Offensive Rookie of the Month. He holds a number of Green Bay Packers franchise records for a rookie that includes most rushing yards in a game (171) and most touchdowns in a single season (7).

The Rabbit versus The Turtle

I remember in elementary school when my teacher taught us the story of the rabbit and the turtle (*hare and tortoise*) that ran a race. Although the rabbit appeared to be stronger, faster and even smarter than the turtle, the rabbit lost the race because the turtle had contentment, commitment, discipline and determination not to give up.

If you are going to win in life, you will have to have the mentality of this turtle. You will have to be content with who you are, have commitment to what you are doing, and discipline yourself enough to stay in your lane. You will make it to the end this way and you will be the winner.

Although, you may hit some rough spots, and go through some storms, speak to some mountains, and cry when you are all alone. You can still make it. You can win, and you can endure until the end.

The Bible says, *"...But he that shall endure unto the end, the same shall be saved." (Mark 13:13)* When you can learn to stand firm, trusting in God and His word, you will accomplish the thing you so desire, because it is God's desire to give you the desires of your heart. (Luke 12:32, Psalms 37:4)

The word **endure** according to the Expanded Vine's Expository Dictionary of New Testament Words, is *hupomeno* or *hoop-om-en'-o* which denotes *to abide under or to bear up courageously.* **Endure** also carries with it the connation of *patiently waiting.* To endure is to rise or bear up under intense pressure. You will not be intimidated, distracted, or manipulated by what you know or don't know; you will only believe for what you are trying to accomplish and you will be persistent in waiting to get your promises.

It was the turtle's consistency that allowed him to complete and win the race. The turtle was constantly the same during the entire race and was not moved by intimidation, distraction or manipulation by the rabbit getting so far ahead. The turtle stayed within his means and although he moved slowly, the turtle understood that he was making progress. Little progress is better than no progress at all. Stay active and keep your mindset fixed on moving forward.

In junior high school, I was a member of the track and field team; my main event was the mile race. My coach would often remind the team runners to watch out for the opposing team's rabbit. The rabbit was a runner whose specific job was to make you burn out, and lose the race.

The rabbits initially would have all the attention on them because they would take off so fast at the beginning of the race, but that was only a manipulation or distraction to make you speed up, only to burn out, getting tired and lose the race. The rabbit would very seldom finish the race. One reason is that you just cannot fly around the track when you start out, you have to pace yourself, and this will give you the endurance to finish the race strongly.

Many people are attempting to be like the rabbit. They are trying to fly through the process of overcoming bad habits; they want microwave (instant) victory but do not understand that sometimes their victory will be the result of them enduring the process.

Another reason the rabbit would very seldom finish the race is that the rabbit was set in place to help its other teammates win. The rabbit could be another form of a guinea pig. The rabbit's sole purpose is to set you up greatly for a big fall.

The interesting thing about the turtle in the race is that he did not fall for any of the rabbit's chauvinistic, facade behaviors. The turtle stayed within the perimeters of what he could do, and did it well, and did not allow all the external situations to influence him to do something that he could not or did not want to do. In other words, the turtle stayed within his means and did not get outside of them.

Staying within your means is going to be one of your main tools to you overcoming the obstacles of life that you may face. Again, you will have to develop determination, contentment and commitment to endure through the tough times. Stay in your lane; do not get upset or jealous because of what you see other people doing. You have to know who you are, what you can do, be content and commit to doing your best. You do your best and let God do the rest.

In his book, *Contentment,* Dr. I.V. Hilliard says,

> *"The root of contentment, the root of this place of peace and satisfaction is linked with me knowing who I am. I have to know who I am because at that point, I am ready to function in Life. When I know who I am and establish my heart in what I know, I break free*

of the negative prediction and manipulative tactics of others and I am free to live out God's exciting plan for my life. When I know who I am and I establish in my heart what I know, then and only then will I break free of every negative prediction. When people say, "You will not make it" and try to keep you down, you will break free..." (P. 17)

The turtle stayed the course and won the race. There is another reason for the turtle winning the race; he **never looked back**. Another main tool in overcoming the obstacles of life is that you cannot look back. The only time you need to look back is when you are reflecting on the goodness that God has done for you in times past. Other than that, you should never look back, especially when you become negative, sad, depressed, when you begin to reject yourself or look down on yourself.

Don't stop because of everything negative in life that has happened to you; you have to keep moving on and do not let your past get you down. On the other hand, the rabbit kept looking back. He wanted to see how far ahead he was of the turtle. The rabbit was so far ahead of the turtle until he decided to take a nap, and while the rabbit slept, the turtle passed by the rabbit and won the race.

Don't Come Up Short

An example of not looking back is when I was at home one night watching a college football game. A defensive back intercepted the football and ran about sixty yards. When he was close to the touchdown line he kept looking back; the opposing team player grabbed him by the back of his jersey and pulled him down at the one-yard line.

The point is this: in life, many people keep looking back and because they keep looking back, it slows them down significantly. The looking back prevents them from crossing over or entering into their greatness. Many times, we are right at the point of entering into what we desire but because we turn back or look back, we come up short.

In order to overcome bad habits you have to get it settled that I am going on, no more looking back, or turning back. I forgive myself and I forgive any and everybody who has done me wrong. You have to be committed and not allow yourself to be concerned about what others think, feel, say or do to you. Don't let them stop you from doing what God said you could do.

What are you looking at?

Let us take an automobile for instance; every automobile has windows and mirrors attached to it. The windows and mirrors that I have chosen to select are as follows; the front window, the back window, the rearview mirror, and the side mirror. When you are going forward, the **front window** is designed specifically to get you to your destination. In addition, not only are you focused on where you are headed (destination), but you have a clear and wide view of what is out in front of you because you are looking ahead.

When you are going forward and you decide for whatever reason to turn around, and look through the **back window**, it becomes impossible for you to stay focused on where you are headed. The reality is that you do not even know where you are headed because you are turned around completely.

When you turn completely around, you lose focus of what is before you; you will be like a wreck going somewhere to happen. When you look back, remember, you lose sight of where you are going. It was once said, *"If you don't know where you are headed then any road will get you there."* In order to get to where you need to be in life, you must have some sense of direction on where you are trying to go.

When you look through your **rearview mirror** you are not physically turning around to look back, but you look back because you have decided to see a small glimpse of what is going on behind you. You never spend the major part of your time looking in the rearview mirror; the rearview mirror is only designed for you to take a glimpse of what is behind you for the moment, then eyes face front, then move in the desired direction.

The **side mirror** is designed for you to be aware of what is going on around you. However, you cannot be so focused on what is going on around you until you lose sight of what is ahead of you. You only need to look in the side mirror to reflect on what is happening around you, and then you put your eyes forward and keep your attention on where you are going.

One of the purposes for windows and mirrors being attached to a car is so that you can safely arrive at your destination; overcoming bad habits has a similar approach. If you want to arrive at your destination in life, you will need to use your available resources appropriately and stay focused on the things that you want to do.

In addition, you should only look back on your life to reflect on good things or things that you can learn or grow from; however, you will have to make it a point that you will not dwell on past disappointments. Dwelling on past disappointments will cause you to criticize yourself to the point of becoming addicted to chaos and confusion in your life. Some people are addicted to experiencing trouble.

The Bible says that you shall be above only and not

beneath and that God will make you the head and not the tail. (Deuteronomy 28:13) The Bible says that God will increase you more and more, and your children. (Psalms 115:14) After reading those scriptures, I am fully persuaded that God's will for your life is that you excel. Bad habits and negative behaviors will stunt Godly maximization in your life.

Again, the Bible says that God will make you the head. The head means that you are the man or woman in charge. When you go through difficult situations, you must understand two things: 1) God is going to get you out and 2) where you are is not where you are going to permanently remain.

God's Blessing during Tough Times

1. **Daniel** was put in a den of lions, but he did not stay in the den because God delivered him out of the den of lions. Daniel had full confidence that God would not allow him to be eaten by the lions. However, those that excused Daniel of doing wrong for praying to his God three times a day, were thrown into the den of lions where the lions ate them to pieces. (Daniel 6:10-24)

2. The **Hebrew boys** were thrown into the fiery furnace because they refused to worship the king's idol. However, they did not stay in the fiery furnace because God delivered them out of the fiery furnace and there was no harm nor hurt to them when they came out of the fire. All their accusers were thrown into the fiery furnace; they were burned to death. (Daniel 3:1-30)

3. **Joseph** was put in a pit, sold into slavery, and thrown into prison, but he did not stay. He got out of the pit, slavery and prison and God elevated him to the second

highest position in all the land of Egypt. God can get you out of whatever you are stuck in. (Genesis 37:23-28, 39:20-23, 41:37-45)

The key to Daniel, the Hebrew Boys and Joseph coming out of everything is that the blessing of God was upon their lives. **The Blessing** is *an empowerment or enablement to succeed.* When you have the blessing of God, you have the favor of God to prosper in life. It does not matter how bad things get or look, God is going to bring you out and take you into your wealthy place.

KEY THOUGHT: You are created by God and for God and there are certain things in life, which can only be accomplished by God. (Isaiah 43:1-2, 10-11)

The Bible indicates in the book of Matthew 6:33 *"Seek ye first the Kingdom of God and his righteousness; and all these things shall be added unto you."* Total restoration and recovery begins and ends with God. You were created by God and for God and there are certain things in life that you cannot and will not be able to obtain until you seek God and discover what He wants you to do. Seeking the kingdom of God is discovering God's way of doing things. God's way is always the right way.

Our own ways often lead us astray and down wrong paths. Note this scripture: *"There is a way that seems right to a man and appears straight before him, but at the end of it is the way of death."* *(Proverbs 16:25 AMP)* This is why it is so important to take every bad habit and every trying situation to God; it is God who will work all things for your good.

In II Chronicles 16:12-13, the Bible says, *"King Asa of Judah was diseased in his feet until his disease was exceedingly great. Yet in his disease he sought not the Lord, but the physicians. Then he died."* The reason for his death is that he did not seek the Lord first. God did not mind the doctors. In fact, God shared with the nation of Israel that because they did not walk in accordance to His commandments and statutes, their physicians was unable to recover the health of the people. *(Jeremiah 8:22)*

God works through doctors and medications that they prescribe: *"A merry heart doeth good like a medicine."* (Proverbs 17:22) However, in this particular situation, the only one that could have healed this king was God. You are created by God and for God and there are certain things that can only be accomplished by God.

The book, *Living Sober,* says:

> *"Some drugs have legitimate value and are beneficial when administrated by knowledgeable physicians if used solely as directed and discontinued when they are no longer a medical necessity." (P. 52)*

There is nothing wrong with taking appropriate medications prescribed by a trained, licensed physician. However, we are not to be dependent upon medications/doctors to make us better. We are to be dependent totally on God. *"I will lift up mine eyes unto the hills, from whence cometh my help. My help cometh from the Lord, which made heaven and earth."* (Psalms 121:1-2)

The reason for King Asa's death is obvious; he did not seek the Lord first. He sought the Lord <u>after</u> the fact. God does not want us to seek Him after we have made a mess. God wants us to seek Him <u>before</u> we make a mess.

This King had a very prominent position...he was the King

of Judah, which indicates that he was over the praise and worship of that particular tribe. Yet in the midst of his dancing and shouting (and for some today, even speaking in tongues) the king died, because he did not put the Lord first.

CHAPTER 3

‖‖‖‖‖‖‖‖‖‖‖‖‖‖‖‖‖‖‖‖‖‖‖

The Keys to Change

KEY THOUGHT: The true essence of change is not found in what a person says but in what a person does. (Matthew 7:20)

An important key to change is **asking people for help.** This key is one of the most important keys to the entire process to change. In order to successfully overcome negative behaviors and to recover from bad situations, you must ask people for help.

Again, asking people for help is one of the major keys to change; there is an old saying that says: *"If you don't know, then ask somebody."* That is true because if you do not ask, in many cases people do not know that you have a need, especially in today's society. People are so busy with their own affairs of life, they do not have time to stop and question your personal struggles. Therefore, you have to make it known that you need help. There is nothing wrong with that.

In Luke 18:1-8, a woman kept asking a judge for help and finally the judge granted help to her. This woman was persistent and she looked in the right place. She went to the judge, although the judge was very selfish, he had the resources that she needed (the authority to set her free) and she seized the moment by taking charge of the rights and privileges that were allotted her.

You have to be strong-willed about what you want to do and let nothing stop you from doing what is right. This woman went to the person who could make a difference in her life and the judge granted the request that she desired.

Many times, people in need of help go to the wrong people and do the wrong things which result in unsuccessfulness. The key is that you have to stay with what you believe God will do for you until you accomplish what you desire. You have to confess and believe that you will receive and are patient enough to watch it happen.

When **Hurricane Katrina** hit New Orleans, Louisiana in 2005, the residents' lives were totally changed. Immediately the state was declared to be in a state of emergency.

A **state of emergency** is *when you are in severe (life threatening) need of help.* Before major help could come to the city of New Orleans the residents had to declare that they needed help. When they declared their inability to recover on their own, immediately people went out of their way to be a blessing.

If the people of New Orleans had refused help, then their ability to overcome a major devastation would have been nearly impossible without the help of others. One thing is certain, it would have definitely taken New Orleans a longer time to rebuild if the residents would have tried to rebuild on their own.

Furthermore, why would you even try to attempt to do something to that magnitude on your own? Many people try to take on things in life that are much larger than they can handle. What these people need to do is precisely what the city of New Orleans did...declare that they need help. When you do that, help will be on the way. Just ask for help—especially, when you have people readily equipped and financially there for you.

Reasons People Do Not Ask For Help

There are at least two reasons why some people don't ask for help: 1) They are too ashamed and embarrassed to let people know that they are not doing so well; 2) They do not want people in their so-called business. I call it pride and arrogance. When you know you need help, there are good people available who would love to help you. Don't refuse to get help; accept their help.

What could possibly be the reason for people not asking for help? Again, it could be shame, embarrassment, pride or arrogance. If you are going to get the help you need, you will have to let your ego go and trust people to help you. Scripture says, "...Yet ye have not, because ye ask not." (James 4:2) You must get others involved in your process of overcoming a bad habit because they will often have the resources readily available to aid in your recovery process.

KEY THOUGHT: If change is to occur and be permanent in your life, you must be willing to change your negative behavior and be determined not to change back into the negative behavior that God brought you out.

Biblical Characters Who Jesus Helped

1. **The Leper** who came to Jesus and asked if Christ would heal him: Jesus' response was I will be clean and the man was healed of his leprosy. (Mark 1:40-42)

2. **The Centurion man** came to Jesus and asked him to speak a word of healing for his servant, Jesus spoke the word of healing over this servant and the servant was immediately healed. (Matthew 8:5-13)

3. **The Apostle Peter** walked on water and lost focus and began to sink, fearing that he was going to drown. He called out to Jesus for help and immediately Jesus helped him by pulling him up to safety. (Matthew 14:28-32)

4. **The Syrophenican woman** came to Jesus for Him to heal her daughter of an unclean spirit. Jesus spoke the word of healing and the woman's daughter was healed. (Mark 7:24-30)

Now if all these people find rest, safety, comfort, healing, deliverance and restoration from their problems, so can you. In addressing the Syrophenican woman in Mark 7:24-30 who came to Jesus for healing, something can be learned from her interaction with Jesus. It is important to note her *consistency*. Remember, consistency is crucial in you overcoming or breaking a bad habit. You cannot give up and you cannot take no initially as a rejection. No, today can be yes, tomorrow.

It is also interesting to note that everyone who came to Jesus received exactly what they were asking for, which indicated that Jesus will do the same thing for you and me today, if you will only call on him for help. Jesus Christ has made a promise that He will hear us and answer our desire.

The Bible says,

> "And this is the confidence that we have in him, that,
> if we ask any thing according to his will, he heareth us:
> And if we know that he hear us, whatsoever we ask,
> we know that we have the petitions that we desired
> of him. (I John 5:14-15)

Another key to change is **awareness.** Before help can come to a person there must be an acknowledgement of the wrong that the person has done. When you are **aware** that means that *you have a clear insight or understanding about the situation.* To be aware is closely related to admitting. The word **admit** means that *you are aware of the truth and are willing to own up* to your responsibility to get it right.

When a person can admit that things are not working the way they should, this admittance means they are fully aware and honest about how they need to do something different in order to produce the results they desire. This admittance opens the door to change.

Dr. Thomson K. Mathew says,

> "Change in a person or ministry is not easy. Although it
> may be a fearful process, it is better to make necessary
> changes, rather than dealing with the consequences
> of trying to maintain the status quo. God can help us
> to make the required changes. As long as we stay in
> denial, we refuse to accept God's help for us. The best
> thing we can do is get beyond denial and acknowledge
> the problems. This process should lead us to seek God's
> help. While denial does not bring healing, admitting
> our problems and seeking God's help will." (P. 92)

When you admit something, that means that you will not shift the blame. You will place the responsibility where it belongs which is upon you. To shift the blame means you will find someone else to fault for your failures, shortcomings or mistakes, when realistically the reason for your downfalls, failures, shortcomings and mistakes, is you.

Let us look at **a case study on shifting the blame**. We will use a married couple as an example. The husband is experiencing great difficulties with isolation from his family. He is overwhelmed with paying the bills, which results in him working more often than he should. This causes the wife to nag and lash out at her husband when he comes through the door after work because he is spending very little time with his wife and children.

This couple constantly argues with each other. His wife says that the husband is to blame and that she has a right to get angry if he does not own up to his manly responsibility. On the contrary, the husband feels that his wife is just not supportive and because she puts him down all the time, he prefers to stay away from his wife to avoid conflict.

Let us examine the case study. First, both members of the couple are to blame for their relationship being in the condition that it is. The wife cannot blame the husband and the husband cannot blame the wife. They are one...even if the wife is 99 percent correct. She still has one percent that she must work on to help improve the marriage.

Just because you may know the contributing cause to the problem, the question must be asked, what you can do to make it better. Often, people focus on others and they fail to look at themselves as having a part to play in the situation.

Second, you must avoid the game *WHO STARTED IT?* The

answer to this question does not matter. Always remember to observe and acknowledge the part that you will play in the situation. Many times, couples get caught up in the fact of who started it and fail to realize that it takes two to tango. Again, one of the best ways to overcome the spirit of blame is to understand the role that you play in the situation.

Third, do not allow your differences to cause frustration for you. One of the ways to overcome the blame game is to try to recognize that people are different. They will not think and do things like you. Many marriages and good relationships have crumbled, fallen apart, because people do not value the importance of difference.

When you recognize your inability and powerlessness over bad habits, that realization opens up the door for God to intervene. He will give you supernatural power to overcome your bad habit because of Him surrounding you with His love, protection and guidance.

Notice this scripture:

> *"Confess your faults one to another, and pray one for another, that ye may be healed. The effectual fervent prayer of a righteous man availeth much."* (James 5:16)

Another definition for the word, **admit,** is to *spill the beans.* Spilling the beans is better known as confession. When you confess, you announce everything that is wrong. You will not be a hypocrite nor water down what is necessary to produce change on your part.

In addition, the word **confession** in the Greek or New Testament of the Bible is *homologeo* which is pronounced *hom-ol-og-eh'-o* which means *to speak the same thing;* you will say or agree with what God's word says about you. You will only say what is good because every good and perfect thing comes from God. (James 1:17) What you say is what will happen to you, therefore, you should not speak words of doubt or words that are going to destroy you.

Scripture says,

> *Let no foul or polluting language, nor evil word nor unwholesome or worthless talk [ever] come out of your mouth, but only such [speech] as is good and beneficial to the spiritual progress of others, as is fitting to the need and the occasion, that it may be a blessing and give grace (God's Favor) to those who hear it. (Ephesians 4:29, AMP)*

There is healing in confession. In many cases, people struggle with confession because they are afraid that once their failures and weaknesses are exposed, they fear people will not look at them in the same way as before the confession. Another reason some people find it difficult to tell their story to others is because they have blocked the things they need to confess from their conscious awareness, and refuse to deal with these things because of the pain and hurt that is associated with their past.

Most people do not understand that in conscious awareness, you deal with the pain that is associated with past hurts; you get to the point to where you will recognize and work through whatever is necessary to make you better. When you admit, you realize and confess what you have done, first to God, then to yourself and then to your fellow brothers and sisters...only when it is appropriate to do so without more injury.

Another key to change is **humility**. Scripture lets us know that if we exalt ourselves, then pride will bring us low. However, if we humble ourselves, God will take us high. (Matthew 23:12) In some cases, people who learned to humble themselves from difficult experiences seem to be more open.

They seem to be more tolerant and behave better, extending themselves in love and compassion to others because they have worked through pain, hurt, bitterness, the fear of disapproval, shame and guilt. The humble person always has reliance and an assurance that God is on their side in everything.

The Bible says:

> *"If it had not been for the Lord who was on our side, when men rose up against us, then they would have quickly swallowed us up alive when their wrath was kindled against us." (Psalm 124:2-3)*

Humble people know that they would not be in the blessed position and place that they are currently in, if it had not been for the Lord, who is on their side. Humble people's confidence is built on nothing less than Jesus Christ and His righteousness.

In his book *"Breaking Out of Trouble"* Dr. Creflo Dollar says,

> *"God wants to exalt you. He wants you submitted under His hand so that* **He may exalt you in due time.** *There's one thing we know about "due season." It always comes. But when will you be exalted? When you get yourself in a position to be exalted. And that position is in humility under the commandments of God." (P. 162)*

One of the ways to overcome struggles is to realize that you are powerless over your situation, and without the help of God, you will not succeed. Humility is a total reliance on God.

The enemy (devil) has blinded many people into thinking that humility is weakness. Humility is not weakness; it is a total surrendering to God's leading.

Notice this scripture:

> *When the other disciples saw what was about to happen, they exclaimed, "Lord, should we fight? We brought the swords!" And one of them slashed at the high priest's servant and cut off his right ear. But Jesus said, "Don't resist anymore." And he touched the place where the man's ear had been and healed him. (Luke 22:49-51, NLT)*

Jesus told Peter not to resist but to permit his arrest; there was nothing weak about Peter cutting off the soldier's ear. Most people would think that Peter was demonstrating courage; however, Jesus demonstrated courage by showing compassion to restore the man's ear that was cut off. One of the things that cannot be overlooked is that Jesus had compassion for people even in the midst of his betrayal and arrest. That's humility.

One of the reasons for Peter cutting off the soldier's ear is that he had a problem with surrendering to God's will. He was unwilling to humble himself at that moment. In addition, if Peter had prayed as Jesus indicated in the Garden of Gethsemane (Matthew 26:36-46), Peter would have been so full of compassion that cutting off the man's ear would never have crossed his mind. Prayer would have allowed Peter to be filled with the love of God. Moreover, God's love motivated Jesus to restore the soldier's ear.

Another very good scripture reference for humility is the Hebrew children who would not bow down to worship King Nebuchadnezzar's golden image. Notice what scripture says:

And these three men, Shadrach, Meshach, and Abednego, fell down bound into the midst of the burning fiery furnace. Then Nebuchadnezzar, the king, was astonished, and rose up in haste, and spake, and said unto his counselors, Did not we cast three men bound into the midst of the fire? They answered and said unto the king, True, O King. He answered and said, Lo, I see four men loose, walking in the midst of the fire, and they have no hurt; and the form of the fourth is like the Son of God. (Daniel 3:23-25)

The Hebrew children humbled themselves; they did not fight, resist or compromise their belief in God. (Daniel 3:14-23) Neither did they fight or resist the king throwing them into the fire; they humbled themselves falling down bound into the midst of the fire, signifying that they had humbled themselves to the will of God.

The Hebrew children humbled themselves, and as a result of them humbling themselves, God was able to deliver them from the fire. If they had had the wrong attitude when they were thrown into the fire, the fire would have burned them alive.

When overcoming bad habits it is important for you to humble yourself. If you refuse to humble yourself when you go through, you could be burned alive. There are times in life, rather than fighting and resisting what you are going through, just humble yourself, submit to God and allow Him to bring you out of what you are going through.

Another important key to change is to **confront your issues.** You will have to come to a point when you stop running from your challenges and begin to deal with them, because those bad habits will not go away. Only until you take authority over certain issues in the name of Jesus will the bad habits be broken.

You have to get to a place where you are fed up with feeling sorry for yourself and begin to do something about it.

In his book, *"Loose That Man and Let Him Go"*, Bishop T. D. Jakes says,

> *"...One truth confronts you: You can never become who you want to be until you can drop who you used to be. If you want to be free, you must be willing to challenge all definitions of your masculinity. You have to be willing to confront issues that other men run from. Freedom only comes when you challenge yourself, when you open up and say things to yourself that you might not have admitted to your wife, to your friend, or to your parents. It is time to confront old issues." (P. 22)*

If your situation is going to get better then you must come face to face with the reality of the truth to allow the process of healing to begin. It is important for you to identify your wrong, and humbly admit that you are wrong. If you do not admit you are wrong, you will get to the point to where you justify one sin and hate another, when the truth of the matter is that all sin is wrong and no sin is to be favored.

> *"The fear of the Lord is to hate evil; pride, and arrogance, and the evil way, and forward mouth, do I hate." (Proverbs 8:13)*

Dr. Bruce Wilkinson says,

> *"To "confront" means to come face to face with; to stand in front of, to bring together for comparison or examination. Originally the word came from the Latin*

confrontare, meaning to have a common border, and
eventually came to mean to bring agreement through
pointing out the boundary that has been overrun."
(P342)

In confronting your situation, you will need to be open to hearing and doing things that you might not like. When confronting your situation, people will sometimes tell you things about yourself that you did not know or maybe you know, but do not want to hear. It is important to be open and accepting so that change can take place.

Naaman's Acceptance

A good biblical example of a person being open and willing to accept change can be located in II Kings 5:19. Naaman, a leper, was instructed by the Prophet Elisha to wash himself seven times in the river of Jordan to be healed of his leprosy. This procedure is important because if freedom, breakthroughs, healing, promotion and increase is going to take place in your life you must be willing to listen and to carry out the instruction that has been given to you.

Now you would think after hearing the words of a prophet of God, you would go forth and do what is said— not so with Naaman. He was very egotistical. However, after being persuaded by his servant that he had nothing to lose, Naaman did as Elisha instructed.

If you are going to be restored, to be set free, and to overcome, you have to put your ego down. You must put your opinions down and do what is required for the process of healing to take place. Whatever God tells you to do, do it, because His instruction is going to work whether or not you feel like it.

Another important thing to note is **God will often work through people to give you what you need**. God has always used mankind as a vehicle to transport His goods. Therefore, you have to listen to spiritual authority, the doctors, the weight instructor, those who are trained, qualified, and placed in a position to help you get better.

If things are going to get better for you... and trust me... things **will** get better, you need to listen and carry out the instructions to make you better. Naaman settled it within himself that he was going to do what was instructed and gave it a try. As a direct result of him listening to the spiritual advisor, he was healed of his leprosy.

His change came because he did what he did not want to do. Naaman was very fortunate that he received his healing. Sometimes people let the answer to what they are going through pass them by. If you do not move in the proper time, you can miss everything that can make the situation right.

Naaman thought that because of his prestigious position and status as a General over the Syrian nation, his position qualified him to have special treatment. One of the reasons that Naaman did not want to submerse himself in the Jordan River is because it was not as clean as some other surrounding rivers.

Naaman preferred to be submersed in the clean surrounding rivers; he felt dipping in a dirty river would make him look bad because he was supposedly, "the Man." Naaman failed to realize that his healing was not in the water that he would wash in, but in the obedience of following God's instructions.

Scripture says, *"For if ye be willing and obedient, ye will eat the good of the land." (Isaiah 1:19)* You must do it God's way if you are going to see the results of the manifestation of change.

In his book, *If You Need Healing Do These Things*, Oral Roberts refers to Naaman:

> "It takes a humble spirit for one to change like that. This is a marvelous thing. It doesn't take long for a man to change if he wants to. But he must want to. When he accepts God's correction, the Spirit of Christ enters him and he is a "new creation" – old things are passed away; behold, all things are become new (2 Corinthians 5:17). Repentance is a change of mind before it becomes a change of heart. General Naaman gave the order and they went to the river. With Elisha's message ringing in his ears, **go and wash**, he plunged into the muddy, yellow water of the famous river Jordan. As he did so, there were only a few ripples on the water revealing that the great man was all under." (P. 45)

Often, people cannot overcome bad habits because they become defensive, angry or resistant when they are confronted with their negative activity. Some people will go as far as trying to use reverse manipulation, attempting to make it appear that something is wrong with you, as an attempt to run away from their own issues.

Again, you cannot run from change you have to be open and willing to do whatever is necessary for positive change to occur. Peter is a good example of a person being open and willing to do things differently in order to produce the results that he desires.

The Bible says:

> "When He had stopped speaking, He said to Simon (Peter), Put out into the deep [water], and lower your

> *nets for a haul, And Simon (Peter) answered, Master,*
> *we toiled all night [exhaustingly] and caught nothing*
> *[in our nets]. But on the ground of Your word, I will*
> *lower the nets [again]. And when they had done this,*
> *they caught a great number of fish; and as their nets*
> *were [at the point of] breaking, They signed to their*
> *partners in the other boat to come and take hold with*
> *them, And they came and filled both the boats, so that*
> *they began to sink." (Luke 5:4-7, AMP)*

If Peter had been rebellious to Jesus' words, Peter would have missed or never experienced the blessing that Jesus had for him. I believe that many people are missing certain break-throughs and having great difficulties overcoming bad habits because they have a problem with confrontation. Confrontation is never to be feared—especially when it is coming from some one who is trying to be a blessing to you, and you know that this person has who has your best interest in mind.

Confronting your issues is important in overcoming bad habits because if you dismiss the truth, you will be blind to what can set you free. In order to receive truth you will have to open yourself to receive what has been told to you.

> *"Wherefore lay apart all filthiness and superfluity of*
> *naughtiness, and receive with meekness the engrafted*
> *word, which is able to save your soul." (James 1:21)*

It will be to your advantage to receive constructive criticism because being willing to hear the constructive criticism will save your soul. Therefore, you will have to put aside your pride and ego and become sensitive to the truth so that you are open to change. Then, and only then, will you break the cycle of addic-tive or negative repeated behavior.

Bishop T.D. Jakes, in his book, *Loose That Man and Let Him Go*, says,

> *"I am not overly concerned about witches, demons, sorcery, or astrology. As bad as crime is, I am not worried about muggers, thieves, rapists, or con artists. I don't want to be their victim, but they are not my greatest dread. Nor do I suffer anxiety thinking about a figure dressed in red with a pitchfork and a pointed tail that peers in the window making evil suggestions to me. If there is anything that I constantly fight against and wrestle with, it is the enemy in me. That is the one I am most concerned about – the enemy "in-a-me"!" (P. 22)*

Another key to change is to **become accountable.** One reason why God's people are very often attacked by wrong influences and decisions is that they are not accountable to anyone. Accountability will help protect, guide, comfort and correct your behavior. (Galatians 6:2)

Many times, disaster and spiritual failure occur because a person has no accountability. People who are accountable produce great life-changing results. Their goals are often achieved because they have others working with them to encourage, support and steer them in the right direction. Failure does not happen with the right kind of accountability.

KEY THOUGHT: If you have to hide or sneak to do something, this thing is wrong.

Unaccountable Christians struggle with making people aware

of where they are and what is going on with them. Their availability to commitment to others is weak; also, they rarely attend church on Sundays, and when they do come to church, they are in a hurry. They live isolated lives from fellowshipping with true believers for fear that negative behavior will be spotlighted.

I have learned that most people who have difficulty with accountability are afraid of exposure; exposure will bring light to inadequate and undisciplined behavior. Therefore, exposure is good because whatever is wrong now has the possibility of becoming right.

In his book, *Over the Top*, Zig Ziglar says,

> *"Speaking of being a team player, if one of your goals is to break a destructive habit like smoking, it's ideal if you can form a partnership with another person who has also decided to quit smoking. Make a commitment to call each other every evening, and discuss how you handled the day. Inquire specifically of the other person if he or she, too, abstained from smoking that day. The fact that you know the call is coming will often be the deterrent you need not to light up that day. Yes, a team effort is very helpful in reaching your goal."* (P. 217)

True partnership or accountability will break the spirit of dysfunction and bring about social structure. True accountability seeks to bring the best out of an individual. People who are <u>not</u> accountable often refuse to make strong commitments and very seldom become involved in special events and occasions.

Lack of accountability opens the door for wrong decision making and for the devil to come in to take the person prisoner. *"And that they may recover themselves out of the snare of the devil, who are taken captive by him at his will."* (II Timothy 2:26)

If you walk under an umbrella on a rainy day and you walk away from the umbrella, there is no doubt that you are going to get wet. That is the way it works in the body of Christ...as long as we stay accountable there is a spiritual covering. The moment we walk away from that covering, we allow ourselves to be exposed to the attacks of the enemy or the negative influences of the world.

Another key to change is that you need to **get a plan and work the plan.** This advice is so important because it gives you something to measure your results. The plan will help you stay focused, setting boundaries to help you do what is right, to prevent you from participating and practicing consistently wrong behaviors. With a good plan in place, you will literally be able to determine your progression.

Pastor Crelfo Dollar, in his book, *SOS! Help My flesh Needs Discipline,* says,

> *"Believing God to break an addiction is no different than believing God for a new bicycle. You must find some Word to stand on. Mediate on that Word. Speak that Word out and keep your mouth from saying anything contrary to that Word. And finally, you must put corresponding action to your faith." (P. 55)*

A good plan will always have corresponding action; corresponding action is what produces the results of the plan that has been set in place to overcome the bad habit or addiction. Without corresponding action, your plan will not work because corresponding action is like the wheels to an automobile. If you take them off you will get nowhere.

Corresponding action is what you do with the information that has been made available to you. If you receive productive information about your situation and you do not apply or implement what you have learned, you will have ineffective results because you fail to apply what you know.

Scripture says,

> Don't fool yourself into thinking that you are a listener
> when you are anything but, letting the Word go in
> one ear and out the other. Act on what you hear!
> Those who hear and don't act like those who glance
> in the mirror, walk away, and two minutes later have
> no idea who they are, what they look like. (James
> 1:22-24, TM)

The book of James in the Bible indicates that those who only receive the words are deceived, because it takes more to getting results in life than just believing and receiving the word. You must apply the word. Those who do not apply the word of God to their situation have not completely obeyed the word of God.

Corresponding action is being a doer of what you have heard. It is a connecting factor between what you know, and what you are doing with what you know. In order to overcome bad habits you must first become aware of what you are doing, then you must gain insight about how you can stop doing what you are doing; next, you must apply (corresponding action) what you know to stop doing what you are doing.

In regards to setting goals, Dr. Mike Murdock in his book *The Making of a Champion* says,

> "Take four sheets of paper. At the top of sheet number
> one, write, "My lifetime dreams and goals." Now write
> in total detail everything you would like to become, do
> or have during your lifetime. Dream your dreams in

detail on paper. Now, take sheet number two and write, "My 12 month goals." Now list everything you want to get done within the next 12 months. Now, take the third sheet of paper and write, "My 30 day goals." Now write out in detail what you would like to accomplish for the next 30 days. Now take a fourth sheet of paper and write "My ideal success daily routine." Now write down the six most important things you will do in the next 24 hours. The secret of your future is hidden in your daily routine. Set your goals." (P.16)

What I mean by getting a plan is setting up approaches and techniques that will successfully stop you from doing what you do not want to do. You will have to come up with some new ideas (your plan) that will work, and then it is equally important for you to carry out your plan.

Many people fail when it comes to setting goals. They know what they should do but for whatever reason they do not get around to doing it until the problem is detrimental or life threatening. You must get a plan and work the plan in order for the plan to work for you.

Dr. Bridget E. Hilliard, in her book, *The Will to Win*, says,

The pursuit of success is always a very personal matter that requires focus, discipline and endurance. We are equipped by God with the potential to raise our productivity and performance through purposeful effort. Behavioral change that equates into performance change is always the product of human effort sustained by divine help. It is through developing a will to win and having an effective strategy for success that goals and dreams can be accomplished. (P. 9)

Why Some People Do Not Change

1. **Inability to control emotions** – Often, when people are under extreme attack, they will allow their feelings to run wild; they will overreact to situations, and later learn that what they were experiencing was not very bad.

2. **Sight is not clear** – People who struggle with breaking addictions and bad habits sometimes see things that are not really happening to them. Their vision is off and many times they make bad decisions because they cannot see clearly. They are very skeptical, experiencing thoughts of paranoia and thinking that people are talking about them or out to get them, when the people are not.

3. **Defensiveness** – When you protect and shield yourself from constructive criticism and view it as personal attacks you open up yourself to become defensive. People who tend to shield themselves have little concern about what others think because they are self-absorbed.

4. **Think you know it all** – When you think that nobody or only certain people can teach you, you are limiting yourself. You know people who have good information that can be beneficial for you, but these people cannot help you because you think you know it all. You must be open and understand that you can learn from anybody, including a tree, if God is trying to get a message to you.

5. **Pointing the Finger** – You cannot recover or overcome bad habits when you blame others for your problems, when in all actuality; you need to point the finger where it belongs...you.

CHAPTER 4

||||||||||||||||||||||||

Jonah's Stages to Change

In the book of Jonah, God told Jonah to go unto Nineveh and preach repentance to the city. However, Jonah refused. He got on a boat and headed into the opposite direction. The reason for Jonah refusing to go to Nineveh is that **he was dealing with an unforgiving attitude**. He refused to forgive Nineveh for their brutal treatment toward other nations.

This is one of the reasons why people cannot be healed of sickness and recover from diseases is because they have not let go of a wrong that was done to them. You cannot hold on to mistreatment. You must give it over to God or it will give you over to a life full of heartaches, misery and pain.

Nineveh, during Jonah's day, was considered a powerhouse city; it contained strong people. Nineveh used very ferocious and inhumane techniques of torture and could gain rapid information from captives very easily. Jonah, no doubt, knew this fact. He hoped this nation would not repent so that God could show no mercy or forgiveness.

Forgiveness is often one of the stages that must be addressed if people are going to change their behavior. Notice this scripture:

"But if ye do not forgive, neither will your father which is in heaven forgive your trespasses." (Mark 11:26) People often wonder why bad things happen to them. It could be their unwillingness to forgive which is causing them to make inaccurate decisions. Jonah's unwillingness to forgive almost cost him his life.

God sent a tremendous windstorm to where the storm began to tear the boat into pieces. Through the process of elimination, the men on the boat found out that brother Jonah was the problem. In an attempt to try to make it better, it got worse.

This leads to the next major point. **You cannot make people change; they must be willing to change for themselves.** These men on the boat exhausted themselves trying to make the situation better. *"Instead, the sailors tried even harder to row the boat ashore. But the stormy sea was too violent for them, and they couldn't make it." (Jonah 1:13, NLT)*

Often, church leaders and counselors become burned out and drained in a needless effort to get people to change. It does not matter how much they plead with people...the church leaders and counselors could sing until the cows come home, if people's mindset does not want to change. If people's minds don't change, then change will not occur. In fact, many times people's situations will get worse before they get better, making the people ripe for change.

The next stage to Jonah's change is that he located himself. If you are going to change, you must **locate yourself.** Jonah understood what was going on around him and why it was happening to him. Jonah identified the contributing factor that was causing the storm. Think about this for a moment...if you are traveling out of town and need directions to your destination, you have to know where you are in order to get to your desired destination.

Dr Creflo A. dollar, in his book, *Claim Your Victory Today*, says:

> *Before you can expect to get from the problem to the*
> *answer, you must first clearly define and understand*
> *the exact nature of the problem you are facing. Is it*
> *Spiritual? Physical? Financial? Emotional? Whatever*
> *it is, the first step in conquering it is facing it head-on*
> *and identifying what it truly is. (P.19)*

When you locate yourself you are identifying the problem that is causing you to do what you do. *"My people are destroyed for lack of knowledge" (Hosea 4:6).* When people locate themselves, not only are they identifying problems but in some cases they recognize and are clearly aware of the contributing factors that are causing the problems.

What I mean by contributing factors is narrowing down what is happening to you. You will know and have a good understanding of what is exactly going on with you. You will work on you and not anyone else. Your focus point for change is all about you.

Notice this scripture:

> *"Wherefore, my beloved, as ye have always obeyed,*
> *not as in my presence only, but now much more in*
> *my absence, work out your own salvation with fear*
> *and trembling." (Philippians 2:12)*

In order to correctly get to where you are trying to go, you must know where you are at the present. You must know where you are in order to get to where you need to be. Jonah located himself: *"Throw me into the sea, Jonah said, and it will become calm again. For I know that this terrible storm is all my fault." (Jonah 1:12 NLT)*

I think it would be very important for me to say this before we continue; **wrong associations with people can produce hindrances and distractions toward your destination.** One reason why people go through a lot of hell here on earth is because they have the wrong people around them. Their associations are all wrong.

The only way these mariners' lives could get back to normal was to throw Jonah overboard. This action indicates that there are some people and things in your life that you will need to throw overboard. Often, struggles and difficulties will not go until you get out of them. In most cases, your situation will get worse if you do not get out.

I drive a car that needed the brakes repaired. When I discovered this needed repair, I thought it was only minor. So I waited a little. When I took my car to the auto mechanic, he diagnosed the problem as major. Not only did I need new brakes, but also I needed new rotors.

If I would have dealt with the original problem immediately, the brake problem would not have been so bad. If I had dealt with it when I felt it needed to be looked at, the result would not have been that bad. In life, you cannot allow things to just go on and on. If you do not fix the problem, it will get so bad until the problem gets worse. What do you need to fix in your life? I would strongly suggest you fixing it immediately.

> *"While he yet spake, there came from the ruler of the synagogue's house which said, Thy daughter is dead: why troublest thou the Master any further? As soon as Jesus heard the word that was spoken, he saith unto the ruler of the synagogue, Be not afraid, only believe." (Mark 5: 35-36)*

Why did Jesus immediately say, to the ruler only believe? Jesus knew that if the ruler had allowed negative talk of doubt and unbelief to go unchecked, the ruler would not have had the faith to see his daughter raised from the dead. Therefore, Jesus dealt with the unbelief quickly; straightened out the ruler's mindset immediately so that he could experience the power of God resurrecting the dead.

As we continue to study Jonah, he is a primary case of a person being arrogant about what he knew until **his stubbornness caused him not to change.** The fact that he was able to locate himself was good, which means that he was aware of his situation and had accepted the responsibility for what was occurring in his life and was not willing to shift the blame towards someone else. However, the fact that he was not willing to change was not so good. This is why: Not only did his flamboyant arrogance almost cost him his life, but it also almost cost innocent lives around him.

After Jonah was thrown overboard at his request, the sea became calm and then a great fish swallowed up Jonah. (Jonah 1:17) Now Jonah goes through hell, hitting the bottom in order to become ripe for change. **Hitting the bottom** is when a person experiences a major crisis knocking him/her off balance, enabling the individual to look at things differently, taking a deep honest inventory of himself/herself, which ultimately causes this person to change.

This idea should serve as a good point because we should not be too quick to bail people out. These folks on the boat lost almost everything trying to save Jonah, and the truth of the matter is, that nothing could have saved Jonah but himself. Jonah needed to get right with God, meaning that Jonah would have had to repent and do exactly what God was asking him to do.

For things to get better for you, you must get right with God to overcome bad habits and chronic addictions. Come unto me is the word of Jesus and He will give the troubled rest. (Matthew 11:28) However, this is something that **you** have to do. *Come to Jesus.* He is the way to get you out of your trouble. (John 14:6)

If Jonah refused to obey God, nothing was going to help him except for Jonah hitting bottom. This fact is important because I have seen people unwilling to repent of sins while church leaders pray for change. Nothing happens...because the person refuses to do what he/she knows is right.

Edwin, H. Friedman says,

> *"Effective healing occurs when the counselor is less anxious to relieve the symptom and instead uses it as a pathway into the emotional system. Then, if changes can be made on that level, the symptom is likely to atrophy" (P.71)*

It is important to have a non-anxious presence with people. A **non-anxious presence** means *that you will sit actively patient with people but you will not move too quickly to bail people out;* you will demonstrate a genuine interest in their concern. However, you must be aware that you are not responsible to fix people's problems—only God can do that. You are responsible to relay the truth so that people can know what to do in order to fix the problem.

I think it is interesting that these mariners or the men on the ship, after they threw Brother Jonah overboard, released Jonah to God. They said a prayer for Jonah; however, they kept on going to their destination. This is not insensitivity; you should pray for people, but do not let people take you down in their mess. Release them to God. **God can do more for a person in five minutes than what you can do in a lifetime.**

Again, now Jonah goes through hell, hitting the bottom, in order to become ripe for change. Notice what he said in *Jonah 2:2 "And said, I cried by reason of mine affliction unto the LORD, and he heard me; Out of the belly of hell cried I, and thou heardest my voice;"* this was a fact that Jonah was at his lowest...he was scared and frightened to death.

This was a good stage in Jonah's life. Again, this idea is not insensitivity. Jonah refused to repent and get things right with God, thus this crisis caused Jonah to be vulnerable. This point of his life was the best chance for change and for him to reflect upon what God had asked him to do. In the midst of his pain, there was hope and promise for Jonah to fulfill the will of God for his life.

Finally, the **acknowledgement of wrong and the confession to make it right** was all a part of the method that Jonah used to recover from his life-threatening situation. Confession has always been known as a person's way of releasing emotional baggage.

If a tea kettle remains over the fire with the lid and cap on, there is no doubt that you will have a mess on your hands because it will explode. This action is what many people do when they have a lot of stress and pressure on them. If they do not get the mess out, they will explode. They will injure themselves and their loved ones. However, when the cap is taken off, the steam releases the pressure and the pressure in the tea kettle decreases.

In order to be successful overcoming or breaking bad habits there must be someone who you can talk with who can help you emotionally drain the pressures of life. You must find a means of release.

Jonah went to God in his time of crisis. God heard and delivered him. (Jonah 2:2, 10) God will do the same thing for you and me today, if we will only come to him and allow him to deliver us from all our fears.

Things to Consider about Jonah

First, God will speak to you when you are in a right relationship with Him, but when you refuse to obey Him; God will become silent to you and will not speak again until you obey Him. After God spoke to Jonah the first time to go unto Nineveh, Jonah willfully refused. God never spoke to him again, until Jonah made up his mind that he was going to do what he knew God wanted him to do.

Notice this scripture:

> *Then the word of the Lord came to Jonah the second time: "Get up! Go to the great city of Nineveh and preach the message that I will tell you." So Jonah got up and went to Nineveh according to the LORD'S command. (Jonah 3:1-3, HCSB)*

The second time God spoke to Jonah, God said the same thing that He had told Jonah the first time...get up and go to Nineveh. Jonah went through all types of problems, literally going through Hell, because he did not do what the word of the Lord instructed him to do the first time.

When Jonah made a decision to come back to God, and to do what God said the first time, he was able to hear the voice of God very clearly. Some people cannot hear God at all, nor can they overcome bad habits, because they are not doing what God has instructed them to do.

If Jonah had not gone to Nineveh the second time, God would not have spoken to Jonah about doing anything else in the ministry because he had not done the first thing that was required of God.

The Bible says,

> *Nevertheless I have this against you, that you have left your first love. Remember therefore from where you have fallen; repent and do the first works, or else I will come to you quickly and remove your lamp-stand from its place – unless you repent. (Revelations 2:4-5, NKJV)*

In this passage of scripture, Jesus was indicating to the Church of Ephesus that He really appreciated their hard labor and patience to the gospel. However, He was very concerned for them because they had fallen away in their commitment to Him. God gave them an admonishment to return to their first work...to love God with all your heart. (Matthew 22:37-38)

The church at Ephesus was very busy warring off pretenders and false doctrines that were trying to infiltrate the Church by the Nicolaitans; they were working hard doing the things of God but they were not spending quality time with God, mainly because their focus had shifted from God to the Nicolaitans. Therefore, Jesus encouraged Ephesus not to forget that their great ministry service is to first minister unto the Lord.

The Interpreter's Dictionary of the Bible says,

> *Nothing is confidently known about the Nicolaitans beyond John's references to them. Their works are hated, but not described, in the letter to Ephesus.*

> *In Pergamum their teaching is held in like manner to those who held the teaching of BALAAM (Num. 25:1-2; 31:16; II Peter. 2:15; Jude 11). In early OT days Balaam had taught Balak, the Moabite king, to cause the Israelites to fall into fornication and idolatry. These same sins were taught and practiced by the Nicolaitans. (P. 547-548)*

Jesus said for the Ephesians to not get so consumed with what the Nicolaitans were doing and lose sight of what God was doing. One of the ways to combat against the spirit of error is just preach and teach the truth. You do not have to try to defend the gospel of Jesus Christ— just live and proclaim it and everything else will be exposed to the truth.

Again, one reason why people cannot advance to the next level in life is because of them struggling to win over bad habits and addictive behaviors; they have not done the first thing that God has asked them to do. God is not like the restaurant Burger King...you cannot have it your way, especially, when He is requiring you to do something specifically His way.

The awesome thing about God's way is that His way is **always** the best way. His way might take you a little longer to get to where you want to be, but you can rest assured, that you **will** get there. When you arrive where God wants you, no one can ever tell you that he/she got you there.

> *But Abram said to king of Salem, I have raised my hand to the LORD, God Most High, the Possessor of heaven and earth, that I will take nothing, from a thread to a sandal strap, and that I will not take anything that is yours, lest you should say, 'I have made Abram rich'. (Genesis 14:22-23, NKJV)*

Abraham refused to receive anything from Melchizedek, lest Melchizedek (king of Salem) would bring up later that he made Abraham the great man that he was. Abraham knew that if he did things God's way, God would bless him with everything that he needed and more. You are made in the image of God (Genesis 1:26) therefore, as little gods, you can do the same thing that God can do because God lives in you.

Second, the ways to go up in life is to stop doing things that are taking you down. **Jonah's life was a downhill spiral once he disobeyed God;** his life kept going down and down until he decided to come up.

Notice the process of Jonah's downward decline: he went down to Joppa, he saw a ship headed to Tarshish and went down in it, he went down into the sides of the ship, he lay down and went to sleep, he was cast down from the ship, he went down into the sea, he went down into a fish's belly, and there went down to Hell.

This example of Jonah's downward progression should serve as a lesson, indicating today that one of the ways to go up in God is to stop doing what is taking you down or away from God. Only when Jonah made a decision to do things God's way did things start looking up for him, and it is going to be the same way with you; only until you start doing things God's way will things start looking up for you.

Third, you need to know whom you are hanging out with because they can rain on your so-called parade. **Jonah had a negative effect on everybody around him,** which means that we do not need to be hooking up with just anybody. Jonah was cursed (empowered to fail). It really did not matter what others did to try to make Jonah's situation better, as long as

Jonah refused to obey God, the curse on him would remain. The only way the curse could be broken was for Jonah to obey God's instructions.

This is the same way that people are empowered to prosper or fail. Jonah, no doubt, was empowered to fail, again and again; he was cursed. The only way Jonah was going to be blessed was by him submitting his will to the will of God. Therefore, it is so important for you to know whom you are hanging around, because they can either curse you or bless you.

Fourth, God's will for us is to love and forgive all people. **The very people who hurt you, God will use <u>you</u> to be a blessing unto them.** Jonah was a racist; he did not want the city of Nineveh to repent because they did cruel and tortuous things to people. Jonah wanted Nineveh to die and go to Hell but God wanted Nineveh to live, to depart from their evil ways so that He could forgive, love and prosper them.

Notice this passage:

> *When God saw that they had put a stop to their evil ways, He had mercy on them and didn't carry out His threatened destruction. This change of plans upset Jonah, and he became very angry. So he complained to the LORD about it: "Didn't I say before I left home that you would do this, LORD? That is why I ran away to Tarshish! I knew that you were a gracious and compassionate God, slow to get angry and filled with unfailing love. I knew easily you could cancel your plans for destroying these people. Just kill me now. LORD! I'd rather be dead than alive because nothing I predicted is going to happen." (Jonah 3:10-4:3, NLT)*

God was teaching Jonah and He is teaching us today that it does not matter what people do to you...God expects you to love and forgive them. No matter what people have done to you, you are not responsible for what people do to you; you are responsible for how you **respond** to what people do to you. Your response should always be one of love and forgiveness. Jesus commands us to love our enemy. (Mathew 5:44)

CHAPTER 5

||||||||||||||||||||||||||

David's Stages of Recovery

Before sharing the recovery process of King David, I would strongly recommend you read the entire chapter of Psalms 51. This chapter expresses King David's repentance, which leads to his stages of recovery after having a sexual relationship (adultery) with Bathsheba and killing her husband (Uriah) in the process of his relationship with Bathsheba. (II Samuel 12: 1-10.)

KEY THOUGHT: In order to recover effectively from your past hurt, you must be willing to work through the shame and guilt that is associated with the past hurt.

In reflecting upon David's statement in the New Living Translation of the Bible located in Psalms 51:3, *"For I recognized my shameful deeds. They haunt me day and night."* **First,** in order for David to recognize where he went wrong, he had to deal with the issues of shame, guilt, and embarrassment.

This recognition is a whopper! Most people cannot get to the healing stage because they refuse to work through their past shame and guilt. **Shame and guilt occur when certain aspects of one's vulnerability of self is exposed.**

Shame has to do with an inferiority complex, an unworthiness of disapproval of others and more importantly to God. When David began to take action of his problem, the haunting in his mind stopped. You must recognize and act on your wrong. *"He that covereth his sins shall not prosper; but whoso confesseth and forsaketh them shall have mercy."* *(Proverbs 28:13)*

David's Recovery Process in Psalms 51:1-19

1. **He repented,** asked the Lord for forgiveness. V1

2. **He accepted,** what was done was done. V2

3. **He acknowledged his wrong,** thereby, not putting it on others. V3

4. **He separated himself,** stopped doing wrong. V7

5. **He received a plan,** if not working to something new. V10

6. **He was restored,** able to recover from his failure. V2

7. **He got back into community,** sharing the love of God. V13

An extremely important factor to keep in mind is that David did not recover alone. God sent Nathan the Prophet (**sponsor/pastoral advisor**) to David, telling him his fault. (II Samuel 12:1-15) In (NA/AA) Narcotic Anonymous and Alcohol Anonymous, a sponsor can make a world of difference.

The Prophet Nathan can be described as a mentor for King

David. Mentors are support advocates designed to speak life over you, and they are used as tools to keep you sharp and functioning properly.

Dr. Barry C. Black, the author of the book, *From the Hood to the Hill*, says that he is the only African-American to ever serve both as United States, Navy Chief of Chaplains and as the first African-American Chaplain of the United States, Senate. He makes this statement about mentoring:

> *Life without mentors would have been exasperating. I was blessed to have people who believed in me, who had an encouraging word that enabled me to believe that tomorrow would be brighter than today. Some were ministers, who saw in me quiescent gifts that I had yet to discover. Others attended my church. "Boy," many would say, "God has given you something special." (P. 22)*

It was the Prophet Nathan who confronted and guided King David through the process of his recovery. Because of King David's willingness to change and make things right, he was able to successfully recover. The fact that King David was willing to repent (change) indicates that he was willing to accept the responsibility for what he had done wrong.

In his book, *So You Call Yourself a Man*, Bishop T.D. Jakes says,

> *"The blame line didn't work for Adam, and it won't work for you. The situation in your life is not the fault of someone else. It's your responsibility. Deal with yourself. And you'll probably find that those you have been blaming are not nearly the problem they were!" (P.96)*

King David was unlike King Saul. When King Saul sinned, instead of Saul owning up to his responsibility, Saul denied and blamed his disobedience on the people.

> *"But I did obey the LORD, Saul said, "I went on the mission the LORD assigned me. I completely destroyed the Amalekites and brought back Agag their king. The soldiers took sheep and cattle from plunder, the best of what was devoted to God, in order to sacrifice them to the LORD your God at Gilgal...Then Saul said to Samuel, I have sinned. I violated the LORD's command and your instructions. I was afraid of the people and so I gave in to them." (I Samuel 15:20, 24 NIV)*

Initially, King Saul was in denial that he did wrong in not obeying the Lord's instructions. God specifically instructed King Saul to destroy the Amalekites, sparing nothing. (I Samuel 15:1-3)

Dr. Creflo Dollar in his book, *Live Without Fear,* **says,**

> *"Saul feared the people. His insecurities and need for approval caused him to violate the clear command of the Lord God Almighty. He fell into the trap of thinking that his position came from pleasing people rather than pleasing God. The result of this was that Saul lost everything: his kingship, his anointing, his calling, and finally, his life." (P. 61)*

One of the major breakthroughs in King David's life is that he moved beyond what people thought about him, unlike King Saul who allowed the people to dictate what he could and could not do. **Truly successful people learn not to be intimidated by others' threats and negative opinions of them.**

King David progressed to the point to where he did not care who knew about the sins he had committed. David was only concerned with getting things right with the Lord, knowing that God would give him grace and insight on how to work out his negative behavior.

Let us look briefly at some biblical characters that broke the habit of trying to please everybody:

1. Jesus —*"But made himself of no reputation, and took upon him the form of a servant, and was made in the likeness of men." (Philippians 2:7)* Jesus was not concerned with winning the Mr. Who's Who award. He did not seek the reputation of mankind. Jesus was only concerned with fulfilling the will of God for his life. Jesus was totally committed to pleasing God.

2. The Apostle Paul–*"At my first answer no man stood with me, but all men forsook me: I pray God that it may not be laid to their charge." (II Timothy 4:16)* When you know what's right to do, you must have enough trust in God to do it—even if it means that you are going to look like a fool in doing it. I would rather be God's fool than to be mankind's robot. Paul was willing to be true and stand for God than to be hypocritical and sit among compromisers.

3. Nehemiah —*"And I said, Should such a man as I flee... And, Lo I perceived that God had not sent him; but that he pronounced this prophecy against me: for Tobiah and Sanballat had hired him." (Nehemiah 6:11-12)* Nehemiah's confidence in God was so strong that not even a lying prophet could persuade him to do differently from what God told Nehemiah to do. You must have both a relationship and a confidence in God to believe that if God said

it, then that settles that—even if church folk are saying differently. (Romans 3:4)

People will tell you to do just about anything; you cannot do everything for everybody. You will eventually become stressed and burned out. Stress and burnout occurs when you become a yes person, saying yes to everybody and everything when you do not have the energy or the time.

In his book, *Stress Less*, Dr Don Colbert says,

> *"Know your own limits. Know when you have enough on your plate. You don't need to be unkind. You can say no in a gentle and respectful way. By not being able to say no, someone else's stress becomes your stress. " (P.119-120)*

One of the greatest words in the English language is the word No. It is okay to say no. There is a familiar slogan about drugs that says, *Just say no.* You should say no, especially when you know that you cannot do something. For you to say yes and not do the thing you said you would, is a lie. Many people are living a lie; they are in bondage to doing things that they do not want to do. They say yes, but deep down within, they know they should have said no.

Saying this lie could be very closely associated with people pleasing. People pleasing is doing what people want you to do, hoping that they will favor or exalt you. The problem with people pleasing is that if people lifted you up then they can certainly bring you down.

That is why you need to put your trust in God (Proverbs 3:5-6), depending on Him to locate you and place you exactly where He wants you to be. Once God lifts you up, there are not enough demons in Hell to bring you down; your biggest downfall will be yourself.

A quote from *The Recovery Book* says:

> *"Shakespeare said it first, but it's a reminder that can't be repeated too often: "To thine own self be true." Self-deception denies your disease. It dodges your responsibilities, neglects the fundamentals of your recovery program, rationalizes unwise actions, and fails to evaluate you (or your good and bad traits) honestly". (P. 543)*

There comes a time when you have to be honest with yourself. You cannot allow yourself to be manipulated, or intimidated by people when you know what they are saying is not true. When asked to do something that is not good, you just flat-out cannot do it. Do not feel badly about it; just say no and move on. Saying no is not being self-centered. Saying no is a way of you setting boundaries to protect yourself from stress and potentially becoming burned out over too much work.

Ray Charles true unto himself

> *"Today we are here to right a wrong that was done to one of our native sons nearly 20 years ago. In 1961 Ray Charles was banned from performing in the state of Georgia because he refused to play before a segregated audience. Thankfully, we have come a long way since then. Some of us has fought for equality through the political process. But Ray Charles changed American culture by touching people's hearts. So on this day March 7, 1979. We the duly elected representatives of the state of Georgia not only proclaim "Georgia on my Mind," our official*

state song. We also offer Mr. Ray Charles a public apology and welcome him back home" (Disc, 1.)

Although Ray Charles was banned from the state of Georgia, he stayed true to his moral values and spiritual truths that segregation and racism was wrong. Ray Charles continued to sing in other states. He was known for helping to integrate Birmingham, Alabama during 1963.

Ray Charles traveled about performing to integrated shows and audiences in America. Heat, snow, bombs or cops, could not stop Ray Charles from singing. Ray Charles knew that God had given him a talent and that God wanted him to be a blessing to others with his singing.

Adam Woog, the author of the book, *Ray Charles*, says,

> *Touring in America, in sharp contrast, was much more difficult. At the height of the civil rights movement in America in the late 1950s and early 1960s, a traveling black musician moved in a volatile atmosphere, especially in the segregated South. Despite his prominence, Charles and his band members were subjected to discrimination and even outright hostility. (P. 68)*

Ray Charles went on to have many number one hits and Grammy awards. Again, although Georgia banned him from the state, they welcomed him back. He performed his song *"Georgia on My Mind"* before the General Assembly in March 7, 1979, and on April 24, 1979, that number one song on the song charts was made Georgia's official state song.

The point I am making about Ray Charles is that he did not allow what people said to him and did to stop him from being who he was and doing what he desired to do. Ray Charles made a difference because he stayed true unto himself; he dreamed big, he stood his ground and did what others could not do because he was not intimidated by people's actions towards him.

Another key to Ray Charles' success as a musician and singer is that he kept doing his thing. In the midst of hate, bomb threats, racism, and discrimination he continued to do his thing; he continued to sing and write music.

The Bible says,

> "Whatsoever thy hand findeth to do, do it with thy might: for there is no work, nor device, nor knowledge, nor wisdom, in the grave, whither thou goest."
> (Ecclesiastes 9:10)

In her book *Shine On,* I like what Gloria Copeland says:

> "You're not called to argue. You're not called to defend your position or your name when men speak evil about you. Just leave all that in the hands of the Lord and continue doing what God has called you to do."
> (P. 7-8)

This means that you have to get busy right where you are to break or overcome a major crisis in your life. Do not get mad or upset; know that God is with you and He is working for you. As you continue to do what God has called you to do, you will discover that things are not as bad as they first seemed because God has taken you to another level.

> "Fear thou not; for I am with thee: be not dismayed; for I am thy God; I will strengthen thee; yea I will help thee; yea, I will uphold thee with the right hand

of my righteousness." (Isaiah 41:10)

Do not be so consumed with what is going on **around** you as much as what you can do to make what is going on around you **better**. Do not complain; do not be disheveled or discouraged about what is negatively happening to you. Do what you know to do, do your best and let God do the rest.

CHAPTER 6

⁝⁝⁝⁝⁝⁝⁝⁝⁝⁝⁝⁝⁝⁝⁝⁝⁝⁝⁝⁝⁝⁝⁝⁝⁝⁝

Joseph's Stages of Recovery

The Bible says,

> *"Joseph could stand it no longer. "Out, all of you!"*
> *he cried out to his attendants. He wanted to be alone*
> *with his brothers when he told them who he was.*
> *Then he broke down and wept aloud. His sobs could*
> *be heard throughout the place, and the news quickly*
> *carried to Pharaoh's palace...but don't be angry with*
> *yourselves that you did this to me, for God did it. He*
> *sent me here ahead of you to preserve your lives."*
> *(Genesis 45:1-2, 5 NLT)*

Joseph weeping was a release to let go of his bitterness and anger toward his brothers. His brothers did several cruel things to him; one was selling him into slavery. Now the emphasis should not be placed on Joseph's weeping, but his willingness to forgive (loose) his brothers of a painful and wrongful hurt.

Joseph, no doubt, knew that he could not fulfill God's will for his life being mad and upset. Joseph did not deserve what his brothers put him through. (Genesis 40:15, NLT) However,

God had a plan to preserve the Israel nation in time of a seven-year famine. The nation was to be preserved through the hand of Joseph.

You need to know that every time somebody does you wrong, and every time things look like they are working against you, know that God is up to something and He will restore, heal, deliver, and set you free from all harm and worries. Just continue to trust Him (God) and stay in a spirit of love and compassion, and God will eventually turn that situation around and cause it to work in your favor.

Bishop T.D. Jakes, in his book, *Women Thou Art Loosed*, says,

> *"God, however has a way of making people who have been forsaken by men and raising them up. In fact, God tends to prefer such individuals, because when they get into a place of power, they are not arrogant like those are who think they deserve to be promoted."*
> *(P. 48)*

If God can restore in a matter of seconds to Joel all the years that the locusts, cankerworms and other insects had destroyed (Joel 2:25) God will do the same for you. God will loose you and set you free from the thing or things that have been trying to consume and choke the life out of you. God can and will do an unheard of thing for you. That is right—God **can** and He **will do** an unheard of thing just to get you what you need.

Let us look briefly at some biblical unheard-of things that God did for His people. **First**, look at Numbers 16:1-34, which I recommend you, read in the *Amplified Version* of the Bible to get the full grasp of what is being conveyed. In this chapter, Moses said that God was going to do a new thing to his enemies; the earth would literally open up and swallow all them who were against what Moses was doing for the Lord.

In this particular chapter, the Bible says that the ground opened...swallowing up all offenders and then, the ground returned to its original state. How can that happen? Easily, God can do it, and He will do whatever it takes to heal, deliver and protect you.

Second, in Exodus, the ninth chapter, God sent a plague of hail and fire mixed together upon Pharaoh and the Egyptian people because they refused to let the children of Israel go from slavery. *"So there was hail, and fire, mingled with hail, very grievous, such as there was none like it in all the land of Egypt since it became a nation." (Exodus 9:24)* Now, if you ask meteorologists about fire and water mixing together, they will tell you that that is humanly impossible. However, God can do it.

God can take a black cow; feed it green grass, and the black cow will produce white milk. God can do it; God **can** and **will** rescue your life. God is willing to do whatever it will take to show Himself strong on your behalf.

Notice this scripture: *"He shall call upon me, and I will answer him: I will be with him in trouble; I will deliver him, and honour him. With long life will I satisfy him and shew him my salvation." (Psalms 91:15-16)*

Third, in II Kings, the sixth chapter, there we will experience another unnatural occurrence.

> *"But as one was felling his beam, the axe head fell into the water; and he cried, Alas my master, for it was borrowed! The man of God asked," Where did it fall? When shown the place, Elisha cut off a stick and threw it in the water, and the iron floated. He*

said, pick it up. And he put his hand and took it. (II Kings 6:5-7, AMP)

How can an axe head swim on top of water? If you look at the physical components of what the axe head consists of, there is no way humanly possible that an axe head is going to float on water. Nevertheless, God can do it; God can and He will restore whatever you have lost, and your situation cannot get so bad to where God cannot put things back together. God has a way of getting you what you need; trust Him and He shall bring the thing that you desire to pass.

In Genesis 45:1-2, God could not bless Joseph until he let go of his hurt. Are you holding on to anything? If so, **the thing that you refuse to loose could be the thing that keeps you from breaking free and overcoming your bad habit(s).** Therefore, you must set your will to forgive by letting it go, no matter what.

Forgiveness is extremely important because if you do not forgive and release people of the wrong that they have done to you, you will never enter into the best that God has for you. Notice this scripture: *"But when you are praying, first forgive anyone you hold a grudge against, so that your Father in Heaven will forgive your sins, too." (Mark 11:25 NLT)*

Hurting people has a tendency to do three things: 1) hurt themselves, 2) hurt others, and 3) make bad decisions. The reason that hurting people do these things is because they are hurting inwardly and therefore, they are only concerned with protecting themselves from being injured again emotionally. You should never make decisions when you are angry, hurting or under a lot of duress, because your thinking is not clear and the decisions you make today can affect you for a lifetime.

Pastor Gregory Dickow in his book, *How to Never be Hurt Again*, says,

> *You can get to a point where, no matter what some-body does to you, it never hurts you. You can get to the point where you can say, "I'll never be hurt another day in my life." Doesn't that sound liber-ating? We can literally be emotionally invincible. That's what God means when He says that noth-ing shall, by any means, hurt us. We can become invincible people. We can become people who are impenetrable. We can become people who cannot be defeated, because real destruction in our lives is not going to come from the outside. It's going to come from within; as is our success." (p.14)*

In looking back at the life of Joseph, his brothers put him into a pit and then sold him into slavery at the age of 17. I am sure most people would have looked at that situation and just wrote off Joseph. (Genesis 45:26-28)

Again, God had a plan and He would work through Joseph's attitude to be a blessing to a nation of people. Many times those who enter into greatness go through extreme difficulties.

One of the major factors to overcome bad habits is that you focus on God, and not the problem. If you talk about the problem more than you talk to God, this could be considered idolatry because you are putting the problem or hurt above God. You must loose the problem or hurt, and be consumed with God's word.

In his book, *Casting Your Cares upon the Lord*, Rev. Kenneth
E. Hagin, says,

> *Some of you are holding onto cares and anxieties.*
> *You're still fretting. In fact, you've even gone beyond*
> *fretting. You're "stewing." And others are possibly*
> *boiling over with anxiety, care, and concern. What*
> *God wants you do is turn it over to Him. No, I didn't*
> *say it was easy, especially if you've been in the habit*
> *of worry for a long time. Get in the habit of faith*
> *instead. Just release the worry habit into His hand."*
> (P. 49-50)

Through it all, Joseph stayed focused on what God had
promised him; he never wavered from it. Joseph spent 13 years
in prison, but God brought him from a pit to a palace. Joseph
was elevated because he was willing to forgive those who hurt
him, and had a right attitude when people did him wrong.

You should deal with all people the way you would want to
be treated. Joseph's brothers had no idea that they would see
their brother again after selling him into slavery, but God did.
Joseph went from a pit, to slavery, to prison to the inner prison
(maximum prison), to becoming the governor of the whole land
of Egypt. There was only one man in all the land of Egypt who
had more power than Joseph and that was Pharaoh, the King
of Egypt.

So when Joseph's brothers came to Egypt for food, they
were shocked to see Joseph still alive and in a most prestigious
position. Joseph could have had them all killed but God had a
plan. Some of you may be going through something right now.
You may be experiencing something that is no fault of your
own. You might have been set up, lied to and abused, but God

can reverse the curse; God can take a wrong and make it right. God can do it.

KEY THOUGHT: Some people are going through so-called hell and experiencing a flow of it because they are not treating people right.

Lessons to be Learned

1. **You must let things go (*forgive*) quickly.** If you do not let them go quickly, then you will prevent God from doing what He wants to do in your life. *"And Joseph called the name of the firstborn Manasseh: For God, said he, hath made me forget all my toil, and all my father's house. And the name of the second called he Ephraim: For God hath caused me to be fruitful in the land of my affliction."* (Genesis 41:51-52)

   Before Joseph could experience the fruitfulness (Ephraim) of God's blessings he had to forget (Manasseh) those who had wronged him. Loose it and let it go.

2. **What you give to people is what you are going to get back.** *"Give, and it shall be given unto you; good measure, pressed down, and shaken together, and running over, shall men give into your bosom."* (Luke 6:38) This scripture refers to more than just money; it refers to treating people with a right attitude. Many people are going through hell and are experiencing an overflow of it because they refuse to treat people right.

3. **Look out for yourself.** *"But think on me when it shall be well with thee, and shew kindness, I pray thee, unto me*

and make mention of me unto Pharaoh, and bring me out of this house." (Genesis 40:14) It was what Joseph said that the butler remembered, which was the word *me*. This was not selfishness. In the process of helping others, make sure you do not cripple yourself. Set limits and boundaries with people so that you can get proper sleep and rest to fulfill the complete will of God for your life and not get burned out.

Many people experience setbacks because they fear telling the truth. They do things they do not want to do for fear of being fired from a job, talked about, misunderstood or looked down upon. The Bible indicates that Jesus was not concerned with what others thought about Him (Philippians 2:7); He was only concerned with the will of God for His life. Everything fell into place under God's will.

4. **Don't allow where you are presently to determine where you will be permanently.** *"I am Joseph your brother, whom ye sold into Egypt." (Genesis 45:4)* Joseph could have become stuck right there in the midst of his past hurts, but he refused to allow his past traumas to set him back. Joseph stayed focused and kept his eyes on what God was doing in his life, which brought him from the pit to the palace.

Again, one of the main things that made Joseph so great is that he never became bitter. He just used everything he went through to make him better. **Do not get bitter; get better.** Joseph, very easily, could have become angry with God. Also, Joseph could have become angry with his father for showing him so much favoritism over his brothers. Joseph's father's favoritism for Joseph enabled Joseph's brothers to be jealous, and provoked them to do the evil that they did to Joseph.

Joseph could have become bitter at Potiphar's wife, who lied on him, and Joseph could have become bitter at Potiphar sentencing Joseph to be imprisoned, but Joseph did not become bitter at people that did him wrong. He shook it off, stepped on it and stepped up. That's what you and I have to do... we have to shake off negative thoughts, past hurts, evil desires, and wrong behaviors, and use negativity and opposition as an opportunity for advancement.

There is a story about a man who had a donkey; the man's donkey was not doing what he asked it to do. Rather than shooting the donkey, the man decided to put the donkey in a deep pit where people throw their trash, thinking that the donkey would just suffocate and die. When people began to throw their trash in the pit, the donkey shook off the trash and stepped on it. This method of the donkey continued many days. Every time someone threw his/her trash in the pit, the donkey would shake it off and step on it.

Dr. Dale Bronner, in his book, *Treasure Your Silent Years*, says,

> *Life is a staircase and you reach the top one step at*
> *a time – whether you are bouncing with energy or*
> *constantly struggling. In the process, the Lord is lifting*
> *us to the next level. (P. 45)*

Finally, with enough shaking it off and stepping on it, the donkey was able to become so high to the point that he was able to walk right out of the mess. The point is this: you can walk out, get out and stay out of whatever keeps you down. Keep the right attitude. Don't get mad, bitter, or angry. **Use** what you go through as stepping stones to get you to where you need to be.

Notice this scripture:

> *"So they appointed taskmasters over them to afflict them with hard labor. And they built for Pharaoh storage cities, Pithoim and Raames. But the more they afflicted them, the more they multiplied and the more they spread out, so that they were in dread of the sons of Israel." (Exodus 1:11-12, NAS)*

The children of Israel became stronger and stronger through the hardship placed on them by the Egyptians. The children of Israel multiplied and grew under the pressure of trouble. *"A righteous man may have many troubles, but the LORD delivers him from them all." (Psalm 34:19, NIV)* In life, you will experience hard times, but that doesn't mean that you pack up and leave or quit, ignoring what God told you to do. You stay in there and believe that your situation will get better. Watch what God can do to make your situation make you better.

CHAPTER 7

Steps to Breaking a Bad Habit

The first step to breaking a Bad Habit is **avoidance**. In order to successfully overcome a bad habit, you have to learn to avoid places, things, and people that cause and draw you to do negative activity (II Corinthians 6:17.) Avoidance is designed to keep you away from high-risk situations, to prevent you from easily being caught up in potential danger.

Pastor Taffi L. Dollar in her book, *The Portrait of a Virtuous Woman*, says,

> *"to transform and maintain areas in your life that need change, you must avoid Satan's attempt to trick you. The Bible admonishes us in 1 Thessalonians 5:22 to avoid the very appearance of evil. In other words, at all cost, avoid those things, people, and situations that get you off track. For example, if you used drugs in the past, avoid your old hangout and old friends who have not decided to change. Or if you're trying to become healthier and lose weight, stop going to the all-you-can-eat food bar. Abstain from things that*

appeal to your flesh (1 Peter 2:11). Instead tap into the power of God's anointing. Say along with Paul, "I can do all things through Christ which strengthens me." (Phil. 4:13) (P. 80-81)

Avoidance is sometimes **changing your environment**, so that you can create a safe place to avoid distractions. A **distraction** is *intrusion of the mind trying to cause confusion.* By avoiding those high-risk situations, you do not have to deal in confusion and the pressure of making the wrong decision that can cause a recurrence of an avalanche of negative behaviors to return in your life.

Moreover, avoidance will help you cut down on the unnecessary conflicts in your life. There are two types of people that will always be in your life: 1) those who will build you up or 2) those who will tear you down. It is your responsibility to recognize who is putting good substance into your life and who is pulling the life out of you. People who you allow to come into your life will either add or subtract; they will assist in helping you accomplish your intended purpose, or they will contribute in sidetracking you from your destination.

Bishop T.D. Jakes, in his book *Saints with Sinners' Problems,* says,

> *"If you had a drinking problem, get rid of everything including the cough syrup that has a high alcoholic content. Flee from those places where you used to hang out. The place is still there, those people are still there, but you must stay away. If cigarettes are a problem, get someone to pray with you for deliverance and make sure you stay away from people who smoke and places where smoking is commonplace. You will*

have to change the circuit you once traveled. If not you
will be setting yourself up for the same old problems
that had you bound before." (P. 20-21)

One of the benefits of avoidance is that it keeps you from physically participating in the negativity. That is not to say, however, that you will not have cravings (strong desires) or withdrawals associated to your detachment from the negative activity or situation. You **can** and **will** overcome, contingent upon the fact that you do not quit and stay with the plan that you have implemented.

The second step to breaking a bad habit is to **come up with new solutions**. You will be replacing the negative habit with a positive one. For instance, if you know that you have a problem with losing weight because of overeating, then you will need, for starters, to change your diet and exercise to lose weight.

In addition, it will not hurt for you to clean out your refrigerator of all unhealthy foods and replace them with foods that are low in fat. What did we just do? We came up with a new solution; we substituted or replaced a bad behavior for a good behavior.

Joyce Meyer, in her book, *Approval Addiction*, says,

"I want to encourage you to replace one addiction with
another one. You are probably thinking, "What sense
does that make?" Actually, I want you to replace all
addictions with one other addiction. I want you to
become addicted to Jesus! You should need Him more
than you need anything else." (P. 116)

If people have a problem with smoking, then they will need, for starters, to get rid of all their cigarettes. Next, they will

133

need to avoid places that allow smoking, then, they will need to find some non-smoking friends, read the Bible and pray. In addition, some may need to buy some Nicoderm, which are patches designed to help stop smoking.

Again, what have we just done? We came up with a new solution; we have put in place preventive techniques to stop old behaviors and implemented new approaches to obtain the goal that is desired.

In his book, *Facing Your Giants*, Max Lucado, says,

> *I had a friend who battled the strong hold of alcohol. He tried a fresh tactic. He gave a few others and me permission to slug him in the nose if we ever saw him drinking. The wall was too tall, so he tried the tunnel. One woman counters her anxiety by memorizing long sections of scripture. A traveling sales rep asks hotels to remove the television from his room so he won't be tempted to watch adult movies. Another man grew so weary of his prejudice that he moved into a minority neighborhood, made new friends, and changed his attitude. (P 107-108)*

Coming up with new ideas and solutions is important because if you do not replace the negative habit with a good one, then you will continue to do the negative behavior and nothing will ever change. That is where we get the word insanity. The word **insanity** is *when you do the same thing repeatedly and expect to get different results.*

The only way you can get different positive results is to do something different. In his book, *101 Wisdom Keys*, Dr. Mike Murdock, says, *"When you want something you have never had, you have got to do something you have never done."* Coming up with a new solution is basically a process of switching it up. If that process is not working, then do something different.

At times, we certainly need to be patient and not move too quickly; patience is an art that we all need to possess. However, when I refer to switching it up, I am referring to the times you know that certain things are not going to get better but only worse, and you still continue to do what is not working, thinking these things are going to get better but they never get better—only worse. That's the time you need to switch it up.

The third step to breaking a bad habit is that **you cannot be stubborn.** Many times, people just need to stop fooling around and do what they need to do, so that they do not have to put up with negative stuff for so long.

A good example of this would be in regards to the men who were on the boat with Jonah. The Bible says,

> *"And he said unto them, Take me up, and cast me forth into the sea; so shall the sea be calm unto you: for I know that for my sake this great tempest is upon you. Nevertheless the men rowed hard to bring it to land, but they could not; for the sea wrought, and was tempestuous against them"* (Jonah 1:12 -13)

I believe that God was setting forth, as an example from brother Jonah and the mariners, that it makes no difference how hard you try to do something if it is not God's will. It makes no difference how hard you try—it just isn't going to work.

Notice this scripture, *EXCEPT THE LORD build the house, they labour in vain that build it: except the LORD keep the city, the watchman waketh but in vain. (Psalms 127:1)*

135

As hard as these men tried to bring the boat to land during the sea storm, they could not. It became a needless effort until they finally realized that the only way their situation was going to get better was for them to do what they did not want to do, which was to throw Jonah overboard. They finally stopped rowing and threw Jonah overboard and immediately the problem stopped; the wind ceased, and their victory came.

So the question is, why did these men continue to row so hard when they did not have to? The bottom line is this: They were stubborn. These men were what you would call good spirited; they were some good ol' boys—they wanted the best for Jonah—which was good.

The problem is that they were attempting a task that they knew they could not do, which made it bad. These men on the boat had good intentions toward Jonah, but just made bad decisions.

They had the answer and knew what was causing the problem, yet they still tried to do something that they were incapable of doing. This is called stubbornness. There comes a time when you have to be honest with yourself and others by letting them know that what you are trying to accomplish is just not working.

The Bible says,

> *"Then Jesus used this illustration: A man planted a fig tree in his garden and came again to see if there was any fruit on it, but he was always disappointed. Finally, he said to his gardener, 'I've waited three years, and there hasn't been a single fig! Cut it down. It's taking up space we can use for something else.' The gardener answered, 'Give it one more chance. Leave*

*it another year, and I'll give it special attention and
plenty of fertilizer. If we get figs next year, fine. If not,
you can cut it down.' " (Luke 13:6-9, NLT)*

If things are not working for you, maybe you should not be doing what you are doing or maybe you need to do something different. (Luke 13:6-9, NLT) There comes a time when you have to submit what you are going through to God. Submitting to God is precisely what these men on the boat eventually did. They finally threw Jonah overboard. Then peace and calm arrived. We need to get with God's programs **immediately** to avoid unnecessary struggles.

I often watch the game of baseball and observe how the manger will take the pitcher out of the game. If the pitcher continues to make mistakes, especially if it is a tight game and they need the win, the manger will get that player out immediately.

On the contrary, in the Body of Christ, we do things and know that the things we are doing are not working, yet, we still stick to what we are doing. We have to stop that. We must have the mentality of the baseball manger; if it's not working then we have to step up to the plate and switch it up or do something different.

The fourth step to breaking a bad habit is that you will definitely need to **educate yourself**. Educating yourself is obtaining the mind of God about your situation. You can read and listen to resource materials to gain the best knowledge possible so that you can have a clear understanding on what you are going through and how you can get out of what you are going through.

God's word says, *"Nay, in all these things we are more than conquerors through him that loved us." (Romans 8:37)* This indicates that anything you go through, God has given you the knowledge, strength and the ability to overcome.

The Bible says that you are more than a conqueror; a conqueror is someone who wins all the time and not some of the time. You win **every** time and **all** the time because God fights your battles (II Chronicles 20:15-17). There is no failure or defeat with God.

Failure and defeat only comes when you turn away from God's instruction about what you need to do. When you do your own thing, God cannot put His stamp of approval upon your own thing. If God has not instructed you to do something, what you are currently doing will have no spiritual benefits because what you are doing is unauthorized by God.

Educating yourself is the process of renewing your mind. Observe what the Amplified Translation says in reference to *Romans 12:2:*

> *"Do not be conformed to this world (this age), [fashioned after and adapted to its external, superficial customs], but be transformed (changed) by the [entire] renewal of your mind [by its new ideals and its new attitude], so that you may prove [for your-selves] what is the good and acceptable and perfect will of God, even the thing which is good and acceptable and perfect [in His sight for you]."*

In accordance with this particular scripture, the way you break a bad habit is to renew your mind by coming up with new ideals and insights to change wrong behavior. Your way of thinking has to change from the old bad behavior to the new good behavior; this is accomplished by renewing the mind. If you are going to break a bad habit, your mind must be renewed in line with the word of God. It must be purged from corrupt thinking.

There is an old saying, *"if you give a man a fish he will eat for a day but if you teach a man how to fish he will eat for life."* Think about this saying for a moment. When you allow yourself to be educated, you can learn techniques and approaches in areas that will benefit you **forever.** Breaking a bad habit successfully will require that you be knowledgeable of what you do and why you do it, then work on how you can stop doing what you don't want to.

"Study to show thyself approved unto God, a workman that needeth not to be ashamed, rightly dividing the word of truth." (II *Timothy 2:15)* It is interesting to note that when you study it will require work, but in the end **you** will greatly benefit from it. Studying helps the person. Studying is important to breaking a bad habit. Again, you must educate yourself on what you do and learn why you do what you do, then determine what you can do to stop it.

What you don't know can hurt you and what you know can help you. Before you get involved in something, it is extremely important to gain as much knowledge as possible concerning the thing. A good example is in Genesis 29:15-30. Jacob made a seven-year agreement to work for Laban in order to marry his younger daughter Rachel. However, at the end of the seventh year, Jacob was tricked by Laban and married the older daughter (Leah) instead of the younger, Rachel. In anger and great disappointment, Jacob confronted Laban about his trickery:

> *"It's not our custom to marry off a younger daughter*
> *ahead of the firstborn, Laban replied. Wait until the*

bridal week is over, and you can have Rachel, too—that
is if you promise to work another seven years for me."
(Genesis 29:26-27, NLT)

Jacob did not know the customs of that town, and because he did not know the customs on marriage, he was challenged with a setback: *"My people are destroyed for lack of Knowledge..."* *(Hosea 4:6)* Here we can see what Jacob didn't know cost him an extra seven years of work.

It is also interesting that Jacob did not use his ignorance (not knowing) as an excuse. You will be held accountable and responsible for what you do not know, just like Jacob. This is why scripture encourages us in II Timothy 2:15 to study, so we can have the full scope of a thing at the beginning.

In regards to educating yourself, you must apply what you know if what you know is going to work for you. Without application, there is no transformation to produce manifestation. Transformation (change) only occurs when you work diligently to accomplish the goals that you have set in place to break the bad habit.

The fifth step to breaking a bad habit is to **get to the root of it**. The majority of the time, bad habits are rooted in deep issues. People bite their fingernails when they are nervous; some people smoke when they are worried; some people lose their temper when they are angry or when feeling threatened. Nevertheless, when a person learns what the bad habit is, he/she has now created a very good opportunity to overcome it.

In his talk series, *Overcoming Bad Habits: When "No" Isn't Enough*, Pastor Crelfo Dollar says,

"We just can't talk about well I got this bad habit,

*send me to a detox clinic. Wait a minute man, if we
don't deal with the root to the issue than the issue will
remain, and maybe you might be free for two months
or so but it won't be long before you get back to the
same source of the problem." (DVD, part 1)*

Anything you deal with on a surface level has the tendency
to return, because you did not get to the root of it. When people
say, you need to get to the bottom of that, basically, what they
are saying is that you need to get to the root or the underlying
issue in order for the bad habit to stop. If you want something
to stop growing in your life, uproot it.

The Bible says,

*Listen carefully: Unless a grain of wheat is buried in
the ground, dead to the world, it is never any more
than a grain of wheat. But if it is buried, it sprouts and
reproduces itself many times over. In the same way,
anyone who holds on to life just as it is destroys that
life. But if you let it go, reckless in your love, you'll
have it forever, real eternal. (John 12:24-25, TM)*

Jesus indicates in this passage of scripture that the way you
make a seed grow is by putting it into the ground and leaving it
alone to sprout and reproduce. On the contrary, the way you get
the seed not to grow is that you do not allow it to take root.

If you allow bad habits to take root in your life, those negative things will sprout and grow. If you do not uproot your
negative behaviors they will continue to grow until you uproot
them. If you do not want negative behaviors and bad habits to
reproduce in your life then you have to get to the root of what
is causing you to do what you do.

Dr. Don Colbert, in his book, *What you Don't Know May Be Killing You,* says,

> *"It's true. Your emotional health is often mirrored in your physical health. Perhaps you've asked your doctor to treat your pain when you would have been better off dealing with the root problem – your deadly emotions." (P. 82)*

Dr. Don Colbert continues to explain what deadly emotions are and what these deadly emotions can do to the body. I have made a list of Dr. Colbert's deadly emotions:

*Unforgiveness	*Anger	*Bitterness
*Hatred	*Resentment	*Abandonment
*Fear	*Shame	*Envy
*Jealousy	*Guilt	*Humiliation

He says that hatred and jealousy can lead to:
* High Blood pressure   * Ulcers
* Migraine Headaches   * Cancer
* Heart disease

He says pride can lead to:
* Mental illness   * Heart attack
* Stroke   * Death

He says fear and anxiety can lead to:
* Heart disease   * Depression
* Mental illness   * Heart attack
*Panic attacks   * Phobias

He says anger can lead to:

*Rheumatoid arthritis	* Heart attack
* High blood pressure	* Stroke
* Heart failure	* Ulcer disease

He says depression can lead to:

* Cancer

* Heart disease

The key to avoiding all of these deadly emotions and their symptoms is just walk before the Lord upright and keep His commandments. Notice this scripture, *"So you shall serve the LORD your God, and He will bless your bread and your water. And I will take sickness away from the midst of you."* (Exodus 23:25, NKJV) God can remove sickness, illness, disease, trouble and complications, as well as prevent them returning, as long as you serve Him.

Normally, when people say that they serve God, in most cases they are speaking of reading the Bible and obeying it, they are speaking of attending church and praying regularly. They also witness to the lost or those who are not born-again, and attend church functions, and maybe even serve the people during those functions. All of these actions are good; however, they are not the <u>only</u> way to serve the Lord.

Other ways you can serve God is to take good care of your body, which means that you will exercise, you will do some form of physical activity to keep your muscles strong and bones healthy. You will eat right, you will put in your body those things that will produce life and that will have a profound effect to make you live much longer.

You will take care of your mind, you will read material that will make you happy, you will do things that will educate and equip you to become a better person and you will get proper rest and sleep so that you can perform your duties and responsibilities to be oriented and alert. Doing these things is serving the Lord holistically.

The Bible goes on to indicate that in Psalms 105:37, *"He also brought them out with silver and gold, and there was none feeble among His tribe."* The word **feeble** means *weakness*; it can be a weakness of mental or physical strength. It can be intellectual deficiency or physical sickness or disease. The thing to note about weakness is that it is always associated with something missing, lacking or unable to function properly.

God allowed the children of Israel to walk in wholeness. When you serve God He will not allow things to work improperly in your life; God will work out whatever it is that you need Him to do. When you serve God, He will heal your body, He will put your mind at peace. When you serve God, He will direct, guide and protect you from all harm and danger. (Psalms 91:10-11)

The sixth step to breaking a bad habit is to **get rid of anything that is causing you to be stuck**. When I use the word stuck, I am referring to those things that keep you bound, those things that repeatedly get you in trouble or repeatedly take you away from the perfect will of God for your life.

> *"And he took the calf which they had made, and burnt it in the fire, and ground it to powder, and strewed it upon the water, and made the children of Israel drink of it."* (Exodus 32:20)

In this particular chapter, the children of Israel made a golden calf and began to worship it; the golden calf that they had made was displeasing both to God and Moses. Now, notice how Moses got rid of the problem. He completed destroyed it by fire, by beating it into powder, and spreading it over the water. These actions assured the children of Israel that they would never be able to encounter that specific problem again.

This is precisely what you are to do today with breaking bad habits or addictions. You are to completely and totally wipe out and bring to an end whatever it is against you, removing any and all possibilities of you ever experiencing the bad situation again. By completely and totally wiping out what is against you, you are getting rid of the problem. You are destroying or getting rid of all connecting association that causes you to deviate from your intended purpose.

In his book *"The Anointing to Live"*, Pastor Creflo Dollar says,

> *"The anointing that Jesus has is designed to remove burdens and destroy yokes. In fact, in Hebrew the word* destroy *means* "to progressively corrode until something is reduced to powder." *The anointing doesn't just break yokes—it disintegrates them. Learning to live in freedom, joy, and power of the anointing is to live in the perfect will of the Father."* (P. 5)

Notice this scripture: *"He that committeth sin is of the devil; for the devil sinneth from the beginning. For this purpose the Son of God was manifested, that he might destroy the works of the devil."* (I John 3:8) Here we see that Jesus destroyed the works of the devil. The word *destroy* means *"to totally wipe out, to bring to an end or to defeat completely."*

145

KEY THOUGHT: When you are undecided
on what to do, do the right thing and you
will never go wrong with God

God can work with you when you do wrong, God just does not want you to consistently and deliberately to do wrong. God can make your wrong right when your intention was to do right. However, you cannot do wrong deliberately and expect God to make it right. You must have a desire to want to do what is right.

Notice what God told Cain before Cain killed his brother Abel:

> *"Why are you so angry?" the Lord asked him. "Why do you look so dejected? You will be accepted if you respond in the right way. But if you refuse to respond correctly, then watch out! Sin is waiting to attack and destroy you, and you must subdue it." (Genesis 4:6 NLT)*

In the above passage of scripture, God was trying to help Cain stay out of trouble. God's remedy for Cain staying out of trouble was to do the right thing. Rather than doing the right thing, Cain did the wrong thing and he suffered the rest of his life because of a bad decision.

One of the major remedies for breaking a bad habit is just doing what you know you ought to be doing. Do not make excuses, do not procrastinate, do not blame others, but do what you are supposed to do. The Bible says in James 4:17, *"Therefore to him that knoweth to do good, and doeth it not, to him it is sin."* The word **good** according to Webster's Dictionary means *to do what is right, proper or correct.*

With that now said, I personally believe that no one has to tell you that you are doing wrong. I believe that God has put in every human being the ability to discern right from wrong. Although, I do believe that some people are better than others at discerning what is right and what is wrong.

Think about this: If a cat knows how to run up a tree for safety when a dog is chasing it; if a fish knows how to swim out of the way when you are cleaning the fish tank; if a bird knows how to fly away if you get too close, why do humans struggle at doing the right thing?

Why does an overeater struggle with eating when he/she knows that he/she should not be eating? What makes an impulsive gambler be willing to lose all of the money, when he/she knows full well that the house payment is due and the baby needs a pair of shoes? How can a person do drugs when he/she knows and is fully consciously aware that doing drugs is going to kill him/her or land him/her in jail or prison?

Why do people smoke cigarettes when they know the label on the back of the carton specifically states that smoking can cause harm, injury or even death? And, yet they still smoke. Why do people do wrong when they know that they should be doing right? I believe one of the reasons is that these people enjoy the sensation of doing the wrong things. Not until they are caught up in the wrong thing and experience so much devastation from the wrong thing, will they want to change and do the right thing.

I think it interesting that when people experience enough headaches and heartaches from doing the wrong thing, their senses come alive. Then, they know what to do and desire to do the right thing. The desire to do the right thing was there in the beginning; it was just that they were so preoccupied with doing the wrong thing that they either did not want to do right, or had no awareness of what was right because they had done wrong for so long.

One way that you can keep the hand of God upon your life and flow in a life of peace and goodness is by making a habit of doing the right thing. When you are undecided on what to do, then do the right thing and you will never go wrong with God. This is what is called character. **Character** is *doing what is right, because it is right.*

This is what King David says in Psalms 51:10 *"Create in me a clean heart, O God; and renew a right spirit within me."* King David knew that the only way to have the favor of God and the blessings of God upon his life was to live right, which would be the result of him doing the right thing.

One of the reasons that people stay bound to things is because they do not take their struggles seriously enough. They do not avoid high-risk situations; they flirt and play around with things they know they should not be doing. This type of behavioral thinking keeps the addiction or bad habit around, and will eventually kill them if they don't gain some type of control over the bad habit.

As a chaplain, I observe many sick people in the hospital. In many cases, the illnesses could have been avoided if patients would have done the things that they should have done. Many times, the illness is the result of not carrying out the doctor's orders, abusing the body, and waiting until the last stages of the disease. Many people wait until things are way out of control, and then decide that they need to do something.

One reason that bad things happen to good people is that good people get themselves involved in bad things. Then, when bad things are consistently done, the good people make themselves look bad because they are not doing what is good.

Negative situations cannot stop if you are constantly involving yourself in negative activities. The Bible says; *"Be not deceived; God is not mocked: for whatsoever a man soweth, that shall he also reap."* *(Galatians 6:7)* You receive what you do, whether you want it or not; whatever you sow is exactly what you are going to reap.

The seventh step to breaking a bad habit is that you must **have a positive view of yourself.** In Numbers 13:33, God instructed the children of Israel to go into Canaan and possess the land that He had for them to enjoy. God said that it was a good land...a land flowing with milk and honey.

Everything that they needed would be in that land. All they had to do was act on what God instructed them to do. They not only had enough; but God had provided more than enough. However, they refused to obey the Lord because they had a poor view of themselves.

> *"But the men that went up with him said, We be not able to go up against the people; for they are stronger than we. And they brought up an evil report of the land which they searched unto the children of Israel, saying, The land, through which we have gone to search it, is a land that eateth up the inhabitants thereof; and all the people that we saw in it are men of a great stature. And there we saw the giants, the sons of Anak, which come of the giants: and we were in our own sight as grasshoppers, and so we were in their sight." (Numbers 13:31-33)*

How you view yourself will determine your success or failure in life. When you have a good self image, you will know and understand that you are able to accomplish whatever is before you. You will know that with the help of God and strong determination, there is no failure or stopping you from entering into God's best for your life.

You should never say that you are not able to do something, especially when God has said that you can do it. The negative image that the children of Israel had about themselves came from the enemy within. God never called them grasshoppers; God calls his people kings and priests, more than conquerors, mighty and great. You are an outstanding achiever, a world changer and history maker!

Dr. Mike Murdock, in his book, *"Wisdom for Crises Times"*, says,

> *The Israelites who left Egypt under Moses never entered Canaan, the land of abundance. You see, they had been peasants and slaves under Egyptian bondage. And they could never shake that slave ship mentality even though they had left Egypt! They thought like slaves. They talked like slaves. They behaved like slaves. They fretted. They fumed. They doubted their capability to overcome giants in the great Land of Promise, Canaan. They even labeled and named themselves as "Grasshoppers" when they saw the giants!" (P. 19)*

The children of Israel did not have a positive view of themselves and it was reflected in what they said, *"...We be not able to go up against the people; for they are stronger than we."* This saying was a disgrace and disservice to the Lord, which resulted in an 11-day journey turning into 40 years of wandering in the wilderness (Numbers 14:34) because they did not have a positive view of themselves.

You have to get it settled; no fear here. These spies saw the bigness of the people and started comparing themselves with the people (II Corinthians 10:12). You cannot compare where you are and what you have accomplished or what you are presently doing with someone else. If God is with you, you can do it; therefore, you do not have anything to worry about because God is going to work things to your advantage. He will not allow you to go under; God will allow you to come out the winner.

Kenneth Copeland, in his book, *Know Your Enemy*, says,

> "One time the Lord showed me a vision of a man holding a big banana. The man began to peel the banana inside, but standing in the bottom was a little man. That man was me! The Lord said, Son that's your attitude toward yourself. It was true. I presented a big front to the world, but actually felt very small on the inside. The Lord told me I needed to change my whole attitude. He began to show me that His Word meant to be in Christ and to have Him in me. I learned that a born-again believer is a limitless creature of God – an unlimited power house of the very life of God himself!" (P. 81.)

You have to see yourself walking in total victory and be able to accomplish whatever you are trying to complete; you have to see yourself walking above your situation and not living beneath it. Scripture says,

> "And the LORD shall make thee the head, and not the tail; and thou shalt be above only, and thou shalt not be beneath; if that thou hearken unto the commandments of the LORD thy God, which I command thee

this day, to observe and to do them:" (Deuteronomy 28:13)

In regards to the *above only* in this passage, it is in reference to mastery. It means victorious living, a life of triumphal jubilant celebration. This can only occur when you have a view of God's mindset concerning you and your situation. Thinking this way will change the outcome of your whole situation.

When people have a poor image of themselves they talk about how bad a person they are; people with a poor self image of themselves will talk a lot about past pain and hurt mainly because they have not received healing. What they fail to realize about talking negatively or contrary to the word of God is what they say about themselves. What you say is what you do:

In her book *"Battlefield of the Mind"* Joyce Meyer says,

> *"Some people see things negatively because they have experienced unhappy circumstances all their lives and can't imagine anything getting any better. Then there are some people who see everything as bad and negative simply because that is the way they are on the inside. Whatever the cause, a negative outlook leaves a person miserable and unlikely of making any progress toward the Promised Land." (P.186)*

You cannot say things like, I am going to always be fat, because you will always be fat. You cannot say things like he or she makes me sick to death because you will become ill and die; you cannot say things like I am always messing up and can't get anything right because your life will be a total mess and you will constantly be struggling with things not working right for you.

*"Let no corrupt communication proceed out of your
mouth, but that which is good to the use of edifying,
that it may minister grace unto the ears." (Ephesians
4:29)*

In this scripture, it is indicating that positive results will
come because of positive speaking. When you say things that
are in opposition to the word of God, God cannot work on your
behalf because God and the Word (Bible) are one. Therefore, if
you want God to help you break a bad habit you have to come
into agreement with God's words.

*"If you abide in Me, and My words abide in you, you
will ask what you desire, and it shall be done for you."
(John 14:7NKJV)*

What you say is what you are going to get. Notice this scripture, *"...According to your faith be it unto you." (Matthew 9:29)*
Your faith is a direct connection to what you say and what you
believe. What you say is what you believe and what you believe
is what you are going to have. Therefore, if you do not mean it,
do not say it because you **will** have what you say.

This type of thinking is different from professional institutionalized treatment centers. In professional institutionalized
treatment centers, they will tell you that you need to confess
what you are. If you are an impulsive gambler they will have
you confess in groups and in different activities several times
a day that you are an impulsive gambler.

The problem with negative confession is what you say and
believe is what you are going to receive, therefore, if you confess
you will always be an impulsive gambler, then you will always
be an impulsive gambler because you have what you say.

The Bible says,

> *"And Jesus answering saith unto them, Have faith in God. For verily I say unto you, That whosoever shall say unto this mountain, Be thou removed, and be thou cast into the sea; and shall not doubt in his heart, but shall believe that those things which he saith shall come to pass; he shall have whatsoever he saith. Therefore I say unto you, What things soever ye desire, when you pray, believe that ye receive them, and ye shall have them."* (Mark 11:22-24)

In this particular passage of scripture, Jesus indicates that we can speak to the mountain or situation and it must obey us. Jesus says that we can take control of an opposing situation simply by the words that we speak. Therefore, if you are speaking negatively, whatever negativity there is will happen to you.

The Bible says, *"And David recovered all."* (I Samuel 30:18) This scripture is in reference to King David recovering all the material things that was stolen from him and his army. However, God is omnipotent (all powerful) and can do all things. This means that God can deliver an excessive alcoholic, a cocaine/crack addict, a prostitute, an impulsive gambler or liar, root worker, over eater, excessive cigarette smoker and devil worshiper; it really doesn't matter what the habit is—God can have you recover from it if you really want him to.

God can move in on a horrible situation and give you total peace, restoration and recovery from all that you are facing. He can give you such a liberation and an overcoming power that when you break free of grips of bondage there will be such a driving force and a conquering mentality never to enter into the addiction or bad habit again.

A secular treatment institution cannot teach the power of God. They can teach religion or spirituality; however, the power of God can only come from the name of Jesus, word of God, Spirit of God, and prayer. Where the name of Jesus, word of God, the Spirit of God, and prayer are so is the ability to recover from chronic addictions and bad habits.

Job said it this way *"I know that thou canst do everything and that no thought can be withholden from thee." (Job 42:2)* That means that God can do for you whatever you need Him to do. However, you will have to be in Him, meaning in a proper relationship with Jesus Christ. Therefore, if you are struggling in a certain area, God can give you total deliverance, restoration and healing, but you have to be aware of what you are saying. You cannot speak contrary to what God's word is saying.

Dr. Frederick K.C. Price says,

> *"If we desire to walk in victory every day of the year, we must form the habit of making a positive confession whenever we speak. Most people think of something bad when they see or hear the word habit, but there are really more good habits than there are bad ones. It is a good habit to bathe, to brush your teeth, to comb your hair, and to use deodorant. Another good habit is to continually confess the right thing." (P. 17)*

Always remember that God can change how you are to you becoming what you expect to be. One of the ways that God can do this is by you speaking the word of God over yourself. *"...Calleth those things which be not as though they were." (Romans 4:17)* If you desire good to come out of your life, you will have to speak good about yourself. Even if things are bad, you have to declare that in the name of Jesus Christ, all things are working out for my good and I am winning because I am more than a conqueror.

If you say negative things about yourself, you will have them and if you say good things about yourself, you will have them. It is interesting to note that in Genesis chapter one, every thing that God said happened. It is also interesting to note that everything that God said was good because He created them. (Genesis 1:31) Let no negative word proceed out of your mouth because you must do the same thing as God. If you want the results of God, you need to do what He says.

Dr. Fredrick K.C. Price, in his book, *Three Keys to Positive Confession*, says,

> *"Confessing the pain will not get rid of the pain. It will only increase it, because pain confessed is pain possessed. Sickness confessed is sickness possessed. Fear confessed is fear possessed. Poverty confessed is poverty possessed. Inability confessed is inability possessed. When you say it, you will have it. (P. 39)*

In my clinical experience, I have had the privilege of working with methadone patients. Methadone is an opioid "agonist" which means, it is used in a way that is very similar to narcotic and other morphine drugs; methadone is used to stop heroin and opioids (certain pain medications) addictions, cravings and withdrawals.

Those patients tell me they are to be on methadone for life and the programs or treatment facilities that administrated this medication encourage the patients to be on methadone for life. The problem is that some of the patients get addicted to the methadone and the methadone addiction is just as bad as their previous drug addiction.

Remember, methadone is a narcotic drug (medication); if not used properly it can and will become addictive. To avoid a life long addiction, these patients will need to believe God to get them off methadone. The longer these patients take medication, the greater the possibility of them staying on the methadone, which is very beneficial for the company's profit.

> "And when he was come into the house, the blind men came to him: and Jesus saith unto them, Believe ye that I am able to do this? They said unto him, Yea, Lord. Then touched he their eyes, saying, According to your faith be it unto you. And their eyes were opened..." (Matthew 9:28-30)

These two blind men believed that they were able to receive their healing by the confession that they made. "They said unto him, Yea, Lord." This indicates that although you do not have something in the natural you can believe God and you can receive what you believe. The first thing you have to do in order to have what you say is that you must put your faith out there—done by confessing the word of God over your life. Now by you saying the Word, God has something to work with to help you.

When Jesus met these men, they were blind. These men refused to stay victims to their blindness. When they heard of Jesus in the house, these blind men got active. That is one of the main keys to overcoming a bad habit; you need to get active in pursuing restoration and recovery. These men came to Jesus; Jesus did not come to them. In other words, these two blind men progressed to a point to where they were fed up with being blind. They also believed that they could make their own way prosperous by pursuing Jesus Christ for their healing.

> *"This Book of the Law shall not depart out of your*
> *mouth, but you shall meditate on it day and night,*
> *that you may observe and do according to all that*
> *is written in it. For then you shall make your way*
> *prosperous, and then you shall deal wisely and have*
> *good success." (Joshua 1:8)*

Another interesting point is that these blind men allowed Christ to speak in their lives; they received what was spoken. In order to receive, you must believe. This also is important because often you go to people for help but when you do or say something that is challenging, or contrary to someone's opinion, often you get offended and shut down—not willing to work through difficulties to overcome your bad habit.

The Blind Man's Recovery Process

In concluding the steps to breaking a bad habit, I would like to finish by looking at another blind man Jesus healed in Mark 8:22-26. The blind man that Jesus healed had a process that he went through that was very significant in order for his healing to take place. I believe that the same process that the blind man used to recover can be very beneficial to helping you overcome what you are going through.

> *They came to Bethsaida, and some people brought*
> *a blind man and begged Jesus to touch him. He took*
> *the blind man by the hand and led him outside the*
> *village. When he had spit on the man's eyes and put*
> *his hands on him, Jesus asked, "Do you see anything?"*
> *He looked up and said, "I see people; they look like*
> *trees walking around." Once more Jesus put his hands*
> *on the man's eyes. Then his eyes were opened, his*

sight was restored, and he saw clearly. Jesus sent him home, saying, "Don't go into the village." (Mark 8:22-26, NIV)

First, we see that the blind man surrounded himself with people who were willing to bring the best out in him. The man was blind but not crippled; although, he was blind, he could walk. Jesus led the blind man. Therefore, do not let what you do not have, stop you from getting what you need.

It is interesting to note that the blind man's friends would not allow the blind man to live comfortably in his blind condition. It is important to have people in your life that will not allow you to wallow and sit in living beneath God's best. Do not accept living below God's best, and do not get complacent with sin, weakness, shortcomings, struggles and inadequateness.

Know that God can make you better; He can heal, restore, deliver and work out whatever needs to be done in your life. You need to know that whatever you are struggling with, or whatever might have you addicted, bound or stuck, is not the will of God. God wants you better.

Second, we see that Jesus took the blind man by the hand; the taking by the hand signifies safety, protection, guidance and direction. Whenever, Jesus has you by the hand, there is nothing that can overpower nor overwhelm you. Scripture says,

He said, "Come ahead." Jumping out of the boat, Peter walked on water to Jesus. But when he looked down at the waves churning beneath his feet, he lost his nerve and started to sink. He cried, "Master, save me!" Jesus didn't hesitate. He reached down and grabbed his hand. Then he said, "Faint-heart, what got into you?" (Matthew 14:29-31 TM)

There are three things, which I would like to point out about Peter getting out of the boat:

1. When Jesus grabs Peter by the hand, Peter was at that moment safely secure and had no doubt, even though he was still out of the boat. God will give you secure comfort as you go through your situation.

   Again, once Jesus grabbed Peter by the hand, Jesus was not going to let Peter go. All of the deliverance, recovery, restoration, and comfort that Peter needed were in the hands of Jesus. Allstate Insurance Company indicates that if you buy their insurance you will be in good hands. With Jesus, if you allow Him to touch you, if you allow Him to hold your hand, not only will you be in good hands, you will be in the **best** hands.

   The psalmist says, *"Though I walk in the midst of trouble, thou wilt revive me; Thou shalt stretch forth thine hand against the warth of mine enemies, And thy right hand shall save me. (Psalms 138:7)* God is bigger and stronger than anything you will ever encounter. The best way to get out of whatever you are going through is to come to Jesus. Let Jesus Christ enlighten you on what you need to do to get your breakthrough.

2. We see that Peter just jumped into the water; Peter did not think about what he was getting himself into. When people make major decisions and do not think about what they are doing, this careless thinking does not turn out well. I have seen people buy cars on impulse, and only months later, have them repossessed because they did not count the cost. They just saw something

they wanted and went after it, even if they paid interest on the car three times the cost.

This is also true of marriages, business deals, job opportunities, real-estate investments and so on. When you make quick, prompt, or impulsive decisions without counting the cost, again, in most cases it will not work out well for you in the end. Think about what you are doing before you do it. Scripture says,

> But don't begin until you count the cost. For who would begin construction of a building without first getting estimates and then checking to see if there is enough money to pay the bills? (Luke 14:28, NLT)

One of the good things about thinking before you do something is that you can get your thought process together about what you have just decided to do. You will be mentally and spiritually prepared to deal with adverse and unexpected situations that may arise from the decisions that you make. When you take your time to think or count the cost about what you are doing, you are eliminating the possibility of failure.

3. We see that Jesus, without hesitation, grabbed Peter by the hand and pulled him out of the water. This gesture indicates that God is always willing and ready to respond to the needs of his people. Scripture says, "I waited patiently for the LORD And He inclined to me and heard my cry. He brought me up out of the pit of destruction, out of the miry clay. And He set my feet upon a rock making my footsteps firm. (Psalms 40:1, NAS)

Reverting to the blind man (Mark 8:22-26), the **third** thing that was very significant in his recovery is that Jesus spit on the man's eyes. This action indicates that healing, deliverance, restoration, and recovery do not always come by conventional wisdom. It is important to be open and accepting of new ideals and different approaches to get you better.

Suppose the blind man would have said to Jesus, now you just wait a minute here! You have to be out of your mind! I know you are the Lord but I cannot let you spit on me. If this blind man had taken that approach, he would have not received his healing. Many times people cannot recover from chronic addiction and bad habits because they are not willing to accept nor adjust from their set way of doing things.

Fourth, we see the blind man was honest about what was going on within him. When Jesus asked the blind man what he saw, the blind man could have settled for partial recovery. The blind man could have said *"I see! Great!"* and walked off with blurred vision, this would have not been God's best. However, the blind man was honest; he was not willing to settle for partial recovery. He wanted to be completely healed. God can completely recover you from whatever you are in if you are honest about your situation.

Fifth, we see how the blind man did not give up just because he did not totally recover on the first attempt. The blind man was willing to reassess the situation with Jesus, so that he could see correctly. This is important. You should not let attempts that did not get you better stop you from trying to get better.

If you don't get what you want on the first attempt, then try again. The Bible is full of people who had to do things repeatedly in order to get the results that they were looking for. Let us look at some of these people.

One, Moses had to go to Pharaoh several times before Pharaoh decided to let the children of Israel go to serve the Lord. Notice this scripture,

> *"But I know that the king of Egypt will not let you go except under heavy pressure. So I will reach out and strike at the heart of Egypt with all kinds of miracles. Then at last he will let you go. (Exodus 3:19-20, NLT)*

Although Moses had to go many times to Pharaoh, Moses did not stop going to him until Pharaoh released the people of Israel. You should never stop trying until you have succeeded at what you want to do.

Two, Elijah the prophet asked his servant to go by the sea seven more times after he went the first time, to determine if the rain was coming to end the drought.

> *"And said to his servant, Go up now, look toward the sea And he went up, and looked, and said, There is nothing. And he said, Go again seven times. And it came to pass at the seventh time, that he said, Behold, there ariseth a little cloud out of the sea..." (I Kings 18:43-44)*

Although initially, this servant went to the sea and saw nothing, he was encouraged by Elijah to continue to return until he saw rain. The rain came and the drought finally ended. Overcoming bad habits work the same way; you will have to stay at what you are trying to accomplish, although, initially, you might see no results of your efforts.

Three, During Jesus' temptation in the wilderness, (Matthew 4:1-11) Jesus set forth an example that even though things or situations might not go or leave immediately, **you just need to keep trying and don't give up. You will overcome.** Jesus consistently spoke the word of God until the devil left him alone. *(Matthew 4:11, NLT)* You need to consistently speak the word of God for the devil to leave you alone.

Although Jesus quoted scripture (Deuteronomy 8:3, 6:16, 6:13) He continually spoke the word of God until he received the victory over the devil. Your recovery is the same way; you will have to keep at it and keep at it, until you get your victory.

CHAPTER 8

The Advantages and Disadvantages Of Treatment Institutions

I believe that there are pros and cons or advantages and disadvantages to attending some treatment institutions. This is not to say that all treatment institutions are bad because they are not, and this is not to say that all treatment institutions are good because they are not. However, one thing is certain— God can heal, deliver and set you free, whether or not you are in a treatment institution.

God has the power (ability to accomplish) to help you overcome, no matter what you may be experiencing. You can, and will be revived, refreshed, renewed, restored and rejuvenated to your proper place in God. Let us look at some disadvantages and advantages of treatment institutions:

Disadvantages

1. The majority of professional institutions are only interested in your money. If you cannot pay, you will not stay, especially, considering inpatient programs. I have seen over the years a lot of non-compliant (acting out) patients get special treatment because they have a lot of money. For the majority of treatment centers there is an old saying, *"money talks."* If you do not have money, you will not be counseled; you will be directed to other facilities that have available resources to help you.

2. A majority of professional institutions find the name Jesus Christ to be offensive. To mention the name of Jesus in an inappropriate setting could be grounds of immediate termination of staff, depending largely upon the setting and whether or not His name (Jesus Christ) was used on purpose or by incidental response. If a patient complains about the name of Jesus Christ, the complainer(s) complaint will definitely be looked into immediately.

3. With some cases, the staff and patient relationship is not genuine; the staff person, in most cases, is only there to receive a paycheck. Therefore, because the staff person is primarily interested in a check, the probability of accidents, non-compliant patients, inaccurate documentation and poor job performance will increase.

Advantages

1. In a professional institution, the staff person(s) are very well trained to handle situations appropriately that may be challenging to the patients.

2. With special cases professional institutions can set up payment plans to help the patients with financial difficulty. In addition, different insurance providers are accepted with a percentage of down payments.

3. A support network is very strong in a professional setting. The patient will receive not only support from staff, but patients, and some relationships with other patients are lifetime relationships.

4. State and federal government agencies provide much material and advice, A tremendous amount of clinical resources are available to the patients.

The main reason for me emphasizing the advantages and disadvantages of treatment programs is to get you to learn to trust God as your major source, whether or not you are in a treatment program; your trust should be in God to get you better. The Bible says, *"It is better to trust in the LORD than to put confidence in a man." (Psalms 118:8)* Again, trusting in the Lord will save you a lot of time, energy and money.

Oral Roberts in his book, *Jesus Sat Where You Sit,* says,

> *"Jesus expects you to look to Him for the hope and meaning of life. And you can. He is your* Source. *He is your only* Source. *He will always be your only* Source. *Let me tell you that Jesus, My personal Lord and Savior, knows every foot of this earth.*

He's walked every foot of it. He's felt every pain.
AND HE NOT ONLY FEELS IT— HE'S READY TO
WALK YOU THROUGH IT." (P. 11)

The Bible provides examples of people who only God could help. Let us take a look at some of these people.

1. **King Asa** – In II Chronicles 16:12-13, King Asa was diseased in his feet until his disease became life threatening. He sought the physician in time of his sickness instead of the Lord and he died. The sole reason for this king's death is that he did not seek God first for his healing.

2. **The lady with the issue of blood** – In Mark 5:25-34, this woman had been suffering from this hemorrhage for twelve years; she sought many physicians over the years and went into bankruptcy from visitations. She never got better but worse. When she met Jesus, though, immediately she was healed.

3. **The boy who was demonic possessed** – In Mark 9:14-29, this boy did not have a mental problem or psychological problem; he had a spiritual problem that began when he was a child. Therefore, no type of medication or special counseling services would have helped this boy; the devil had to come out of this boy before he could get better. The only way the devil could come out was through the name of Jesus accomplished through prayer and fasting.

On the contrary, many people try to recover on their own from bad habits and they find themselves unable to overcome or break their negative behavior. This is when the treatment programs or professional institutions are beneficial for recovery.

Ruth Turk, the author of the book *Ray Charles: Soul Man*, says,

> *In August 1965, Ray checked himself into St. Francis Hospital outside of Los Angeles. Ray refused the usual treatment for Narcotics withdrawal. He would not take pills, sedatives, or tranquilizers to ease the difficulty of withdrawal. For the first few days he was very sick, but he had promised himself he was going to make it on his own. He stayed in his room and concentrated on overcoming the pain and misery with every bit of willpower he could collect. Not convinced that Ray was seriously going "cold turkey" – withdrawing from narcotics suddenly and completely-hospital employees searched Ray's room and belongings. They could not find drugs hidden anywhere. Finally, they gave him several tests that proved he was clean. Ray had broken a 17-year addiction. (P. 87-88)*

Ray Charles was able to overcome his bad habit and break the cycle of his chronic addiction by checking himself into a treatment program/professional institution. This institution proved very beneficial for Ray Charles because he was able to successfully overcome his bad habit.

Another reason that people do not like to go to institutionalized programs is that they do not want to be associated with what, some call, the crazy house. Many people are misinformed and uneducated when it comes to professional recovery.

Admitting yourself into a professional institutional program does not qualify nor identify you as a crazy. I have more respect for people who are willing to get help because they know they need help, than for people who need help and know that they need help, but refuse for whatever reason, to get help. God can't help you if you do not want to be helped.

When you are addicted and the situation continues to get worse, and you cannot recover on your own, then get professional help, or at the least, tell a friend about your condition. You will need someone to walk you through the process of how you can obtain and maintain your sobriety. Make no doubt about it; your situation is not going to get better if you do not take action to do something about the out-of-control behavior. Your situation will get worse.

Addictions or bad habits are designed to take you as low as you can go, while good habits are designed to take you as high as you can go. Therefore, you will have to decide whether or not you can quit the negative behavior on your own; if not, look into getting help from a professional institution. Whatever way you choose, always remember that it is God who is going to make you better. He works through people to get you better.

CHAPTER 9

||||||||||||||||||||||||||||

What to Do When Under Attack

"...But David encouraged himself in the Lord his God.
And David said to Abiathar the priest, Ahimelech's
son, I pray thee, bring me hither the ephod. And
Abiathar brought thither the ephod to David. And
David inquired at the Lord, saying, Shall I pursue after
this troop? Shall I overtake them? And he answered
him, Pursue: for thou shalt surely overtake them, and
without fail recover all." (I Samuel 30:6-8)

In this particular chapter while King David and his army
were away, the Amalekites (enemies) had invaded the South,
conquering King David's place of residency, taking captive all
their wives, children and all their material possessions. King
David's army was so devastated, they cried themselves powerless; their thoughts were to kill King David for having them
away from their families.

King David, deeply wounded and basking in a pool of tears,
quickly got himself together. King David who was the leader
over this army no doubt knew that he needed to do something
quickly about this matter. If you do not deal with your problem,

your problem will conquer you; it will not get better until you take authority over it.

There are some basic principles that King David used when he was under attack: **First, he encouraged himself in the Lord.** What was he encouraging himself about? God was good and God was going to work this situation out for his good and that no weapon that is formed against him shall prosper. Whatever is wrong; God was going to make it right.

Encouraging yourself in the Lord is where you get the inner strength from God that will produce self-motivation and stimulation to believe that you can win. It is important that you have no doubt that the Lord will allow you to win. Below, I have listed **words of encouragement** that are essential for success and spiritual growth.

You can	Be blessed	God is able
That's powerful	Winner	Genuine
Success	Happy	Love
Looking good	Empowerment	Super
Vision	Focused	Teachable
Smile	Responsible	Patient
You're the best	Knowledge	Healed
Forgiveness	Open-mined	Vision
Kindness	Humbleness	Joy
Encourager	Discipline	Motivated
God's favor	Honesty	Excellence
You will	Consistent	Caring
Good thinking	Acceptance	Outstanding
Congratulations	Good going	Thanks
Correct	Impressive	Awareness
Believe	Great job	Grace
You're intelligent	Wisdom	Integrity
Increase	Good work	Peaceful

When you encourage yourself in the Lord, you will begin to see the bigness of God and the littleness of your problem. You will begin to believe that you can receive everything that you have spoken and it will happen according to Mark 11:24. You must believe that you have it **now**, you believe it **now** and you possess it **now** because faith is *now* according to Hebrews 11:1.

Biblical Evidence of Encouraging Yourself in the Lord

1. Paul and Silas praised God in jail. (Acts 16:25-26.) *"And at midnight Paul and Silas prayed, and sang praises unto God: the prisoners heard them, and suddenly there was a great earthquake, so that the foundations of the prison were shaken: and immediately all the doors were open, and everyone's band was loosed."*

2. Job's wife wanted him to denounce God and die, after the death of their children, servants and cattle. (Job 2:9-10) *"Then said his wife unto him, Dost thou still retain thine integrity? Curse God and die. But he said unto her, Thou speakest as one of the foolish women speaketh. What? Shall we receive good at the hand of God, and shall we not receive evil? In all this did not Job sin with his lips."* **Job understood that if he could not pray his way out he was going to praise his way out. God blessed him with double and increased his latter years greatly. (Job 42:10, 12)**

3. Jehoshaphat praised the Lord before entering into battle, *"And when they began to sing and to praise, the Lord set ambushments against the Children of Ammon, Moab, and mount Seir, which were come against Judah; and they were smitten." (II Chronicles 20:22-23)*

4. **Nehemiah and the people rebuilt the walls of Jerusalem because they focused on praising God,** *"...for the joy of the Lord is your strength."* **In other words, the joy of the Lord produced super-natural sustaining ability for them to hold up under the pressures of quitting.**

If you are going to successfully overcome when you are under attack then you will need to rejoice and encourage yourself in the Lord. You can set your will to be encouraged...no matter what.

In Acts 26:2, Paul says, *"I thinketh myself happy."* When looking at Paul's situation from a logical viewpoint there was nothing that Paul should have been happy about; he was in chained custody and headed toward house arrest, while the Jewish government was trying to take his life (kill him) for preaching the gospel. (Acts 23:12)

Paul set his will to be happy no matter what. We cannot control certain things or situations from happening to us; however, we can control how we will deal with those things and situations that are happening to us.

> *"I call heaven and earth to record this day against you, that I have set before your life and death, blessing and cursing: therefore, choose life, that both thou and thy seed may live: That thou mayest love the LORD thy God, and thou mayest cleave unto him: for he is thy life, and the length of thy days..." (Deuteronomy 30:19-20)*

You have a choice, you can choose to be happy or you can choose to be sad. You can choose to be positive or you can choose to be negative. You can choose to believe that you can receive promotion, increase, deliverance and total life prosperity, in abundance, to the full, and until it runs over, or you can choose to do nothing and just allow the best to pass you by.

The **second** thing King David did while under attack was that he came to the point to where **he had had enough.** King David had had enough of his folks crying, complaining and putting death threats on his life. Often, change will not occur in people lives until they get to the point of having enough of what they are going through. **Discontentment is one of the catalysts to produce change.** King David stopped crying and decided to do something about his situation.

To overcome bad habits and to deal productively with things coming against you, you must stop seeing yourself as the victim and start visualizing yourself as the victor. Again, you will not look to the bigness of your problem but you will look to the biggest of your God.

Rosa Parks

A modern day person who came to the point to where she had had enough of being picked on was Mrs. Rosa Parks. She refused one day to give up her seat to a white man, and go to the back on a transit bus in Montgomery, Alabama, where Negroes were required to sit or stand at the back during that time period in American history.

Rosa Parks had had enough of social injustice, and did not think that it was constitutional for a black woman to be forced to stand in order for a white man to sit down. Therefore, she took courage, taking action by stepping up and speaking out. What she did set in motion a revolution, and to this very day, has changed the history of race relationships in America forever. All races of people are now given the right to sit where they choose... all this occurred because a woman came to the point to where she had had enough of social injustice.

Douglas Brinkley, the author of the book, *Rosa Parks, A Life*, says,

> *That changed on December 1, 1955, when Rosa Louise Parks, a prim, bespectacled, forty-two-year-old mulatto seamstress, made history by refusing to give up her seat on the Cleveland Avenue bus to a white man. Her courageous act touched off a 381-day boycott of the city's bus system, led by Dr. Martin Luther King, Jr., and is now considered the beginning of the American Civil Rights Movement. (P. 2)*

Mrs. Rosa Parks came to the point to where she had had enough of the back-of-the bus syndrome. She did not fight back physically, but she fought back mentally, politically, and spiritually. In June 15, 1999, Mrs. Rosa Parks was awarded the Congressional Medal of Honor, a tribute to recognize the courage of one single woman who influenced the nation.

Another example of Mrs. Rosa Parks being fed up or having had enough of social injustice is the Scottsboro Boys. In her book *Quiet Strength* Rosa L. Parks, says,

> *Mrs. Rosa Parks worked courageously for the release of the Scottsboro Boys, a group of nine young black men who were wrongly accused of raping two white women in 1931. They were found guilty and condemned to die for a crime they did not commit. They did not die, thanks to the effort of many. Anyone who supported them had to meet in secret. To do anything openly for this cause could mean death. And yet Parks,*

alone with the NAACP, fearlessly pursued justice for these men. (P. 46-47)

To be fed up or to have enough of something and you do not take active endeavors to change the structure that is causing chaos and confusion is not being an activist. An activist is a person who is fed up with how negative things are and acts to change the situation to make things better.

The Children of Israel

A similar situation occurred with the children of Israel. They were facing the Red Sea and their enemies the Egyptians were traveling fast to destroy them. (Exodus 14:9, 15) God said *go forth* which indicates that **you have to get to a point to where you move on.** This is where the process of overcoming a bad habit really begins. You make a decision that you have had enough and you will not put up with the worries, pains or hurts any longer. So, you decide to not stay at that point anymore; you go forth.

In overcoming bad habits you have to get to a point where you have had enough of bad experiences; you have to make a quality decision that you have had enough junk in your life, and you will not go through it any longer. You decide to move on to bigger and better things for your life.

The Four Lepers

In II Kings 7:3-9, the four lepers had to make a quality decision whether or not to live or die by entering Syria (the enemy city) for food during the famine. If they stayed outside the city they would die because there was no food.

They made the choice to enter the city, and their enemies,

the Syrian army, had departed the city because the Lord made the Syrians hear a noise of chariots and horses and a great number of people coming to destroy them; so, the enemy left their camp leaving all their goods behind and the lepers' dreams became a reality.

They gained unlimited access to all the city resources; they had more than they could have ever imagine, which was a dream that came true. All because of a quality decision that they made to enter into the city! You have to **make the quality decision to go after what you desire** and God will give you the strength to overcome.

Nelson Mandela

I believe that an excellent example of a person who was intolerant of wrong behaviors and who worked overwhelmingly, demanding change, is Nelson Mandela. Remember, change can only occur when you take constructive action to deal with what is wrong. **Whatever you are willing to tolerate, you cannot change.** Nelson Mandela and others had come to a point to where they had had enough of injustice and mistreatment and decided to do something about them.

As recipient of the 1993 Nobel Peace Prize, President of the African National Congress, Nelson Mandela had to under go a numerous series of things before he could see change within the nation of South Africa.

In his book, *Long Walk to Freedom,* **Nelson Mandela, says,**

> *Africans were desperate for legal help in government buildings: it was a crime to walk through a White Only door, a crime to ride a White Only bus, a crime to use a White Only drinking fountain, a crime to*

walk on a Whites Only beach, a crime to be on the
streets past eleven, a crime not to have a pass book
and a crime to have the wrong signature in that book,
a crime to be unemployed and a crime to be employed
in the wrong place, a crime to live in certain places
and a crime to have no place to live." (P.149)

Nelson Mandela, simply put, was a freedom fighter through-out his life; he experienced intense cruelty, social injustice, discrimination, and racial prejudice. As a freedom fighter, he fought for South African blacks to have the right to vote, the right to buy land, and the right to repeal all discriminatory leg-islation. He was investigated, arrested and went to prison many times for advocating the right for fair treatment and equality among all African people.

Nelson Mandela says this about prison life:

"At 7:15, we were taken into a tiny cell with a single
drainage hole in the floor which could be flushed
only from the outside. We were given no blankets,
no food, no mats, and no toilet paper. The hole regu-
larly became blocked and the stench in the room was
insufferable...At six o'clock we received sleeping mats
and blankets. I do not think words can do justice to a
description of the foulness and filthiness of this bed-
ding. The blankets were encrusted with dried blood
and vomit, ridden with lice, vermin and cockroaches,
and reeked with a stench that actually competed with
the odiousness of the drain." (P. 240-241)

The courts banned him several times from talking to more than one person at a time, he was banned from attending meetings of all kind, not just political ones, and he could not even attend his own son's birthday party. As a lawyer, Nelson Mandela confronted the court system on clear violations of court practices.

The amazing thing about Nelson Mandela is that he was able to see change. On April 27, 1994 he witnessed South Africa having its first ever non-racial voting election. For the first time in South African history, the black majority could go to the polls to elect a president!

He lived to experience the freeing of political prisoners who were incarcerated for nonviolent activities. He was the only man in South Africa's history to serve 27 years in prison and to be elected the President of the African National Congress.

He was able to see the same laws, rules and relegations that he was once beaten, jailed, imprisoned, harassed, threaten, banned, and assaulted for change right before his very eyes. These corrupt and detestable laws, rules, and relegations changed because Nelson Mandela and others had come to a point to where they had had enough of social injustice and inequality. They demanded change; change did occur.

Here are three additional biblical references, which I would like to give you about people who had had enough of experiencing wrongdoing, and moved to do something about it. These people include the following:

Jesus

> *Jesus entered the temple area and drove out all who were buying and selling there. He overturned the tables of the money changers and the benches of those selling doves. "It is written," he said to them, "My house will be called a house of prayer, but you*

are making it a den of robbers." The blind and the
lame came to him at the temple, and he healed them.
(Matthew 21:12-14, NIV)

What made Jesus become so angry to where he started turning over the tables and benches in the temple of God? Jesus had had enough of people using the temple of God as a money-maker. Even though the tradition of that time period said the moneychangers had a right to be in the temple, they were not to become so preoccupied with making a profit, thus forgetting the true purpose of the temple—a place of prayer.

Those who sold their merchandise only for profit had no respect for God. The temple was designed for prayer, but the people had turned it into a shopping center. When Jesus cleansed the temple, the people immediately received healing. Jesus healed the blind and the lame. Jesus' actions brought about the reason that the temple was built...to focus on God through prayer.

Joseph

Joseph could stand it no longer. "Out, all of you!" he
cried out to his attendants. He wanted to be alone
with his brothers when he told them who he was.
Then he broke down and wept aloud. His sobs could
be heard throughout the palace, and the news was
quickly carried to Pharaoh's palace. I am Joseph!" he
said to his brothers. "Is my father still alive?" But his
brothers were speechless! They were stunned to real-
ize that Joseph was standing there in front of them.
Come over here," he said. So they came closer. And
he said again, "I am Joseph your brother whom you
sold into Egypt. But don't be angry with yourselves

*that you did this to me, for God did it, He sent me
here ahead of you to preserve your lives. (Genesis
45:1-5, NLT)*

Again, Joseph was a man of love and forgiveness; he did
not want to be away from his family any longer. Joseph had
had enough of being separated from his family; he loved them
and chose at that point to reveal himself to his brothers. This
revealing of himself to his brothers was not to punish, pay back
or gloat over the fact of how God has blessed him. No, it was
none of that.

Joseph revealed himself because he was ready to be with the
ones he loved, which was his family. Therefore, Joseph was willing to forgive his brothers and salvage their broken relationship
which was only possible when Joseph came to a point to where
he had had enough of hiding in pain and hurt; he chose to be
restored to his family instead of being separated from it.

David

*"Don't worry about a thing," David told Saul, "I'll
go fight this Philistine!" "Don't be ridiculous!" Saul
replied, "There is no way you can go against this
Philistine. You are only a boy, and he has been in
the army since he was a boy...So David triumphed
over the Philistine giant with only a stone and sling.
And since he had no sword, he ran over and pulled
Goliath's sword from its sheath. David used it to kill
the giant and cut off his head. (I Samuel 17:32-33,
50-51, LNT)*

The question must be asked, why did David take on the challenge of killing Goliath? David had come to a point to where he

had had enough of this giant Goliath, abusing, and dishonoring both God and the people of God. Therefore, David stepped up to do something about it.

The interesting thing about David taking on the challenge to kill Goliath is that God never told him to do it. There are some things in life that God just expects you to do. If the things you are doing are blocking, stopping, hindering or in opposition to God, then God wants you to deal with them. He expects you to do something about them.

David, no doubt, understood that anything that is opposing God or in direct conflict with God is not of God and is viewed as an enemy of God. Anything that you do that does not bring glory to God will eventually kill you. You have to take control of it.

When you are with God, God is always with you. (II Chronicles 15:2); David had served God faithfully, he walked spiritually upright and as a result, he knew that God would exonerate him over Goliath.

Now, we will continue to look at some of the principles that King David used while under attack. The **third** thing that King David did when he was under attack was **separate himself** of high-risk situations. What do I mean by high-risk situations? It means getting caught in things that can easily persuade you in the wrong direction; you have to avoid those things. One way of doing that is to just separate yourself from any negative influence.

Dr. Leroy Thompson says,

> *"Do not let habits and bondages hold you back from the things of God and the blessings of God. Live clean and holy. Consecrate yourself. The prophets of old – Isaiah, Jeremiah, Ezekiel, and others – would go before*

the people and say, "Consecrate yourselves before God!" We do not hear a lot about consecration in our society today. But consecration is an important part of walking in the blessings of God and overcoming the challenges of life that would try to rob you of those blessings. So strip away those things that are causing you not to bring glory to God's Name." (P. 103,104)

If King David had not separated himself and prayed, he could have easily become full of anger, depression and overwhelmed by the troops wanting to kill him. He could have said or done the wrong thing that could have possibly cost him his life, but, instead, he avoided a high-risk situation by separating himself; he prayed, instead.

If you want to be elevated, you will have to separate yourself and be with God; elevation is the result of separation. *"But when you pray, go away by yourself, shut the door behind you, and pray to your Father secretly. Then your Father, who knows all secrets, will reward you. (Matthew 6:6, NLT)*

When you separate yourself from a high-risk situation, God will allow you to see, in secret, what other people cannot see openly. John, the revelator, was isolated on the island of Patmos (Revelations 1:9-10) and observed things that no other man could see because he separated himself to God.

In addition, King David in I Samuel 30:7 asked for the *ephod*, the ephod represented consecrating oneself before the Lord. The ephod was similar to a "skirt" which had two shoulder straps, to which the golden breastplate was attached, and a belt to tie in the front. It was part of the dress of the high priest (Exodus 29:5-6, etc). It is here that King David sought the mind and the will of God, because whatever God tells you to do, it is always with the intent of prospering you.

If you really desire to overcome a bad habit, begin by consecrating yourself to the Lord. This is where you can get the wisdom on what to do and how to do it. David, no doubt, knew that if he was going to recover all that was stolen from him, he had to be in a place of total saturation before God. Saturating yourself before God will no doubt open up your heart and mind to receive from God. It is at this point that King David focused totally on the Lord's will for his life, thus avoiding all distraction and confusion that could have tormented his mind.

Now let us examine the definition of the word **separate**. It means, *"to divide, or set apart."* If you are going to walk in freedom, you must understand that God requires you to set yourself apart unto him. Several names can describe God. One of them is **Jehovah M'kaddesh,** which is *the Lord God your Sanctifier.*

One of the greatest ways to stay out of trouble is just to stay sanctified; the word **sanctify** is *hagiazo* or *hag-ee-ad'-zo* which means *to make holy, purify, or separate for the consecration of God.* It is literally becoming one with God. In other words, you will do what God likes to do, and you will say what God likes to say. The word **sanctify** carries with it the connotation of sameness. You will become one with the word of God and the spirit of God to successfully fulfill and complete the will of God.

Notice this scripture,

> *Sanctify them [purify, consecrate, separate them for Yourself, make them holy] by the Truth; Your Word is Truth. Just as You sent Me into the world, I also have sent them into the world. And so for their sake and on their behalf I sanctify (dedicate, consecrate) Myself, that they also may be sanctified (dedicated, consecrated, made holy) in the Truth." (John 17:17-19, AMP)*

The word of God is the answer, if you can get a hold of the Word when you are going through difficult times, you will overcome. The word of God will sanctify you, clearing your mind so you can be mentally alert to have holy, keen, astuteness to be led in the right direction to prosper and experience good success.

The best way to break strongholds, overcome chronic addictions and bad habits is to get full of the Word and live holy. The word of God will cleanse you of all toxifications; it will purify your body so that you can be strong enough to resist diseases, sickness, and illnesses.

Most people think that sanctification is women wearing long dresses, wearing no make up on their face or having long beautiful hair. For men, some think sanctification is wearing loose fitting clothes, no jewelry and keeping their hair cut short. Sanctification is more of an inward manifestation, not an outward manifestation. You can wear all of the right things; your appearance can look like its holy, yet you can still be full of hatred and evil.

Notice what Jesus said about the religious leaders and some of the so-called sanctified churchgoers of his day,

> "Woe unto you, scribes and Pharisees, hypocrites! For ye are like unto whitened sepulchers, which indeed appear beautiful outward, but are within full of dead men's bones, and of all uncleanness. Even so ye also outwardly appear righteous unto men, but within ye are full of hypocrisy and iniquity." (Matthew 23:27-28)

Jesus was saying that these religious leaders were pretenders, although they might seem to have it all together, spiritually,

Jesus knew better. Jesus had peeked at their hearts and knew exactly how they were. These religious leaders acted as though they had no relationship with God; they did not behave as a child of God should.

Observe this quote:

> When you follow the desires of your sinful nature, your lives will produce these evil results: sexual immorality, impure thoughts, eagerness for lustful pleasure, idolatry, participation in demonic activities, hostility, quarreling, jealousy, outbursts of anger, selfish ambition, divisions, the feeling that everyone is wrong except those in your own little group, envy, drunkenness, wild parties, and other kinds of sin. Let me tell you again, as I have before, that anyone living that sort of life will not inherit the Kingdom of God."
> (Galatians 5:19-21, NLT)

When you have these negative characteristics or behaviors in your life, it does not matter how you dress, what you wear or how you look or smell, if you are participating consistently in negative activity you are a bad example of God. God loves you, but you are a bad example of Christ. Remember, whatever you yield yourself to long enough; you will become addicted to it, whether good or bad.

In Matthew 23:27-28, Jesus knew that these religious leaders were not what they were professing to be, because there were no inward signs of transformation (change). When a person has changed, no one will have to tell you, you will know by what is said and done.

The Bible says that Satan (Devil) was beautiful, wise, rich, influential, possessing great trading skills and had an ability to produce excellent music, but he was dishonest, defiled and corrupt. Thus, he was kicked out of heaven by God for insubordination. These characteristics can be located in Ezekiel 28:1-19, and Satan's fall, Isaiah 14:12-17.

You can look good on the outside, but be corrupt on the inside. You can look, smell and dress good yet be all wrong if you do not change within. One of the ways that you detect a sanctified person is by what comes out of them and what they do around you. What they say and do will be godly.

The Bible says, *"Ye shall know them by their fruits..."* *(Matthew 7:16)* what you do is who you are, regardless of what you say or how you act. Jesus said that you would be able to identify fakes and phonies simply by how they act. Just like you can recognize a fruit on a tree; you can detect what type of fruit a person is bearing.

The Bible tells us what type of fruit we should produce in Galatians 5:22-23,*"But the fruit of the Spirit is love, joy, peace, longsuffering, gentleness, goodness, faith, meekness, temperance: against such there is no law."*

Everything that exists concerning you is wrapped up in love; love will never fail, it will never let you down (I Corinthians 13:8). The Bible says, *"God is love."* (I John 4:8) When you can learn to walk in the love of God, love alone will dismiss a lot of misfortune in your life. Love will enable you to forgive, care, be gentle and kind to others, as well as yourself. When walking in love, it will keep you from many disappointments, headaches, slips, pitfalls, and setbacks in your life.

Notice this scripture:

> *"I beseech you therefore, brethren, by the mercies of*
> *God, that ye present your bodies a living sacrifice,*

holy, acceptable unto God, which is your reasonable service." (Romans 12:1)

One of God's standards for living is holiness. Living holy is living right. Living right is following God's word; it is becoming one with God and His word (the Bible). God has called every born-again believer to live holy. There is nothing wrong with living holy. Scripture declares, *"Be you holy because God is holy."* One of the ways you get close to God is to stop deliberately sinning, and consistently living holy and pure in mind, body and spirit.

Dr. I.V. Hilliard, in his book, *Mental Toughness for Success*, says,

> *"When my heart is right toward God, He is obligated to orchestrate the circumstances, the events and situations of my life to bring me into the knowledge of the things and the people I need to know that are critical for the fulfillment of my purpose and destiny in my life." (P.25)*

One of the best ways to overcome a bad habit and stay free of demonic activity in your life is to keep your heart right by living holy and staying away from all activities that are associated with sin. *"For the wages of sin is death,"* (Romans 6:23); sin will bring evil spirits into your life attempting to destroy everything about you. The devil's purpose is to rob the body of Christ of its identity (John 10:10); if the body of Christ does not know who they are; the body of Christ will never be free to achieve God's best.

Dr. Leroy Thompson Senior, in his book, *What to do When Your Faith is Challenged*, says,

> *"Do not let habits and bondages hold you back from the things of God and the blessings of God. Live clean*

and holy. Consecrate yourself. The prophets of old
– Isaiah, Jeremiah, and Ezekiel, and other – would
go before the people and say, "Consecrate yourself
before God!" But consecration is an important part of
walking in the blessings of God and overcoming the
challenges of life that would try to rob you of those
blessings. So strip away those things that are causing
you not to bring glory to God's Name." (P. 103)

The **fourth** thing King David did when under attack is that
he took authority over his situation. King David did not just sit
there and cry about all the bad things that had happened. He
stopped crying, worrying and even waiting; once he got the
answer from God, he began to move. This is big in breaking
negative behaviors, because you must get to a point to where
you do something about your problem, if your problem is going
to get better.

David began to go after his enemies, which means that you
do not have to be taken away or pulled under by life's disappointments; you can take control of your bad situation. David
went after his family, which indicated that he was not going
to sit idle and allow things to just be, but David began to will
that things would get better by him choosing to make them
get better.

It is here that King David began to make his own way to
prosperity (Joshua 1:8). When you do for yourself, you help
yourself, but only God can get the credit for your success. Many
people sit around and wait for others to give them words of
wisdom, money, direction, hope or peace, when everything
they need is in Jesus. *"For in him we live, and move, and have our*
being..." (Acts 17:28) Your deliverance, security, freedom, and
everything you need to live is in Jesus.

The Bible says,

> *"According as his divine power hath given unto us all things that pertain unto life and godliness, through the knowledge of him that hath called us to glory and virtue." (II Peter 1:3)*

Jesus has given us everything that pertains to life. In other words, Jesus has given us the keys, tools, principles, gifts, strengths, and talents to unlock the greatness in our lives, and to come up out of whatever is trying to keep us down.

It is important to note that if you do not go after your desires, then things are not going to get better, but they will get worse. David heard from God, and then went after what he desired. When you are under attack, God will allow you to experience His victory.

Joyce Meyer in her book, *Eight Ways to Keep the Devil Under Your Feet*, demonstrates how to take authority over your situation:

> *"God has lots of good things stored up for His people— but in order to receive them, we must do something. In order to live in the good land He has set aside for us, we must be willing to go in and take possession of it." (P. 10)*

Your victory will be contingent upon you not complaining, caving-in, giving-up or quitting. *"And let us not be weary in well doing: for in due season we shall reap, if we faint not." (Galatians 6:9)* There are two things that must be done to overcome opposition. **One**, you can't quit, you cannot give up; you will never experience the joy of overcoming if you quit or give up.

Two, you must become active; if you want things to shift into your favor, you must become active doing something to make your situation better. You have a right to exercise your authority; you are a recipient of all the benefits and blessings that God has bestowed upon you through his son Jesus Christ.

> *David and the six hundred men with him came to the Besor Ravine, where some stayed behind, for two hundred men were too exhausted to cross the ravine. But David and four hundred men continued the pursuit. (I Samuel 30:9-10, NIV)*

Notice that King David had 200 men who stayed behind because they were weak; they were weak in body and, more importantly, they were weak in mind and spirit. The 200 men who stayed behind did not experience the joy of total restoration and recovery from all that the enemy had stolen from them. The reason? They stayed behind.

Another thing to consider about the 200 men is that they were too weak to pursue the enemy. Those who went with King David conquered the enemy; they refused to allow the weak, 200 men to have a part in the victory.

> *Then answered all the wicked men and men of Belial, of those that went with David, and said, Because they went not with us, we will not give them aught of the spoil that we have recovered, save to every man his wife and his children, that they may lead them away, and depart." (I Samuel 30:22)*

These weak 200 men almost lost out on everything except their families; that is precisely what happens when you don't become active and pursue what you know to do; ultimately you will lose out in the end. This is why you must become active, take authority over your situation because with God on your side you cannot lose; you are more than a Conqueror (Romans 8:37).

The **fifth** thing King David did when under attack is that **he was very compassionate and kind to the people.**

> *They found an Egyptian in the field and brought him to David, and gave him bread and he ate, and water to drink, And a piece of cake of figs and two clusters of raisins; and when he had eaten, his spirit returned to him, for he had no food or drunk any water for three days and three nights. "I Samuel 30:11-12)*

It was this Egyptian man who was dying of starvation who would give King David and his army the directions and insight to where their enemy was camping. If King David and his army would have been rude or unprofessional to this Egyptian man, the man could have become upset and would not have told them anything. However, by David and his army showing mercy, they received mercy, *"Blessed are the merciful: for they shall obtain mercy" (Matthew 5:7)* King David and his army took time to **be kind during tough times.**

Remember, whatever you want to happen to you, you have to make it happen for others. Do unto others as you want done unto yourself. Whatever good you do to others, you set yourself up for that same good to boomerang right back to you.

This man who King David helped was able to give King David and his army all the accurate information they needed to locate their enemy, thus recovering all that was stolen from King David and his people. In addition, David's compassion and kindness is seen when he convinced the 400 men who went to war to share their wealth with the weak 200 men who stayed behind. (I Samuel 30:22-25)

When under attack you cannot become angry, rude or cold with people because often the people you are angry, hard, or cold with could be the very people who God uses to bless and steer you in the right direction. Therefore, be kind to people and do not be afraid to ask people for help because they can point you in the right direction.

A major oversight that many people make when they are struggling with bad habits and addictions is they are not kind and compassionate. Rather, than being happy and kind to people, they get angry and frustrated mainly because things are not working quite the way they want them to.

When you are nasty and hateful to people, you are hurting yourself because most people will help you. In fact, when you are really acting out negatively, many people do not even want to be around you because they can clearly see that you have some issues going on and they refuse to be a part of your negative behavior.

The Hospital Visit

When you are angry, you really hurt yourself. People will not help you. My wife and I visited a patient in the hospital who was recuperating from an illness for a few days. We were asked by the patient's family to give this patient a visit since the hospital was near our home.

As we were traveling to the hospital, the Spirit of the Lord told me to go by the bank and get some money to bless this patient. When my wife and I walked into the room, immediately we were unwelcome; the patient who knew us very well was very rude and disrespectful.

The patient who knew my wife extremely well was saying things to my wife that I just did not like. Therefore, after listening approximately five to 10 minutes of this person's anger toward us, my wife and I agreed to leave. While going home, I remembered that I forgot to give the person the money that I received from the bank.

I allowed the person's anger to throw me off track. That is precisely what anger will do; it will throw you off track. I did not want to upset the patient; therefore, in a hurry to get out of the room, I forgot to give the patient the money which was intended for them. Anger if misappropriated, will cause hypertension, and distractions; it will throw you off from your intended purpose.

God told me that when people get angry, their blessing passes them by. I wanted to be a blessing to this patient but could not because the patient was mentally hurting too badly to receive it. This patient was so angry, hurt and torn by what she was going through that the patient's anger caused her not to be helped. Do not run God and people off when you are hurting; be humble and kind to people and they will help you.

When you are rude and ugly with people, you will run people off. The Bible says, *Make no friendship with an angry man; And with a furious man thou shalt not go: Lest thou learn his ways, And get a snare to thy soul." (Proverbs 22:24-25)* again, this person was so disrespectful; it wasn't until I had left the hospital that I remembered about the money God told me to give. Anger improperly managed causes destruction and confusion. God is not the author of confusion, but peace. (I Corinthians 14:33)

Pointers to Controlling Your Anger

1. **Change Your Environment** – Try hanging around people who are calm. When you begin to associate with calm people on a consistent basis, you will learn their ways on how to be calm. Also, pull away from those things that infuriate and make you feel trapped. People become angry when they are doing things they don't like to do; find out what you like to do and do it.

2. **Change how you think** – Angry people have a tendency to be very critical and negative. Very often do they see or say anything good. Try replacing those critical and negative thoughts with words that are encouraging and inspirational. Start reading material that focuses only on building you up. Share with others those positive things that you have learned from your reading.

3. **Schedule your time appropriately** – People often get overwhelmed when they take on more than they can handle. Try scheduling your time to where you are not always in a hurry. When you are constantly in a hurry, you forget things and become upset when people appear to be slowing you down. Manage your time more wisely: If you have a problem with traffic jams, try leaving early or take another route to get to where you need to be comfortably.

4. **Express Yourself** – There is nothing wrong with you expressing yourself in an assertive, not aggressive or demanding way. Expressing yourself appropriately is healthy because you get what is in you, out. Thereby, you keep yourself from exploding and mild episodes of anger. When you express yourself, you are preventing

pressure from building up in you and giving your anger a way of escape so that you won't blow up.

The **sixth** thing that King David did when under attack was that **he recovered all.** That is right...he recovered all and so will you when you decide that you will maintain the right attitude and do things God's way. When you do things God's way, God will give you total restoration and recover from all that the enemy has stolen.

> *"David recovered all that the Amalekities had taken and rescued his two wives. Nothing was missing, small or great, sons or daughters, spoil or anything that had been taken; David recovered all. Also David captured all the flocks and herds [which the enemy had], and the people drove those animals before him and said, this is David's spoil." (I Samuel 30:18-20, AMP)*

In this scripture passage, we see that King David did not allow a bad situation to get the best of him. He maintained the right attitude and trusted God. Whatever situation you may be encountering today, do not allow the bad to get the best of you; take authority and become the person who God created you to be.

In addition, we see the God of the overflow working in king David's life; not only did King David recover all that was stolen from him, but he recovered all that the enemy had. That is **El Shaddai,** which is the (*God that is more than enough*), with the emphasis being on <u>more</u>.

I say unto you my brother and sister whatever state you may find yourself in, you can recover all and you can reap the benefits of everyone who caused you trouble and heartaches.

Notice this scripture:

> *Instead of your [former] shame you shall have two-fold recompense; instead of dishonor and reproach [your people] shall rejoice in their portion. Therefore in their land they shall possess double [what they had forfeited]; everlasting joy shall be theirs. (Isaiah 61:7, NLT)*

Whatever you gave up and whatever you thought that you have lost because of bad habits; God says that you do not have to worry because He is going to return to you everything that you thought you would never see again. Not only is God going to give it back, but he is going to give you more than what you had before; He will give more grace, strength, money, joy, wisdom, favor and healing. He will give in abundance, to the max, and what He gives will overflow in every part of your life so that you can experience the God of recompense.

||||||||||||||||||||||||||

CHAPTER 10

Laws that Govern Overcoming a Bad Habit

When I mention the word *law* I am referring to the law as an established set principle. A **law** is *an established principle that will work the same way every time for anyone who chooses to become involved.* Take for instance, the law of gravity. If you go up on a roof and jump off, you will come down. That's a law meaning that it is an established principle. If you choose to get involved in the established principle, it is going to work the same way no matter who you are.

Let's take a person who likes to eat all the time; if that person does not get control or gain some type of restraint over his/her eating habits, this person will continue to get bigger. The more you consume, the bigger you will become, because the law of sowing and reaping indicates that what you do is what you are going to get. Eat a lot and you get big; eat less and you get smaller.

I like what Dr. Fredrick K.C. Price, said in his book, *Faith, Foolishness or Presumption:*

> *"A lot of people have the silly ideal that they can overeat and not get fat. My wife and I were having dinner with some people one time. We could look at one girl, and tell that she was overweight. And when she prayed over the food, she cast out the calories... Praying over your food, saying, "In the name of Jesus, I cast these calories out. Come out in Jesus' name," is pure foolishness. You need to bring your body under subjection. It's not Faith to think you can pray and eat whatever you want." (P.97, 99)*

This is why it is so important to understand the laws that govern overcoming a bad habit. The law of sowing and reaping in the Bible says,

> *"Don't be misled. Remember that you can't ignore God and get away with it. You will always reap what you sow! Those who live only to satisfy their own sinful desires will harvest the consequences of decay and death. But those who live to please the Spirit will harvest everlasting life from the Spirit." (Galatians 6:7-8, NLT)*

I believe most people fail to realize that sowing and reaping goes beyond just giving of finances; sowing and reaping covers how you treat yourself and others. If you do well, then good will come; if you treat your body and mind in a negative manner, then you will destroy your body and corrupt your mind.

My point is whatever you do, it is going to come back at ya; if you smoke cigarettes or abuse drugs and don't quit, you will get cancer and eventually die. If you are an overeater, the law (established principle) says that you will become overweight. The only way to overcome negative activities in your life is to become involved in the law of life that is in Christ Jesus. (Romans 8:2)

The **first** thing to understand about the laws that govern overcoming a bad habit is that **things just do not happen.** That is true...things just do not happen; if you are going to break addictive struggles, you will have to get a plan and work the plan.

Here is a scripture example of what I mean:

> *"So he went and did according unto the word of the Lord: for he went and dwelt by the brook Cherith that is before Jordan. And the ravens brought him bread and flesh in the morning, and bread and flesh in the evening; and he drank of the brook." (I Kings 17:5-6)*

The key thing to note is that Elijah did exactly what the Lord said and he prospered. Elijah had to go to the brook; God did not go for him. Again, this is generally a major oversight by many Christians, thinking that things just happen or that God is just going to bless them.

That kind of thinking is far from the truth. You will be responsible for the outcome of the decision that you make, whether good or bad, right or wrong. Ultimately, you will be responsible and God will get involved when you make the decision to do your part.

Scripture says, *"Then Isaac sowed in that land, and received in the same year an hundredfold: and the LORD blessed him." (Genesis 26:12)* Isaac was responsible for his harvest by sowing. When he sowed, it allowed God to get involved by putting his Hand on his seed that was sown. This enabled Isaac to receive a hundred times what he gave.

You have to give God something to work with "...*But be ye doers of the word, and not hearers only, deceiving your own selves.*" *(James 1:22)* The old saying is *"you can lead a horse to water, but you can't make him drink."* In other words, the horse has to decide for itself whether or not to drink the water. God gave Elijah the strength to go to the brook; however, Elijah had to settle in his mind that he was going to put forth the effort and go.

If the Prophet Elijah had not gone to the brook, he would have died of starvation...just like everyone else. However, Elijah put forth the effort to get there and God gave him the strength to get there. Everything that Elijah needed was right there at the brook because he was right where he was appointed to be. This same thing will happen in your life when you put forth the effort to get to where you are supposed to be. God will give you everything that you need.

The **second** thing to understand about the laws that govern overcoming a bad habit is that **you will have to let go or be dragged**. When you let things go, you are casting all your worries and cares on God.

> "*Cast the whole of your care [all your anxieties, all your worries, all your concerns, once and for all} on Him, for He cares for you affectionately and cares about you watchfully.*" (I Peter 5:7, AMP)

Dr. Creflo Dollar, in his teaching series on *The Hand of God*, says,

> "*Take that heavy burden, difficulty or challenge, that you are carrying. The one that has arisen due to circumstances that has created hardship and struggles*

in your life and fling those worries and anxiety over onto the back and hands of the Lord. Let him carry them for you. The Lord is extremely interested in every facet of your life and is genuinely concerned about your welfare." (DVD, Part 2)

KEY THOUGHT: If you cannot seem to forgive, try letting it go.

When you let go you release quickly what is on you, off you and put it into the hands of God who is equipped, and designed to handle what you cannot handle. When I was a boy, I remember one day touching the hot stove. When my hand touched the hot burner, immediately I released my hand from the burner. I released or let go of the hot burner because the human hand is not designed to handle or bear the burning, torturing pain of the hot object.

On the contrary, when a cooking pan is placed on the hot burner, the cooking pan has no problem with taking on the heat and the intensive pressure of the fire, because the cooking pan is specifically designed to take on the hot burner.

This is also true with overcoming a bad habit. Instead of going through the torture of holding on to deep-rooted issues, try letting them go by casting them on Jesus and allow Him to carry what He has been designed by God to do. (I Peter 5:7)

When I speak of letting go, I am referring to giving up the struggle, turning the bad habit over to God, and getting to the point to where you are willing to release your issues to God. You have to come to a point to where you are ready to let go of the issues or you will get dragged.

Notice this scripture,

> *"For the wages of sin is death; but the gift of God is*
> *eternal life through Jesus Christ our Lord." (Romans*
> *6:23)*

The point I am conveying is that if you do not let go of your addictions or negative behaviors they will, according to verse 23, drive you to your grave. Sin produces death, both spiritually and physically. The Enemy wants you to enjoy sin, not God. God knows that sin will produce death; therefore, if there is any sin in your life, it must be confessed and released to God.

God's desire for people is life in abundance, to the full and overflowing. *"The thief cometh not, but for to steal, and to kill, and to destroy: I am come that they might have life, and that they might have it more abundantly." (John 10:10)* Satan desires that your bad habits consume you to the point of death, demoralizing you and making you ineffective to the point of handicapping you from all kingdom of God progression and productivity.

The devil wants people to concentrate on the negatives more than the positives. I often go to the YMCA to play basketball. One particular day while playing, I noticed that a friend of mine was on a team that won four games back to back. My friend's team finally lost the fifth game. When he came over to sit down beside me, I made the comment to him, *"Man you guys did really well today, you won four games straight!"*

His reply was, *"Ya, but we lost the last one, and that is what I am focused on."*

I thought, *how sad*; he could not enjoy his four victories because of losing one. Satan often works the same way; he wants people to focus all of their attention on their failures, instead of focusing on godly success. God want us to focus on our victories and not our failures; God wants us to focus on the good and not the bad. If you focus on the good, then you will have the outcome of the good.

CHAPTER 11

IIIIIIIIIIIIIIIIIIIIIIIII

Confession Steps

Step One: I acknowledge by confession that my bad habit is not pleasing to God and it is setting a bad example in my personal life and in the life of others; therefore I make a quality decision to lay down my bad habit and change my behavior. (Galatians 5:1, Hebrew 12:1)

Step Two: I am fully, consciously aware that only God can help me get my life back on track. It is my confidence in God that is going to remove the burden and destroy the yoke of my impulsive and addictive behavior(s). (Psalms 121:1-2, 118:8-9)

Step Three: I make a decision to accept Jesus Christ as Lord and Savior of my life. I make a decision to serve Him and to live a life that is pleasing to Him according to the Bible (The Word of God). (Romans 10:9-10, Matthew 4:10)

Step Four: I make a decision to evaluate my lifestyle on a continual basis, asking God to help me stop negative behaviors and removing all character defects that is not pleasing to Him, to work on purifying and maximizing the will of God for my life. (II Corinthians 13:5, Hebrews 9:13-14)

Step Five: I forgive myself of all wrong and I forgive others who have wronged me. I make a decision to love every person—this includes those who hate, hurt, discriminate and isolate themselves from me. (I John 1:9, Mark 11:25-26, Matthew 5:44-45,)

Step Six: I now commission the hand of God to be upon my life. I declare that I am blessed, healed, restored, and empowered to be a blessing to all those with whom I come into contact with. (Isaiah 45:11, Deuteronomy 28:1-13, Psalms 91:15-16)

Step Seven: I make a decision that I will go to church on a consistent basis; I will come under the authority of the church by becoming accountable. I will be faithful, diligent, and prompt, on time and ready to serve. I will read my Bible, and I will pray to maintain a proper relationship with God and others. (Hebrews 10:25, Romans 13:1-5, Hebrews 13:7, II Timothy 2:15)

Step Eight: Now, after having all of my defects, shortcomings, faults, and failures removed by the blood of Jesus and the love of God, I make a commitment to serve God with all my heart and to carry the message of the gospel of Jesus Christ my LORD and savior to others. (Matthew 22:37-40, Mark 16:15-20)

CHAPTER 12

Things Most People Ignore when Breaking a Bad Habit

First, most people ignore the fact that, saying *I am sorry* **to a person is not enough.** You will have to stop making excuses for what you do and learn to do the right thing. When a person says that they are sorry about something, this is very good. However, saying I am sorry is not the end, but only the beginning to the process of change. Eventually, the person who apologized, must move from saying *I am sorry* to work on not saying and doing things that makes him/her sorry.

> *But when he saw many of the Pharisees and Sadducees come to his baptism, he said unto them, O generation of vipers, who hath warned you to flee from the wrath to come? Bring forth therefore fruits meet for repentance. (Matthew 3:7-8)*

The word **repentance** means in this particular verse of scriptures a *reversal in decision* or *to change the way of thinking.* When a person truly repents there is a change or a turn from old behavior to positive, new behavior. John the Baptist was interested in the religious leaders demonstrating manifested results (proof) that they had turned from sinning and turned to living holy and righteous for God. Therefore, John was looking for the true mark of repentance.

Some people can become addicted to making excuses; they say that they are sorry, but never demonstrate any signs to validate that they are sorry or that they have changed.

Dr. Bridget E. Hilliard, in her book, *The Will to Win*, says,

> *The major step that must be taken is the mental step of eliminating all excuses from remaining in your present, unfulfilled state. Excuses are the crutches for the uncommitted, and just beyond your excuse is the effort you need to win. Excuses are the smoke screens of the self-deceived! Unfortunately, only you feel your fabricated reason for remaining in your state is justifiable; others who know you know that your flimsy reason is just an excuse."* (P. 9)

If a person is constantly offending another person, then the person who constantly offends needs to get help. If a person is verbally or physically abusive to someone, the abused person is not interested in you saying *I am sorry*; this person is only interested in you no longer being the abuser. Therefore, saying *I am sorry* is not enough.

Again, while it is perfectly all right to apologize, the offender must desire not to offend. Remember this; people will always remember you more for what you **do**. You can say all the right things, but end up doing all the wrong things.

Second, most people ignore the fact that **you will need to fast at times** to overcome bad habits and break the cycle of chronic addictions. There is an old saying that says, *"A way to a man's heart is through his stomach."* This particular saying has taken many men to their graves; many people are eating themselves to death.

As a former hospital chaplain, I observed many people coming into the hospital and dying not because they where sick, but mainly because they were overweight, or did not properly take care of their bodies, thus illness or sickness killed them.

Fasting creates self-discipline. You need discipline to overcome bad behaviors that try to overcome you. It is important to note that fasting does not change God. The Bible says, *"Jesus Christ the same yesterday, and today, and for ever." (Hebrews 13:8)* Fasting will change you. When you are fasting for the right reasons, there is a certain yoke that will be destroyed in your life. Bad habits and chronic addictions will be removed. Fasting will break the chain or the cycle of repetitive and excessively negative behaviors.

Isaiah 58:1-14, the Bible tells us the purpose of the fast is to undo the yoke, that is...unlock the grip that is around the neck that one is incapable of getting out. The yoke is that thing that has you bound; it totally has you submerged under its control and it is humanly impossible to break; fasting creates a discipline to where you can have the strength to break free.

The Bible says,

> *Is not this the fast that I have chosen? To loose the bands of wickedness, To undo the heavy burdens, And to let the oppressed go free, And that ye break every yoke? Is not to deal thy bread to the hungry, And that thou bring the poor that are cast out to thy house? When thou seest the naked, that thou cover*

him; and that thou hide not thyself from thine own
flesh. (Isaiah 58:6-7)

Another aspect of this word **yoke** is in references to the
Assyrian Empire forceful grip (yoke) on Israel. Isaiah the
prophet, was prophesying that God was going to break the
yoke, undo the heavy burdens and let the people go free of their
oppression and mistreatment from the Assyrian nation.

God's people, Israel, at this time in history, had stepped away
from obeying God's laws and serving Him as a monotheistic God
(One and only true God). Therefore, in Israel's rebellion to serve
God, the Assyrian nation conquered Israel and defeated them,
taking Israel captive because of Israel's disobedience to God.

Vernon J. McGee, in his commentary, *Thru the Bible*, elabo-
rates on Isaiah 58:6:

> *This is tremendous—it gets right down to the nitty-*
> *gritty, right down where the rubber meets the road.*
> *God says in effect, "If you really want to fast, let Me*
> *tell you what to do: Instead of fasting and going around*
> *with a pious look, stop your sinning. Stop your gos-*
> *siping. Stop the things that reveal the wickedness and*
> *the evil in your hearts. Demonstrate your faith in Me*
> *by your conduct. Start being honest in your dealings.*
> *Be truthful in what you say. Instead of seeing you in*
> *sackcloth and covered with ashes, I'd like to see you*
> *clean on the inside." (P.328)*

After a time, God would hear his people cry and move to
have compassion on them. God would remove the burdens and
destroy the yokes of the Assyrian nation so God's people could
be free to serve God.

This is important because whatever has you yoked up and addicted, God's purpose of releasing you is so that you can serve Him. God will release you so that you can tell your story to someone else so that He (God) can release others the same way that He released you. This is the power in being a witness. (Isaiah 43:1-21, John 15:16, Acts 1:8)

When you talk about what God has done for you, others will want to experience that same goodness from God, so that God can do the same thing for them. God uses people as vehicles to transport what He wants said and accomplished in and throughout the earth.

The Bible says,

> *Now therefore, behold, the cry of the children of Israel is come unto me: and I have also seen the oppression wherewith the Egyptians oppress them. Come now, therefore, and I will send thee unto Pharaoh, that thou mayest bring forth my people the children of Israel out of Egypt. (Exodus 3:9-10)*

God used Moses as a channel to go unto Pharaoh and communicate specifically to him that God said," *Let my people go, that they may serve Me.*" Egypt, just like Assyria, was a yoke to the children of Israel; these nations kept the children of Israel in bondage.

Furthermore, If Moses would not have obeyed the Lord, God; Moses would have positioned himself for a yoke and a heavy burden to come on him that only God could remove. God will use both your body and mouth to reveal and make known to others who He is. Again, that is the power of the witness, which Israel had moved away from, thus causing them to be yoked up. Later, they returned to God, thus the burden-removing, yoke-destroying, power of God freed them from captivity.

You have to understand that there are certain things that you cannot, and will not overcome with self-will power. **Self-will power is not the answer; you must have a dependence on God.** If you have not submitted your bad habits and chronic addictions to God in times of weakness, then you will give in and participate in the sin. God cannot do anything for you until you do something to get Him involved. One of those things that you can do to get God involved is to fast.

Fasting allows God to supernaturally get involved in your life. What I mean by *supernatural* is God exceeding beyond human ability and expectations (Ephesians 3:20). I would strongly recommend you to read my book on *Breaking Free* to learn more about how prayer and fasting can commission the hand of God to work on your behalf.

The supernatural power of God is revealed in Mark 9:14-29; a man brought his son to Jesus' disciple to cast out a demon. The disciple could not do it. Jesus' response to the situation was *"this kind can only come by prayer and fasting."* There are certain kinds of things (bad habits) in life that must be addressed only spiritually or supernaturally through prayer and fasting.

This boy did not have a mental problem; he had a spiritual problem which began when he was a child. Therefore, since this boy had a spiritual problem, natural means could have not helped him. *Natural* is when you do things without God; you will go to the hospital, and you will take medications, or visit a psychologist or clinical therapist who knows nothing about God.

These natural resources can work. However, you will only get a temporary fix—especially when your problem is spiritual! When your problem is spiritual, no natural resources are going to work. That is when fasting comes into play; you can use fasting as a spiritual weapon to break chronic addiction and bad habits in the natural.

When there is no apparent cause or reason for sickness or pain that you are experiencing, when you go to the doctor and they cannot determine what the problem is, that is when you need to look beyond the natural and begin to look toward the spirit of God to make you better. The only one to make you better, in this case, is God.

One of the ways that God can make you better or give you clear insight and direction is by you fasting. Therefore, many people are bound in pain, worry, insanity, drugs, alcohol, and mental disorders to certain addictions and bad habits all because they refuse to come unto the one (Jesus Christ) who can do any and everything for them..

In addition, you cannot allow things to go unchecked for a long period. If you allow problems to persist, the situation will not get better, but worse. This is where we get the word **stronghold** (yoke); a stronghold is something that has a forceful or intense grip on the mind, body, or spirit of an individual. The key to overcoming strongholds is consuming the word of God, and to commit oneself to prayer, and fasting.

Scripture says,

> *And it shall come to pass in that day, That his burden shall be taken away from thy shoulder, And his yoke from off thy neck, And the yoke shall be destroyed because of the anointing. (Isaiah 10:27)*

Another traditional aspect of the word **yoke** was *a crossbar with two U-shaped pieces that encircle the necks of a pair of oxen or other draft animals working together.* The point is this—once the yoke is attached firmly to the animal, it has no way from getting out. The yoke had complete control of the animals (or slaves).

In addition, the yoke is placed between the animals, attached to a pole of the vehicle, or sometimes chains were used to drag the load. God said that with fasting, He breaks the yoke, that thing that has you tied down, bound, twisted up or in a head-lock, God is going to break it; God said that He would break the yoke and remove the burden and allow you to go free.

When the yoke was taken off the oxen, immediately there was a release. The oxen would go freely wherever they wanted. They felt the same way a dog feels that has been chained up for so long, and when it is freed, it runs all over the place because it is used to being tied down.

Well, I have good news for you; the thing that has had you tied down, God will release it from you. God will release you from every satanic bond, every negative behavior and every chronic addiction so that you can be free to serve Him.

God has allowed you, through the blood of Jesus, to break loose of anything that has you tied down; God has already released you through His son Jesus Christ. All power has been given unto you, (Matthew 28:18-20, Luke 10:19) You must make the decision to walk away, tear down, and break free, thus coming out of all sin, and past failures and enter into what God has for you.

Third, most people ignore **speaking scripture over what they are going through.** The Bible indicates that you will have what you say. (Mark 11:23) There is another scripture that indicates, *"Let the redeemed of the LORD say so, whom he hath redeemed from the hand of the enemy." (Psalms 107:2)* In the wilderness, (Luke 4:1-13) every time the devil pressured Jesus with temptation, Jesus would verbalize the word of God and win.

One of the ways to overcome bad habits is to verbalize the

word of God when you are under intense pressure. You do not have to speak loudly; you can speak very softly where no one can hear you, but you must speak the Word. Jesus spoke to Satan and He told Satan what to do, "Get away from me." Satan left Jesus for a season.

"And when the devil had ended all the temptation, he departed from him for a season." (Luke 4:13) This **season** that the Bible refers to is *a period of time,* which means that negative things will go but they have a way of resurfacing. When they do, you will have to speak the Word in order not to fall into temptation.

Notice this scripture, *"And they overcame him by the Blood of the Lamb and by the word of their testimony; and they loved not their lives unto the death." (Revelations 12:11)* If you want your bad habits and chronic addiction to leave you, then you will have to speak the Word over your bad habits or chronic additions and tell them to go:

> *"Speaking to yourselves in psalms and hymns and spiritual songs, singing and making melody in your heart to the Lord." (Ephesians 5:19)*

Speaking the word of God over yourself or someone else, does not mean that your are crazy; in the same way you say a blessing over your food, that is the same way you speak a blessing about your situation. You speak the word of God over them and believe that God's word is the key that is going to make whatever you need happen.

I find it to be very interesting that when people are in severe, unexpected sudden danger, they welcome the calling on God. They will say things like, *"O Lord save me! Jesus, help! O my God, Lord have mercy!"* Other people have a tendency to say bad things such as using the name of the Lord God in vain.

The point I am attempting to make is this—if you can speak a Word during unexpected danger, why not speak the word of faith to make you feel better, to make you motivated about overcoming bad habits.

When King David was dealing with depression, he talked to himself. He said, *"Why am I so depressed? Why this turmoil within me? Put your hope in God, for I will still praise Him, my Savior and my God" (Psalms 42:5)* There is nothing wrong with you saying unto yourself that you are a good person, that God loves you, and that you are more than a conqueror. Saying that would be better than saying all kinds of nasty and evil things about yourself.

One of the key things in overcoming bad habits is that you must find a scripture to stand on. Notice this scripture, *"And Jesus answering said unto them, Do ye not therefore err, because ye know not the scriptures, neither the power of God." (Mark 12:24)* The reason that it is important to find a scripture to stand on is because it is the word of God that is going to uphold you in times of trouble.

Fourth, most ignore the importance of **sowing a seed to meet a need.** Scripture says, *"Don't be misled. Remember that you can't ignore God and get away with it. You will always reap what you sow." (Galatians 6:7)* A person's harvest in life depends solely upon the seed he/she has sown; if you do not give into the kingdom of God, there is no harvest that can come from God; the measure of your return in life is dependent upon how much you are willing to give.

The Bible says,

> *For God so loved the world that he gave his only begotten Son, that whosoever believeth in him should not perish, but have everlasting life. (John 3:16)*

God gave his one and only son as a sacrifice to die for the sins of the world, and the return was that the whole world <u>could be</u> saved through the name and blood of His one and only son, Jesus Christ. God demonstrated his love for the world by His gift; when you love God you will always give. You will not have to be pushed, pumped, probed or encouraged. Actually, cheerful givers look for opportunities to be a blessing.

When I speak of sowing a seed, it is precisely your money, time, and energy that has been given or invested into the things of God. When you give into the kingdom of God, you must remember that God has promised to give back to you.

> *Give, and it shall be given unto you; good measure,*
> *pressed down, and shaken together, and running over,*
> *shall men give into your bosom, for with the same*
> *measure that ye mete withal it shall be measured to*
> *you again. (Luke 6:38)*

When you give into the kingdom of God, you never give anything away. God will always make sure that you get it back in abundance, to the full and overflow in your life. You should always expect and pray for a harvest on your return. Some people will have you to believe that you should give and expect nothing in return. Scripture differs from that way of thinking.

Think about this for a second, if a farmer plants apple seeds, the farmer is planting those seeds for a reason—a return of juicy apples at harvest time. Because of the seeds that were planted, the farmer knows and fully understands that harvest time is always going to come. He/She looks forward to the harvest.

> *While the earth remaineth, seedtime and harvest, and*
> *cold and heat, and summer and winter, and day and*
> *night shall not cease. (Genesis 8:22)*

When the farmers sow or plant their seed, their minds are already thinking about the harvest of the seed that were sown. They believe that they will receive something. If a return does not come from the seed, then they know that something was wrong. The problem could be because of how the seed was planted, or it could be because of how the seed was cared for. Nevertheless, the seed sown will determine the harvest.

Your money is a seed, your time is a seed, and more importantly, the word of God is a seed. (Luke 8:11) When you sow your seed, you give God something to work with; if you do not sow a seed, then you will not get your needs met. If you go into work, you expect to be paid because you have sown your time and energy. When you give, God promises to bless you, both spiritually and financially. God will not only give back to you, but he will increase your return, phenomenally.

> *Remember this—a farmer who plants only a few seeds will get a small crop. But the one who plants generously will get a generous crop. You must each make up your own mind as to how you should give. Don't give reluctantly or in response to pressure. God loves the person who gives cheerfully. And God will generously provide all you need. Then you will always have everything you need and plenty left over to share with others. (II Corinthians 9:6-8, NLT)*

My brother and sister, God is saying the same thing today; when you give, you should expect a return. If you do not get a return, you are doing something wrong. Again, you will receive from your giving. If you give a little, you will get a little; if you give a lot, you will receive a lot. That's what the word says. One thing is clear...when you give, you will get.

When you give, it must be given with the right attitude; you cannot give and wish you could have kept your money. It cannot produce effective results when you regret that you gave. God loves a cheerful giver, a giver who is enthusiastically excited about giving money to the kingdom of God. God loves the person who is joyously overwhelmed with faith in giving.

The Widow Woman in Need

> But she said, "I swear by the LORD your God that I don't have a single piece of bread in the house. And I have only a handful of flour left in the jar and a little cooking oil in the bottom of the jug. I was just gathering a few sticks to cook this last meal, and then my son and I will eat it and die." But Elijah said to her, "Don't be afraid! Go ahead and cook that 'last meal,' but bake me a little loaf of bread first. Afterward there will still be enough food for you and your son. For this is what the LORD, the God of Israel, says; There will always be plenty of flour and oil left in your containers until the time when the LORD sends rain and the crops grow again!" So she did as Elijah said, and she, Elijah and her son continued to eat from her supply of flour and oil for many days. For no matter how much they used, there was always enough left in the containers, just as the LORD had promised through Elijah. (I Kings 17:12-16, NLT)

A good example of a person sowing a seed to meet a need is the widow woman. She gave her last piece of bread and water and experienced an overflow to where her supply of bread and water never ran out. There are a few things that can be learned from this widow woman's behavior:

One, you must obey the word of the Lord. This woman obeyed the word of the Lord that came from the prophet; she prospered. It is important to obey God with your giving. Whatever God instructs you to do with your money, that is exactly what you are to do.

It is also important to note that God is never going to ask you to give below your tithes. The word **tithe** means tenth. (Numbers 18:24, 26, 28, Malachi 3:8-12) You cannot give an offering until you have first given your tithe.

The tithe or tenth is to be given first, then you give your offering as the Lord leads. When you give, whether your tithe or offering, you give because you love the Lord. When you love the Lord, you will give Him your best. This means that you will give over and beyond the tenth because you love the Lord and want to see the kingdom of God promoted.

Two, the widow woman gave as unto the Lord. Although she gave to the prophet, her giving was as unto the Lord. The Prophet Elijah told the widow woman that if she gave to Him, God would give back to her in abundance, to full and overflowing.

> "And they rose early in the morning, and went forth into the wilderness of Tekoa: and as they went forth, Jehoshaphat stood and said, Hear me, O Judah, and ye inhabitants of Jerusalem; Believe in the Lord your God, so shall ye be established; believe his prophets, so shall ye prosper." (II Chronicles 20:20)

This widow woman was obedient in giving to the Lord; as a result, her flour bowl was never empty and her jar of oil never ran out. People were dying of starvation all over the land, but not this woman and her son. She had plenty in the midst of a drought, all because she believed the words of a prophet and gave unto the Lord.

Three, the widow woman gave out of a need. She could have refused to give anything to the Prophet and she and her son would have died. The reason she would have died is that she would have been disobedient to the word of the Lord. It was her obedience to the word of the Lord, spoken by the man of God, that resulted in sustaining her life and causing her to prosper.

This woman knew that it was better to give out of her need, than to hold onto her seed. **If you do not have enough to meet your need, then turn your need into your seed and reap the harvest of your seed.** This woman knew what little she had she could give to God. He would blow on it and make what she barely had more than enough to where she could even give some food away.

Notice this particular scripture, *"Than Isaac sowed in that land, and received in the same year an hundredfold: and the LORD blessed him. (Genesis 26:12)* Again, God will bless you when you give and it does not have to take you long to see the result of the seed that you have sown. Isaac sowed during a famine and received back more than he had. You cannot allow negative circumstances and situations to dictate what and how you should give:

> Cast thy bread upon the waters: for thou shalt find it after many days. Give a portion to seven, and also to eight; for thou knowest not what evil shall be upon the earth. If the clouds be full of rain, they empty themselves upon the earth: and if the tree fall toward the south, or toward the north, in the place where the

*tree falleth, there it shall be. He that observeth the
wind shall not sow; and he that regardeth the clouds
shall not reap. (Ecclesiastes 11:1-4)*

Isaac gave when everybody else was holding onto their
seeds, which means that when the harvest time came, Isaac
would be the only one to receive. God will tell you how to keep
financially secure when the stock market drops. God knows
how to cause increase when all other resources around you has
taken a nosedive and plundered to the bottom. God can have
you invest in something that appears insignificant, but later
becomes something great.

You cannot wait on perfect conditions to sow; Isaac planted
a seed unto the Lord and God multiplied the seed sown. When
Scripture says *cast thou bread,* it is indicating for you to put
your money out there. Bread is just another usage for the word
money; do not be afraid to give your money, because when you
generously give, your gift will come back to you later. Therefore,
you have to keep in mind that what you get in life is a direct
result of what you did. (Galatians 6:7)

Lastly, the widow woman gave into good ground. This
woman knew that the prophet Elijah was a man of God and
because she gave to the man of God, God gave back to her.
What this means is that when you give to a man or a woman of
God, you have a right to receive the anointing from that man or
woman of God because of your association with them.

There are at least three ways that you can get God's anointing from a man or woman of God; 1) You must hear the man or
woman of God's words; 2) You must give money to their ministry; 3) You must physically support or serve in their ministry.
This will release what is on them to come on you. This is called

a transferal anointing. A transferal anointing can only take place with a deposit. When you deposit your time, money and energy into the man and woman of God, you then set yourself up for a withdrawal that comes from God.

You need to be selective with your giving; just because people are asking for money does not mean that you have to give it to them. You must know to whom you are giving. You must ask the questions...are they honest? Are they accountable? Are they living in right standing with God? Do they walk in integrity? If the answers are *yes* then they are good ground.

You should never give just because there is a need. Some people have a need because they are living in sin, and it really does not matter how much you give unto them or their ministry, your money will not yield a return because it is bad ground. So, when you give, make sure you are giving unto good ground; good ground will always yield a return.

CHAPTER 13

||||||||||||||||||||||||||||||||

Things You Need to Know

You can do it

> *"I can do all things through Christ which strength-*
> *eneth me." (Philippians 4:13)*

> *"Jesus said unto him, If thou canst believe, all things*
> *are possible to him that believeth." (Mark 9:23)*

You can do all things through Christ because He will give you the wisdom and strength to succeed. The reason that you can successfully overcome a bad habit is because there is no failure in God; because there is no failure in God, God dwells in you. Thus, there is no failure in you which means that your confidence has to be in God. *"The Lord shall be thy confidence, and shall keep thy foot from being taken." (Proverbs 3:26)*

Dr. Creflo Dollar, in his book, *Confidence: The Missing Substance of Faith*, says;

> *"When the Bible uses the word confidence it means*
> *"assurance" or complete and total "persuasion." It also*

> *closely parallels that mean of "trust." When you trust*
> *something, you have confidence in it." (P. 2)*

Often, people fail because they are not confident in God and they are not willing to endure. Wether you can do it is determined upon the fact that you are confident in God and that you are willing to endure. *"And let us not be weary in well doing: for in due season we shall reap, if we faint not."* (Galatians 6:9) The Bible gives the solution to making things work, which is faint not.

Simplified, the word **faint** means to *cave-in, give-up, and turn coward to the point of quitting,* however, the word faint does mean much...much more than that. I will explain why in just a moment. Nevertheless, people often desire change to happen right away in their lives and they fail to realize that change, sometimes, will take time.

Change is a process, and in some cases you will not arrive instantly at your desired level of change. However, in the process of change, it is extremely important to stay focused, disciplined, and do not give up. Again, everything is subject to change except for the word of God.

The word **faint** in its original language (Greek) in Galatians 6:9 is *ekluo* pronounced *ek-loo'-o* which means *to loose or release;* it carries with it the connation of becoming *to relax.*

I like the original translation of the word faint because it indicates why the person caved in, gave up or turned coward and quit. The reason is that they became too relaxed, which resulted in them caving-in, giving up, turning coward and progressing to the point of quitting.

I shared in a previous chapter about the story of the rabbit versus the turtle in a race. You would think from a logical perspective that the rabbit would surely win the race because of its speed. However, because the rabbit become overly confident about being so far ahead, it became *too relaxed.* In fact, the rabbit became so relaxed that it went to sleep during the race, thus losing its intended goal.

Esau Madness

Again, another aspect of the word **faint** in its original language is to *release.* When you release something, you turn it over. A good example of this is the story of Esau's birthright. (Genesis 25:29-34):

One day Jacob cooked a pot of stew; Esau, his brother, came in from hunting and was extremely hungry. Esau asked for some stew but his brother refused to give him any unless Esau sold (*released*) his birthright to Jacob. Esau released his birthright signifying that he cared very little for it.

A **birthright** is *an inheritance* – which all the children had a right to share (Luke 15:11-13) – however the portion of the firstborn child's was to be two times bigger than all the other children's inheritance. If there were three children, the inheritance would be divided in four parts. The firstborn child was to receive two parts, and the remaining two children were to receive one part each. (Deuteronomy 21:17)

The point I want to make about Esau is that when he released his birthright this started an avalanche of psychotic behaviors that drove Esau to the point of almost losing his mind. Esau actually thought that Jacob deceived him into selling his birthright, but realistically, Esau chose to release it.

Notice this scripture,

> "Esau replied, "My brother deserves the name Jacob
> because he has already cheated me twice. The first

time he cheated me was out of my right as the first-born son, and now he has cheated me out of my blessing." Then Esau asked his father, "Don't you still have any blessing left for me?" (Genesis 27:36, CEV)

Esau eventually became so mad and angry with his brother Jacob that he wanted to kill him. (Genesis 27:41) Esau felt that Jacob had cheated him twice, but actually, Jacob had only cheated him once, which was out of his father's blessing. For whatever reason, Esau failed to deal with the fact that he sold his birthright to Jacob for a pot of beef stew.

Esau is the responsible party, not Jacob. When Esau sold his birthright, it was no longer stolen because he had turned it over to Jacob. Esau released to Jacob all of the blessings that would be associated with the first-born inheritance.

Apparently, Esau never let the anger go of selling his birthright because later he accuses Jacob of stealing. Again, this lie indicates addictive behavior on Esau's part because he never owns up to his own responsibilities. In addition, if Esau had admitted giving Jacob his birthright, things would have been better inside Esau.

In a nutshell, all of Esau's problems evolved out of the fact that he became too relaxed; he released his blessing to his brother. Therefore, because Esau could not handle the fact that he turned over his blessings, he got mad, resulting in him wanting to just cave in, give-up and quit.

I have experienced people who appear to be very successful for a long period, then all of a sudden, they hit bottom. Everything appears to fall apart or go wrong in their lives. I believe that these people became too loose and relaxed; they felt that because they had arrived to success, they did not have to do anything to keep their success.

Notice this scripture: *"Therefore we ought to give the more earnest heed to the things which we have heard, lest at any time we should let them slip." (Hebrews 2:1)* When you start letting things slip and slide by, that is when you set yourself up for a fall; the disappointments of life often occur when you become to relax. How can an individual know when they are slipping? When you no longer are doing the things that made you successful.

When you faint, you become stagnant; you lose your grip on your focus and start slipping. In boxing terms, you drop your guard. You become too tired or relaxed, which can result in the possibility of a knock out.

The Bible tells us,

> *"be well balanced (temperance, sober of mind), be vigilant and cautious at all times; for that enemy of yours, the devil, roams around like a lion roaring [in fierce hunger], seeking someone to seize upon and devour."*
> *(I Peter 5:8, AMP)*

When you faint, you relax until you do not do anything, which opens the door for whatever you are struggling with to come on you and overpower (*seizing or devouring*) you to the point of you shutting down, making you have no desire to continue.

The way to overcome when you feel like giving up is to keep doing what you know to do. You have to stay with it; you cannot allow the immediate discomfort or dissatisfaction to cause you to lose heart and quit. Sometimes in life you will just have to ride things out; you just have to stick with it and enjoy the ride, making the best out of a not-so good situation.

The Storm

Let me give you an example of what I am talking about when I say staying or sticking with it. I remember a time when traveling home from seminary in Cleveland, Tennessee. Right before I came to North Carolina it began to rain very hard. The rain was consistent and would not let up. I knew that I had an appointment to make and I needed to get there. Therefore, I slowed down, turned on my headlights and flashers and continued to move forward very slowly. Within less than five minutes, I was out of the storm.

Now let us diagnose the storm situation. Life struggles are the same way: **First,** we decide that we are going to make it. Although the storm was bad, I slowed down because it was not bad enough for me to stop. That is important because your situation cannot get so bad that God cannot get you through it. I think I need to say that one more time...your situation cannot get so bad that God cannot get you through it.

The important thing to note here is that you have to keep on moving forward. You cannot allow negative opinions and difficult situations to cause you to stop, turn or derail you from what God wants to do in you. I like what Oral Roberts says about the difficulties that was surrounding him when building Oral Roberts University located in Tulsa, Oklahoma.

In his autobiography, *Expect a Miracle*, Oral Roberts says,

> *"Despite what anyone may think or believe, God Himself called me to build Him a university, build it on His authority and the Holy Spirit. I am not leaving the healing ministry; it is my life. But God doesn't operate in a vacuum. He is constantly moving forward, and I have learned we must move with God." (P. 166)*

One of the main things that will get you through the storms of life is that you will keep on moving forward. Although you might not have it all together, and things might even appear not to be working for you, know that God is with you. He will lead you safely through the storms of life.

Second, in regards to life struggles you have to learn how to make adjustment. What I mean by adjustment is doing something different that will ultimately make you come out ahead. Adjustment does not mean that it did not work, but you have to do something different in order to obtain the results you are looking for. That's awesome. Rather than calling your attempts that came up short, failures, why not call them opportunities for advancement.

I often watch college football and with this one particular game, the quarterback was having his challenges that day. The game was about mid-way into finishing; the quarterback had thrown three interceptions and had fumbled one time.

The announcer of the game kept saying, *"They must get the quarterback out, they have to get him out of there if they're going to have a good chance at winning this game."* Well sure enough, the coach pulled the quarterback out of there, and the team came back and won the game, all because they made the necessary adjustments.

My point is this—in life just because things are not working that well at the moment does not mean you throw in the towel and quit; maybe you need to do like the announcer said about the quarterback—switch it up or do something different. Many times when things are not working, it is because we have not made the necessary adjustment to get it right; therefore I encourage you to get it right.

Often, people do not achieve or receive because they do not believe in God or themselves. **You can do it** is based on the fact that you will believe in God and yourself no matter what. *"And Jesus said, [You say to me], If You can do anything? [Why,] all things can be (are possible) to him who believes!" (Mark 9:23, NLT)* It does not matter what you hear, see, know, or even feel. God is able to do the great and awesome thing in your life, if you will only believe Him.

The **third** thing I did in this storm was that I stayed the course; I did not turn back. I did not even pull over to the side of the road. I slowed down and proceeded with care and safely went through. Just because things happen in your life that you do not like, you cannot allow those things to get you off course. You must stay the course because you can do it. You cannot quit, because on the other side of the storm the sun is shining and there is a brighter day.

The songwriter says,

> *"Though the storm keeps on raging in my life, and sometimes its hard to tell the night from the day, Still that hope that lies within is reassured as I keep my eyes upon the distant shore. I know He'll lead me safely to that blessed place He has prepared, but if the storm doesn't cease and if the wind keeps on blowing, my soul has been anchored in the Lord."*

I would like to point out two additional keys to getting through the storms of life. **First**, the storm does not have to keep on raging in your life. You can do something about it. **Second,** you must take authority over the storm and tell it what to do. Therefore, if you do nothing then nothing is going to happen; you must demonstrate action to obtain the things that you desire.

*"And there arose a great storm of wind, and the waves
beat into the ship, so that it was now full. And he was
in the hinder part of the ship, asleep on a pillow; and
they awoke him, said unto him, Master, carest thou not
that we perish? And he arose, and rebuked the wind,
and said unto the sea, Peace, be still. And the wind
ceased, and there was a great calm." (Mark 4:37-39)*

Jesus took action over what was opposing them (the storm);
He woke up and did something about the situation. If you do
not appreciate the results that you are getting in life then do
something about that dissatisfaction. Jesus encouraged his disciples not to be afraid. If they would take action just as He did,
they would have had the results that they desired.

The Bible says in Luke 10:19, *"Behold, I give you power to tread
on serpents and scorpions, and over all the power of the enemy:
and nothing shall by any means hurt you."* The storms of life can
cease by you speaking and acting on what you know to do. That
is right—you can speak to the storm or the mountain, and you
can tell it to be still or be at peace; what you say will happen,
according to Mark 11:23-24.

KEY THOUGHT: Struggle is the indicator
that you have not stopped moving.

---

*"Yea, though I walk through the valley of the shadow
of death, I will fear no evil; for thou are with me; thy
rod and thy staff they comfort me." (Psalms 23:4)*

There are two things to note about this verse:

1. You will only go through for a certain period of time; you will come out when you go through. You are only going through temporarily and not permanently. You do not pitch a tent and settle down in your challenges. When you go through, your eyes should be firmly locked to where you are going and not what you are going through. Struggle is the indicator that you have not stopped moving.

   Dr. Crelfo Dollar, in his book, *How to Trouble Your Trouble*, says,

   "The ultimate weapon against trouble is the knowledge that trouble is only temporary. No matter what the devil brings against us, it is subject to change! The apostle Paul had more trouble during his ministry than most of us can even imagine. But Paul was not troubled by his trouble, because he knew the trouble was only temporary. And he knew he had a shield against trouble which would never fail him–the word of God." (P.195)

2. You do not have to fear what you are going through because God is with you, and because God is with you no weapon formed against you shall prosper. (Isaiah 54:17) Fear is the enemy of faith. Where fear is present, faith is absent. When you know that God is with you, He will protect, guide, comfort and deliver. God will give you the strength to make it through.

Jesus' Experience in the Garden of Gethsemane

"Then Jesus went with them to a place called Gethsemane, and he told his disciples, Sit down here while I go yonder and pray. And taking with Him Peter and the two sons of Zebedee, He began to show grief and distress of mind and was deeply depressed. Then He said to them, My soul is very sad and deeply grieved, so that I am almost dying of sorrow, Stay here and keep awake and keep watch with Me. And going a little farther, He threw Himself upon the ground on His face and prayed saying, My Father, if it is possible, let this cup pass away from Me: nevertheless, not what I will [not what I desire], but as You will and desire. And He came to the disciples and found them sleeping, and He said to Peter, What! Are you so utterly unable to stay awake and keep watch with me for one hour? All of you must awake (give strict attention, be cautious and active) and watch and pray, that you may not come into temptation. The spirit indeed is willing, but the flesh is weak. Again a second time He went away and prayed, My Father, if this cannot pass by unless I drink it, Your will be done. And again He came and found them sleeping, for their eyes were weighed down with sleep. So leaving them again, He went away and prayed for the third time, using the same words. Then He returned to the disciples and said to them, Are you still sleeping and taking your rest? Behold, the hour is at hand, and the Son of Man is betrayed into the hands of especially wicked sinners [whose way or nature it is to act in opposition to God]. Rise, let us be going: behold he is at hand that doeth betray me." (Matthew 26:36-46, AMP)

There are at least **three very important things,** which Jesus did in regards to his experience in the Garden of Gethsemane. Those things are as follows:

One, he watched. You have to keep your eyes open to see what is happening around you so that you can avoid trouble and to see clearly where you are headed and observe what you need to do. *"A wise man will see trouble afar and will go into another direction, but a fool will walk into it."* Jesus watching while praying is scriptural; the Bible instructs us to watch and pray.

Two, he prayed. It was prayer that allowed and enabled Jesus to submit to the will of God. When Judas and the soldiers came to arrest Jesus and to take him away, Jesus was not moved at all by his arrest. In fact, Jesus was so in tune with his life through prayer that nothing caught him off guard. Furthermore, Jesus foreknew that his time was at hand to be arrested; Jesus prophesied that Judas, one of the disciples, would betray him for 30 pieces of silver. (Matthew 26:23-25)

The ones who were really shook up about Jesus' arrest were his own disciples. One of the reasons they were so shook up and moved with anger, grief and disappointment was because they had not spent much time in prayer prior to Jesus' arrest. They were asleep. Prayer, supported by the Word, will find all of the answers and solutions to your challenges.

Three, Jesus kept going forward. Jesus kept praying; He did not stop until He received his breakthrough to get Him through his death, burial and resurrection. Again, Jesus kept praying and praying until He prayed through everything that He would go through. It was prayer that kept Jesus' mind focused on going forward to obtain the will of God for his life.

In the same manner it will be prayer that will keep you focused on going forward to obtain the will of God for your life.

> The spirit of God will lead you but it is prayer that is going to keep you.

There are **two things about prayer:** 1) Prayer will allow the Spirit of God to lead and guide you. 2) Prayer will keep you. Prayer will keep you from entering into temptation. Temptation is going to come to you; no one can get away from that. However, when temptation comes to you, you do not have to fall or give in to the thing that is tempting you.

Scripture says, *"Then was Jesus led up of the spirit into the wilderness to be tempted of the devil." (Matthew 4:1)* The important thing about Jesus' temptation in the wilderness is that He overcame. Again, the spirit of God will lead and guide you, but it is prayer that is going to keep you. Jesus did not give in to temptation. Jesus was able to resist everything that the devil tempted Him with because He had already prayed about it.

The motivating factor to hearing from God and being led by the Holy Spirit is spending time in quality prayer. Prayer is a direct communication with God; it is prayer that will allow the Spirit of God to come into union with a person's Spirit, where the person becomes a supernatural individual. Prayer will enable you to become a superwoman or a superman. Prayer will give you the ability to do in the Spirit what you can not do in your own natural strength and intellectualism.

Scriptural References on the Spirit of God Leading and Guiding

1. For as many as are led by the Spirit of God, they are the sons of God. (Romans 8:14)

2. After they were come to Mysia, they assayed to go into Bithynia: but the Spirit suffered them not. (Acts 16:7)

3. But I say, walk and live [habitually] in the [Holy] Spirit [responsive to and controlled and guided by the Spirit]; then you will certainly not gratify the cravings and desires of the flesh of human nature without God). (Galatians 5:16 AMP)

4. Oh, there is so much more I want to tell you, but you can't bear it now. When the Spirit of truth comes, he will guide you into all truth. He will not be presenting his own ideas; he will be telling you what he has heard. He will tell you about the future. He will bring me glory by revealing to you whatever he receives from me. All that the father has is mine; this is what I mean when I say that the spirit will reveal to you whatever he receives from me. (John 16:13, NLT)

5. And the Spirit bade me go with them, nothing doubting. Moreover, these six accompanied me, and we entered into the man's house. (Acts 11:12)

6. While they were worshiping the Lord and fasting, the Holy Spirit said, "Set apart for me Barnabas and Saul for the work to which I have called them." So after they had fasted and prayed, they placed their hands on them and sent them off. The two of them, sent on their way by the Holy Spirit, went down to Seleucia and sailed from there to Cyprus. (Acts 13:2-4, NIV)

The Bible says,

> "AND JESUS being full of the HOLY GHOST returned
> from Jordan, and was led by the Spirit into the wilder-
> ness, Being forty days tempted of the devil. And in
> those days he did eat nothing: and when they were
> ended, he afterward hungered." (Luke 4:1-2)

The only thing the devil could do to Jesus was tempt him.
The word **tempted** in Luke 4:2 is *peirazo* which is pronounced
pi-rad'-zo; it means to *test*, *try* or *prove*. It is important to say,

> "Blessed is the man who perseveres under trial,
> because when he has stood the test, he will receive
> the crown of life that God has promised to those who
> love him. When tempted, no one should say, "God is
> tempting me." For God cannot be tempted by evil, nor
> does he tempt anyone; but each one is tempted when,
> by his own evil desire, he is dragged away and enticed.
> Then after desire has conceived, it gives birth to sin;
> and sin, when it is full-grown, gives birth to death."
> (James 1:12-15, NIV)

According to scripture, God does not tempt anyone; however,
the devil is very different. His purpose is to examine and challenge your faith in God, to destroy every potential promise of you
becoming great in God. The devil plans to get people addicted to
drugs, alcohol, cigarettes, perversion, unlawful sexual activities,
overeating, lying, killing, cheating, anything that is evil or causes
death. The devil's plan is to get you tangled up in despair until
you believe that there is no hope to live any longer.

When you yield yourself to certain bad habits, you become
the slave to them; in other words, the thing you surrender

yourself to is the thing that will be responsible for bringing you down or lifting you up. Scripture says, *"Know ye not, that to whom ye yield yourselves servants to obey, his servant ye are to whom ye obey; whether of sin unto death, or of obedience unto righteousness?" (Roman 6:16)* The thing to note about you yielding yourself to bad habits is that the sole cause for the catastrophe in your life is you.

This is vital to know because you cannot blame the devil or people, although the devil or evil spirits do work through people, nevertheless, people cannot make you do anything. You have to be aware of how people can be used; people are used by the devil to get you into bondages, addictions, and bad habits. Some people may be smart, good-looking, and even intelligent, but if Satan is behind their actions, He will ultimately destroy them and you. (John 10:10)

Temptation begins in the mind. This is why you need to guard what you see, hear and think because those things can have negative effects upon what you do. The thing about bad habits is that they will try to trigger or stimulate you to do the things you see, hear and feel, although you know that it is not right for you to be doing those things. Just because things look, sound, or feel good does not mean that they are right, especially when they contradict the word of God.

It is also important to note that the devil had no power or control over Jesus' life. Jesus was able to overcome every lie, every manipulative tactic, and every trickery maneuver of the devil. (Luke 4:3-13) Therefore, you can overcome; you can overcome every negative desire and chronic addiction that attempts to take you away from the will of God for your life. You do not have to hit bottom, you do not have to lose everything. God has designed you to be a winner; God has designed you to bounce back, to get up and to go to your victory.

Notice this scripture: *"The Lord shall increase you more and more, you and your children." (Psalms 115:14)* The word **increase** means to *add up*, it means *(enlargement, escalation, multiplication, to heighten or widen, and to expand.)* That is what God desires to do in your life; He wants to increase you with good. The Bible says that you are more than a conqueror. (Romans 8:37) No weapon formed against you shall prosper, (Isaiah 54:17) and nothing by any means shall hurt or harm you. (Luke 10:19)

In his book, *Not Guilty*, Dr. Creflo A. Dollar, says,

> *God's commitment to you and to me is that He will not let the devil put pressure on our flesh, or tempt us beyond our ability to overcome that temptation. The temptations we face are according to our ability to overcome them. If you and I do not have the ability to overcome a certain temptation, God's commitment is that we will not be tempted in that area. So when you are being tempted, rejoice because you have the ability to overcome it." (P. 128)*

In the Garden of Gethsemane (Matthew 26:51-53), Jesus was not tempted to fight during his arrest, but Peter was tempted to fight and this was clearly demonstrated by Peter cutting off the soldier's ear. Immediately Jesus restored the soldier's ear because Jesus is love, restoration, forgiveness and healing.

During the time of Jesus arrest, He spent quality time in prayer. The reason Peter was confused and angry was because he spent very little time in prayer. Peter was sleeping when he should have been praying.

The Benefits of Prayer

1. **King Hezekiah,** The prophet Isaiah came to him and informed him to get his house in order because he was going to die of his sickness. King Hezekiah, immediately prayed to God and God heard the King and added 15 more years to his life; if the King would have not prayed, he would have not lived 15 extra years. (II Kings 20:1-6)

2. **Jonah** was physically going down to Hell and called on God. God heard him and delivered him. The prophet's life was spared from death because he prayed to God. (Jonah 2:1-10)

3. **Peter** was released from prison because prayer was made fervently and consistently by the Church. (Acts 12:5-16) When you pray, it will enable God to get involved to release you from everything that is attempting to keep you in prison or locked down.

The Forgiveness Study

Dr. Don Colbert, in his book, *Deadly Emotions,* says,

> *"A scientific project conducted at the University of Wisconsin was simply called "The Forgiveness Study." The study demonstrated that learning to forgive may help prevent heart disease in middle-age subjects. The incidence of heart disease was higher in those who admitted they could not forgive. The risk of heart disease was much lower in those who reported an ability to forgive easily. These researchers concluded that a failure to forgive is a greater predictor of physical health problems than hostility." (P. 169)*

This research on the forgiveness study can be affirmed and accurate by examining the life of **Judas Iscariot's unforgiving attitude;** Judas was one of the 12 disciples that Jesus Christ selected to follow Him while on his earthly ministry. (Matthew 10:2-4)

Initially, when Judas started out in the ministry as a disciple I am sure he had no idea or intentions of betraying Christ for money; however, because his heart was not right with God, it was not right with money. He made a bad money decision, one of which was selling out Jesus for 30 pieces of silver.

Judas felt so bad about his betrayal until he was unwilling to forgive himself; it was not that he was unable to forgive himself, but it was that he **refused** to forgive himself. The Bible says, *"If we confess our sins, he is faithful and just to forgive our sins, and to cleanse us from all unrighteousness." (I John 1:9)* That means that God is willing, ready and able to forgive you, contingent upon the fact that you will ask Him to forgive you and then believe that He has forgiven you.

> *"I have sinned," he said, "for I have betrayed innocent blood." "What is that to us?" they replied. "That's your responsibility." So Judas threw the money into the temple and left. Then he went away and hanged himself." (Mathew 27:4-5, NIV)*

Again, Judas became so obsessed with guilt from betraying Jesus until he began to have suicidal thoughts, his suicidal thoughts became so strong that he tried to kill himself, and he acted on what he thought. Judas killed himself as an attempt to relieve the pain and guilt that was associated with his betrayal. The point is that because Judas chose not to forgive himself, his unforgiving attitude became so dark within his heart until he killed himself.

An unforgiving attitude will break you down; it will stunt and handicap you from maximizing your potential. This kind of attitude will destroy your body causing it to become dysfunctional. The thing to note about an unforgiving attitude is that you do not have to accept it. You can make the decision to forgive. You chose whether to forgive yourself and others.

The ability to forgive can be seen in the life of the apostle Peter. Like Judas, Peter sinned against Christ but **Peter forgave himself** and received restoration from God for all that he did wrong. Peter denied Christ when Jesus was arrested, Peter denied that he even knew Christ, and when confronted about his connection to the ministry of Jesus, Peter acted out with very inappropriate behavior.

When Peter was questioned about his relationship with Jesus, not only did Peter lie one time, but he lied three times, denying and disowning that he ever knew Jesus. In fact, Peter disowned Jesus in the presence of Jesus. The Bible says,

> *"Then began he to curse and swear, saying, I know not the man and immediately the cock crew and Peter remembered the word of Jesus which said unto him, before the cock crow, thou shalt deny me thrice. And he went out and wept bitterly." (Matthew 26:74-75)*

Peter literally began both, to curse himself, and to use the Lord's name in vain. In addition, he began to use excessive profanity and inappropriate language to convince the people into the lie about him not knowing Jesus. Dr. Archibald T. Robertson, says, *"He repeated his denial with the addition of profanity to prove that he was telling the truth instead of the lie that they all knew."* (P. 220)

After the rooster crowed, Peter remembered the words of Jesus and he repented. True repentance will always make you feel better. God is not interested in beating you down; He is interested in lifting you up so that you can joyously fulfill His will for your life. Peter weeping and asking God for forgiveness was the turning point in his life not going under. Peter's life was restored from destruction, all because he released his guilt, shame, and hurt to God.

Dr. Dale Bronner, in his book, *Pass the Baton,* says,

> *Fortunately, you have been created with an eraser to help you correct your errors. It's been placed on the top (in your head) so you can rub out what needs to be removed. This is a three part process: 1. Admit it! 2. Quit it! 3. Forget it! Without question, you are going to make some marks you'd rather forget, but a loving God gives you the ability to wipe the slate clean.* Repentance not only erases, it treats the mistake as though it never happened. *The Lord knew in advance we would say things we did not mean and behave in ways we knew were wrong. That's why He provided the means to correct the errors-through mercy, forgiveness and repentance.* (P. 31)

When Judas Iscariot betrayed Jesus, he acted out of selfishness; he refused to come to God for forgiveness. He took matters within his own hands. He became so self-absorbed and overwhelmed by his betrayal of Jesus until he just could not overcome the negative thoughts of what he had done, but rather chose to kill himself.

Notice this scripture:

> *Come to me all you who labor and are heavy-laden*
> *and overburdened and I will cause you rest. [I will*
> *ease and relieve and refresh your souls.] Take My*
> *yoke upon you and learn of Me, for I am gentle (meek)*
> *and humble (lowly) in heart, and you will find rest*
> *(relief and ease and refreshment and recreation and*
> *blessed quiet) for your souls. [Jer.6:16.] For My yoke is*
> *wholesome (useful, good – not harsh, hard, sharp, or*
> *pressing, but comfortable, gracious, and pleasant), and*
> *My burden is light and easy to be borne." (Matthew*
> *11:28-30, AMP)*

When you come to Jesus, you are not going to feel badly about yourself because God does not feel badly about you. Again, God is not interested in beating you up. God loves you, and when you ask for forgiveness, God will not be hard, sharp and cold with you; God will only expect you to turn from the wrong and move into doing what is right.

Control Your Emotions

If you do not take control of your negative emotions then your negative emotions will carry you in the wrong direction. What happens when you go in the wrong direction? You get farther and farther away from where you need to be. Negative emotions will get you in to a place that God did not intend for you to be. You can spend several years recovering from a bad decision that you made under the influence of your wrong emotions.

> *"And the Lord said to Cain, Why are you angry? And*
> *why do you look sad and depressed and dejected? If*

you do well, will you not be accepted? And if you do
not well, sin crouches at your door; its desire is for
you, but you must master it." (Genesis 4:6-7, AMP)

One of the keys in this verse is the word *it*, what is it that God wanted Cain to master? It would be his uncontrollable emotions (anger and envy) leading him eventually in a direction that would take him out of the will of God for his life. God told Cain that **you must master it** because if he did not master his uncontrollable emotions, they would cause him to do something insane, and then later on, he would regret his decision. You must master your emotions or your emotions will master you.

If your emotions do not line up with the word of God, or if they go against the word of God, then your emotions are not from God. In his book, *Taking Charge Of Your Emotions*, Pastor Gregory Dickow says,

> *"Emotions are feelings on the inside caused by pain or*
> *pleasure trying to move us in a certain direction. Jesus*
> *had emotions, yet His emotions did not have Him!*
> *There were times, however, where He was tempted, as*
> *we are, yet without sin. (Hebrews 4:15)." (P. 13)*

What is an emotion? An emotion clinically speaking has to do with an intense feeling of cravings or a strong desire for something whether or not it is right or wrong. According to the American Heritage Dictionary, an **emotion** is defined as *the part of the consciousness that involves feelings and sensibility.* Emotions will begin in the mind (consciousness) that is psychological, and then they will move you into a reaction caused by feelings of expression, which is physiological.

Amnon's Uncontrolled Emotions

A good example of the definition of emotion can be located in (II Samuel 13:1-5, 12, 14, 18, 23, and 32.) I strongly recommend that you read this chapter in its entirety to grasp its full meaning of what I am communicating.

> *"And it came to pass after this, that Absalom the son of David had a fair sister, whose name was Tamar; and Amnon the son of David loved her. And Amnon was so vexed, that he fell sick for his sister Tamar; for she was a virgin; and Amnon thought it hard for him to do anything to her. But Amnon had a friend, whose name was Jonadab, the son of Shimeah David's brother: and Jonadab was a very subtle man. He said unto him, why art thou, being the king's son lean from day to day? Wilt thou not tell me? Amnon said unto him, I love Tamar, my brother Absalom's sister. And Jonadab said unto him...And she answered him, Nay my brother, do not force me; for no such thing ought to be done in Israel: do not thou this folly...Howbeit he would not hearken unto her voice; but being stronger than she, forced her, and lay with her. Then Amnon hated her exceedingly; so that the hatred wherewith he hated her was greater than the love wherewith he had loved her. And Amnon said unto her, Arise, be gone...Then his servant brought her out, and bolted the door after her...And it came to pass after two years, that Absalom had sheepshears in Baal-hazor, which is beside Ephraim: and Absalom invited all the king's sons...and Jonadab, the son of Shimeah David's brother, answered and said, Let not my lord suppose that they have slain all the young men the king's sons;*

*for Amnon only is dead: for by the appointment of
Absalom this hath been determined from the day that
he forced his sister Tamar."*

First, Amnon's love was lust. Amnon's love for Tamar was
built on an emotional fatal attraction and not a genuine commitment. This was displayed when he received what he wanted
(sexual relations) by forcing her, and then afterwards, beginning
to hate her. Love does not hate nor will it hurt. Love always
desires the best for another person and love will never think
of doing evil. (I Corinthians 13:4-8) Therefore, the question to
be asked is what made Amnon hate Tamar? It was his uncontrollable emotions; his spirit of lust overpowered him causing
Tamar shame, and Amnon, eventually, death.

Bishop T.D. Jakes, in his book, *Women Thou Art Loosed*, says,

*"Many women feel guilty about things they had no
control over. They feel guilty about being victimized.
Often their original intention was to help another,
but in the process they are damaged. Tamar was the
King's daughter. She was a virgin. She was a "good
girl." She didn't do anything immoral. It is amazing
that her own brother would be so filled with desire
that he would go to such lengths to destroy his sister.
He thought he was in love. It wasn't love. It was lust.
He craved her so intensely that he lost his appetite
for food. He was visibly distorted with passion. Love
is a giving force, while lust is a selfish compulsion
centralized on gratification." (P.48-49)*

Uncontrollable emotions will always get you into situations
that you did not intend to get into. Amnon had no idea that

Absalom would eventually kill him over his sister. I am sure Amnon had no idea that he would violate Tamer sexually. That is the trick of uncontrollable emotions; they will set you up to have short pleasure, but after the thrill is gone the devastation of the consequences that follow are never pleasant. The death of Amnon could have been avoided if Amnon would have controlled his negative emotions.

Second, Amnon listened to wrong advice. *"Blessed is the man that walketh not in the counsel of the ungodly." (Psalms 1:1)* The Amplified states; *BLESSED (Happy, fortunate, prosperous, and enviable) is the man who walks and lives not in the counsel of the ungodly [following their advice, their plans and purposes].* It was very ungodly what Ammon's friend (Jonadab) told him to do. Therefore, by Amnon acting on his friend's wrong advice, it cost him his life. Who are you listening too? What they say to you could be a matter of life and death.

In the Garden of Eden, (Genesis 3:1-11) Adam and Eve had sinned and discovered that they were naked. Immediately God asked the question, who told you? God knew that they had listened to the wrong advice thus this wrong advice caused separation between them and God. This wrong advice resulted in Jesus Christ dying for humanity to reestablish a spiritual connection between God and man. (I Timothy 2:5-6)

Third, your uncontrollable emotions will affect others around you. Whether or not you are aware of your uncontrollable emotions, they will affect the people in your life. Amnon's decision to violate his sister-in-law made his extended family angry with him. Absalom, his brother, was affected by his decision so badly until he ordered Amnon killed at the time that Amnon thought everything was calm and forgotten.

On the contrary, in (Genesis 41:1, 9) the Bible says that the butler remembered Joseph's dream two years later because it had a positive, life-lasting effect on him. Joseph and the butler were in prison together; Joseph did something for the butler that he would never forget. Joseph showed the butler kindness by interpreting his dream and showing him comfort until the king released the butler.

When the butler was released from prison and the king needed his dream interpreted, immediately the butler remembered Joseph. This is how Joseph came out of prison; he made a mark, a positive effect that would be life-lasting for the butler to remember.

Dr. Mike Murdock says, *You will only be remembered for two things: the problems you solve or the ones you create." (P. 6)* Amnon's bad decision was remembered two years after he sexually abused his sister and was killed for it, however, Joseph was remembered two years later because of what he did for the butler. He was rewarded by being released from prison and promoted to the second highest position in Egypt—the governor. (Genesis 42:6)

You will definitely be remembered for something. Both Joseph and Amnon were remembered for their actions, one was remembered for his good action and the other was remembered for his bad action. What will you be remembered for?

It is also important to indicate that emotions have to do with you making the right or wrong decisions under the influence of intense feelings of pressure applied to the mind. When I say intense feelings of pressure applied to the mind, I am conveying that you will feel emotions, such as fear, anger, guilt or intimidation and will have to work hard and be consistent at doing the right thing, even though your emotions are telling you to do the wrong thing.

Fourth, your uncontrollable emotions will have consequences. We see that because of what Amnon did; his uncontrollable emotion cost him his life, which means that you will have to give an account for what you do. You cannot do wrong and get away with it.

The Bible says,

> "Don't be misled. Remember that you can't ignore God and get away with it. You will always reap what you sow! Those who live only to satisfy their own sinful desires will harvest the consequences of decay and death. But those who live to please the Spirit will harvest everlasting life from the Spirit, so don't get tired of doing what is good. Don't get discouraged and give up, for we will reap a harvest of blessing at the appropriate time." (Galatians 6:7-9, NLT)

As a believer, if you are doing wrong and think that you can continue to do wrong and can get away with it, that is criminal thinking. Your actions always have consequences; this is why you want to develop good habits. Good habits produce good consequences and good consequences are always the results of a good decision that was made.

Adam and Eve's Uncontrollable Emotion

> "NOW THE serpent was more subtle than any beast of the field which the LORD God had made. And he said unto the woman, Yea hath God said, Ye shall not eat of every tree of the garden? And the woman said unto the serpent, We may eat of the fruit of the trees of the garden: But of the fruit of the tree which is in

the midst of the garden, God hath said, Ye shall not eat of it, neither shall ye touch it, lest ye die. And the serpent said unto the woman, Ye shall not surely die: For God doth know that in the day ye eat thereof, then your eyes shall be opened, and ye shall be as gods, knowing good and evil. And when the woman saw that the tree was good for food, and that it was pleasant to the eyes, and a tree to be desired to make one wise, she took of the fruit thereof, and did eat, and gave also unto her husband with her; and he did eat. And the eyes of them both were opened, and they knew that they were naked; and they sewed fig leaves together, and made themselves aprons. And they heard the voice of the LORD God walking in the garden in the cool of the day: and Adam and his wife hid themselves from the presence of the Lord God amongst the trees of the garden. And the LORD God called unto Adam, and said unto him, Where are thou? And he said, I heard thy voice in the garden, and I was afraid, because I was naked; and I hid myself...So he drove out the man; and he placed at the east of the garden of Eden Cherubims, and a flaming sword which turned every way, to keep the way of the tree of life." (Genesis 3:1-10, 24)

There are some things that can be learned as a result, of Adam and Eve being emotionally ruled in the Garden of Eden. **First, indulging in the wrong thing will make you act the wrong way.** If you eat too much, you will get sick. If you worry too much, you will get depressed. When people get under the influence of wrong behaviors, they do and say things that they would never do or say if they were not under the influence of wrong behavior.

Notice that Adam and Eve hid themselves because they saw that they were naked. Their uncontrollable emotion to gratify their flesh caused them to respond in a way that was unnatural; they saw things that God did not want them to see. That is what bad habits will do to you; they will cause you to act and do things that are unhealthy or unnatural for you, ultimately destroying your life if you do not regain control of your emotions.

Second, do not make impulsive decisions. Many times people get into trouble when they make impulsive decisions, especially when they do not know the person(s) or the product that is luring them. It is extremely important to talk with someone about the major decisions you make.

Notice this scripture: *"Where no counsel is, the people fall: But in the multitude of counselors there is safety." (Proverbs 11:14)* Adam and Eve fell into sin because they did not bounce their decision off God whether or not to eat the fruit. If they would have checked it out with God first, they could have avoided eviction from the Garden of Eden and the consequences of eating the forbidden fruit.

It is important to note that the devil came to Eve asking her questions about what God said; making it appear that God was not telling the truth and that God was withholding something good from Adam and her. The same manipulative approach that the devil used with Adam and Eve is being used in today's society, by people from all types of occupations to promote and sell their products. If you do not know what you need, you can buy things or get involved in things that will cause you to suffer and experience great loss, taking you away from the will of God for your life.

Pastor Greg Powe, in his book, *Success Habit,* says,

> *"Don't' buy things in a hurry just because someone is pushing you. Don't make an important decision when you feel pressured. You'll be stuck with the outcome because you came under the control of someone's pressure."* (P. 134)

Before you make any decision that is in opposition to the information that you know to be true, you should not buy or commit to anything. Let people know that you will get back with them after you have prayed about the situation. If you seemed pressured at that point to make an immediate decision, then that's not God. Do not make any decisions under the influence of pressure. I have seen sales people pressure people into purchasing things that they do not need and the purchaser struggle to keep the merchandise purchased—if not lose it.

Again, Pastor Greg Powe in his book, *Success Habit,* says,

> *"I always said it like this: investigate before you invest. Before you invest your life or your life's saving, investigate, because your losses can be very heavy if you don't. You can experience losses that you may never recover. Some people end up so damaged and bruised that they can never again trust another person. Don't become the walking wounded. Take the time you need to make wise choices."* (P. 137)

People who come into your life will either help you or set you back. Wrong association will keep you addicted and bound to what you need to be set free from. In other words, it is important for you to be **self-differentiated,** not taking on others' advice when you know exactly what you need to do. When people tell you to do things contrary to what's right, when you are self-differentiated, you can say no, stepping away, feeling no sense of guilt or responsibility to anyone.

Third, it is important to check out your association with people. *"And we beseech you, brethren, to know them which labour among you..." (I Thessalonians 5:12)* When you know people because of association, you are aware of what they are capable of doing and what they are not capable of doing. Before Adam and Eve made any decisions about the fruit they ate, they should have sought God about the devil's credibility. They should have done a background check on the devil. This would have provided them with accurate information to determine if what the devil was saying was true.

Here are four biblical references regarding the importance of association: (1) Lot was blessed because of his association with his uncle Abraham. (Genesis 13:5-6) (2) The mariners were cursed because of their association with Jonah. (Jonah 1:12) (3) Laban acknowledged that he was blessed because of Jacob. (Genesis 30:27) (4) Joshua and the nation of Israel were cursed because of their association with Achan. (Joshua 7:1-26)

> *"And everyone that was in distress and everyone that was in debt, and every one that was discontented, gathered themselves unto him; and he became a captain over them: and there were with him about four hundred men." (I Samuel 22:2)*

One of the ways to get the blessings of God upon your life is to get connected with blessed people. King David was blessed by God; people knew this by gathering themselves unto him. The people knew that King David had a yoke-destroying and burden-removing anointing. The anointing that was in King

David's life spilled over into their lives. This is what you call **increase by association**. The same way you can increase by right association, you can decrease by wrong association.

The word **bless** is an *empowerment to prosper*. It is a way of God enabling you to produce effective results. It is an ability to get the job done and to get the job done right. The word **curse** is an *empowerment to fail*; it is an inability to produce effective results. The curse is associated with Satan and its result is always failure. If you do not want the curse, you will have to disconnect from cursed people and cursed things. Therefore, your association with people will do two things; either it will bless you or curse you.

Learn the Vocabulary of Silence

"To everything there is a season, and a time for every matter or purpose under heaven...a time to keep silent and a time to speak." (Ecclesiastes 3:1, 7)

According to this particular passage of scripture, it is indicating that there is a time and a season for everything. That means that there is a time to deal with complicated issues and a time to leave them alone. There is a time to voice your concern and a time to leave them alone. To everything, there is a time and a season.

An example of understanding the vocabulary of silence was when I was called and asked to help serve at a **home going celebration**. A home going is not a funeral; the word funeral has the association of sadness, hurt and grief. When a believer goes home to be with the Lord you should be excited for them; they are in a better place, a place of no more pain, sorrow, hurt or inabilities, therefore, there is nothing to be sad, hurt or in grief about. (Revelation 14:13, 21:1-5)

However, the family needs to be both comforted and supported during this time. In addition, the family needs to implement some techniques and approaches to deal with the separation or detachment of no longer being physically able to be present with their loved one.

I was asked by one of the leaders of the home going ministry to have all the volunteers for the service to arrive one hour before the service started. On the day of the home going, I spent a good amount of time that morning in prayer. I was uncertain if I were going to attend because of my work schedule. Nevertheless, I felt the prompting of the Holy Spirit to go and serve during the home going.

Upon walking through the door and getting in my position to serve, immediately one of the volunteers of the home going ministry walked up to me and began to let me have it. This person was loud and was very disrespectful to me. This person was upset because I had asked this person to arrive one hour before the service started to set up and to make sure everything was in place.

I told the person that I was instructed by the authority over me to have everyone arrive at that particular time. This person refused to hear any of that, and said that I was to tell the exact time of the home going so they could arrive when the home going would start. In addition, this person told me other things that I chose not to write.

Because this person was unreasonable and intolerant, I became silent and walked away, mainly because I was tired of being disrespected in public. There were many people walking around us that day.

During the home going service, I noticed that some of the family and friends were walking in and out. I went out of the service to comfort a young man. After talking with this man for about five minutes, he accepted Jesus Christ as Lord and Savior outside of the church. He became born-again before he returned to the service.

I observed another young man walking out of the service. This man told me that he was there when his friend died. He saw and heard things that he felt no one else could understand but him, because he was with the person when they breathed their last.

This brother also accepted Jesus Christ as Lord and Savior of his life, and returned to the service saved, born-again, forgiven, healed, and restored.

KEY THOUGHT: Silence communicates loudly and can never be misquoted.

The point I am making in saying this is: At the beginning of the home going service a volunteer member was very disrespectful and embarrassing to me. This person's attitude included derogatory words and they did not feel or sound good, but I kept my mouth shut.

I refused to become a victim of those negative words that were spoken to me. I used the vocabulary of silence. I knew that if I could just walk away and not argue, but pray in the Holy Ghost to myself, I would be keeping myself in the love of God. (Jude 1:20-21) This would keep me sensitive to the move of God to be a blessing to the people of God.

Dr. I.V. Hilliard, in his book, *Living the Maximized Life*, says,

"In order to live a maximized life you must quickly learn the important principle of maximizing your

mouth. Most people are highly developed in what I call "victim vocabulary" and negative talk, but they don't realize that their negative speech becomes a self-fulfilling prophecy. The scriptures clearly teach that the words we speak really do matter. Our words are spiritual containers that impact both the natural realm and the spiritual realm." (P. 146)

The key to successfully using the vocabulary of silence is to keep you from saying the wrong words and to keep your mind on God. Scripture tells us to set our affection on things that are above. (Colossians 3:1-2.) Setting your affection on things that are above is mentally and spiritually establishing what you say and do to be uplifting, which can be done by you understanding the importance of your words.

Many people talk themselves out of the blessings of God. They speak negatively or they are amassed in negative activities that distract them from the presence and blessings of God. Distractions cause them to lose focus of God's intended purpose. During the home going service I stayed focused and God was able to show His strength through me to help two young men turn their lives over to Him (Jesus Christ).

These two young men became born-again because I controlled my tongue; I exercised the vocabulary of silence. If I would have argued with the disgruntled volunteer, or would have become angry or shut down, I would not have experienced the blessing of God using me.

The Message Bible says, *"I am determined to watch steps and tongue so they won't land me in trouble. I decided to hold my tongue as long as Wicked is in the room." (Psalms 39:1, TM)* There are times when you hear negative things (wicked); you need not respond, but just keep your mouth shut and pray softly to yourself.

Joyce Meyer, in her book, *Me and My Big Mouth*, says,

> *"All of us get upset when we have our plans made,*
> *then something comes along to upset them. When that*
> *happens to me, I have learned to take a deep breath,*
> *shut my mouth for a minute, get control of myself,*
> *then go on with my life." (P.173)*

Again, God could not have used me if I would have been caught up in a spirit of anger, bitterness, or unforgiving attitude with this volunteer member. *"Let no corrupt communication proceed out of your mouth, but that which is good for the use of edifying, that it may minister grace into the hearers."* (Ephesians 4:29) Often, when people get mistreated they get mad and their tongues are like loose cannons. If you cannot say something good about a person, it is better to not say anything at all.

> *"Wherefore, my beloved brethren, let every man be swift*
> *to hear, slow to speak, slow to wrath." (James 1:19)*

Some people need to learn the art of just keeping their mouths shut; they then would receive deliverance and breakthroughs. It is the mouth that often gets people in trouble. Therefore, silence is an art that the Christian's Body definitely needs to master.

The Bird and the Frog

There is a story about a bird and a frog. They both needed to go south for the winter. The frog came up with an idea as to how the bird could possibly get him there. The frog suggested to the bird, "If you would allow me to grab your legs with my mouth, then you can flap your wings and the both of us could fly south for the winter."

The bird thought about that statement in amazement, wondering how the frog came up with such a good idea. The bird shook his head in agreement and said, "Okay. I can do that." The frog grabbed the bird's legs with his mouth and off they flew, flying south to enjoy the heat.

As they were flying south, a farmer was working in the field. He noticed the bird was flying and how the frog was holding on to the bird's legs with his mouth; they were both successfully flying south for the winter. As the bird and the frog continued to fly south, the farmer thought out loud and said; *What an ingenious idea, that is just brilliant! I wonder who could come up with such an ingenious idea?* And about that time the frog opened its mouth and said its mi————ne, its mi————ne and fell right to the ground and splattered.

The moral of the story is this **if you open your mouth at the wrong time, it can cost you.** This is oh so true in overcoming a bad habit because there are times that you need to keep your mouth shut and just believe God; everybody does not need to know your business. In most cases, the only time some people are aware of your struggles is when you tell them.

Another interesting thing to note about the frog is that the frog forgot the old saying that says, *"Think before you speak."* If the frog could have just only implemented the think before you speak technique, the frog would not have died.

There were times when Jesus did not even respond to people. (Matthew 27:12, Luke 22:64) I believe one of the reasons Jesus did not respond to some people's questions is that it was not necessary to respond, and some times if you respond to foolish questions, your answer will only complicate the matter.

The Bible says, *"But avoid foolish questions, and genealogies, and contentions, and strivings about the law; for they are unprofitable* and vain. *(Titus 3:9)* Many people, often, are caught up in the mouth trap; their mouths often get them into situations that they do not want to be in. Therefore, in those situations it is better to just keep quiet.

In regards to watching what comes out of your mouth, Dr. Dale Bronner, in his book, *Guard your Gates,* says,

> *Here is a life-changing scripture:* **"Whoso keepeth his mouth and his tongue keepeth his soul from troubles" (Proverbs 21:23).** *Think of the heartaches you could have avoided had you simply closed your mouth! If some people had learned to seal their lips, they would still have their job and their marriage would be intact. When a fire is raging, you don't try to douse it with gasoline. Instead, you cut off the supply of oxygen and extinguish the flame...I don't always agree with Confucius, but I concur with his words on this topic. He said, "The wise man speaks because he has something to say. The fool speaks because he has to say something." (P. 17-18)*

Think about this for a moment. The only reason a fish is hooked is that it opens its mouth. The fish getting hooked has nothing at all to do with the sophistication, expensive fishing bate or the expertise of the fisherperson. The fish is hooked solely because the fish opened its mouth. I do not compare anyone to an animal, but Jesus often used animals and nature to better paint the picture of what he was attempting to communicate.

Notice how fish respond when they are caught—they resist, pull back, kick, and flop all over the place. So, what is happening? The fish is in a situation that it does not want to be in; if the fish had it to do it all over again, it would definitely keep its mouth shut. Therefore, when you keep your mouth shut, and learn the vocabulary of silence, being silent will keep you from being hooked or caught up in things you do not want.

When most people are going through or experiencing great difficulties; it is very seldom that they say anything good. They are very negative about themselves and very negative about others:

> "So the men Moses had sent to explore the land, who returned and made the whole community grumble against him by spreading a bad report about it – these men responsible for spreading the bad report about the land were struck down and died of a plague before the LORD. Of the men who went to explore the land, only Joshua son of Nun and Caleb son of Jephunneh survived." (Numbers 14:36-38, NIV)

God held these negative men's mouths responsible; God took the bad report of these men so seriously that they all died the same day they spoke negative. Only Joshua and Caleb survived because they set a watch over their tongues. *"Those who love to talk will experience the consequences, for the tongue can kill or nourish life. (Proverbs 18:21, NLT)* Your mouth will hold you responsible before God; you will have what you said whether or not you are conscience of it, what you say will grow and develop, thus you become what you say.

God gave humans two of just about everything; He gave them two feet, two legs, two arms, two ears, two eyes, two hands and two holes in the nose, but interestingly, a human's mouth, God gave only one. Could it be that God in His Omniscience (*all knowing ability*) knew that man would run his mouth twice as much as he would work with his hands and hear with his ears?

Scripture indicates for us to be *"slow to speak..."* *(James 1:19)*.

What you say affects how you think, and what you think affects what you do. What you do is what you are going to have. This is why the Bible says,

> *"For verily I say unto you, That whosoever shall say*
> *unto this mountain, Be thou removed, and be thou*
> *cast into the sea; and shall not doubt in his heart, but*
> *shall believe that those things which he saith shall*
> *come to pass; he shall have whatsoever he saith."*
> *(Mark 11:23)*

You cannot say things like *"I am always messing up,"* because you will always mess up. You have to say what you desire, and not confess the negative stuff you are presently experiencing. If you say, *"I will never recover,"* or *"I will never get out of this,"* then you won't.

If you can consistently speak that you believe that you will receive healing, restoration, freedom and recovery, then that is what you are going to have. Therefore, you can recover and you do not have to be anything that God's word says that you are not.

Another example of understanding the vocabulary of silence is when my wife and I were traveling home one evening from Birmingham, Alabama. We were traveling through the Woodlawn area when a police officer pulled us over for going through a traffic light that was on yellow and turning red. When the officer came up to the car, I was completely quiet and did not talk until I was spoken to.

The officer indicated that I needed to stop when the light was yellow. He also went on to say that it was a nice truck that I was driving and he would hate to see it get hit. The officer concluded by telling me to have a nice day.

What the officer did not know is that on that day, I did not have my driver's license with me. Although I did have some form of identification and my wife had her driving license and other identification, it was not necessary to use any identification at that time because of the vocabulary of silence.

Allow People to Help You

At the beginning of this book, I said that you must ask God for help. Not only must you ask Him for help, but equally important, you must allow people to help you.

> "O Jerusalem, Jerusalem, thou that killest the prophets, and stonest them which are sent unto thee, how often would I have gathered thy children together, even as a hen gathereth her chickens under her wings, and ye would not!" (Matthew 23:37)

Jesus Christ was indicating in this particular passage his desire to heal and restore Jerusalem. He was always willing and open to help remove burdens and destroy yokes, even to the point of doing whatever was needed for them to break negative behaviors and overcome bad habits, but they would not allow Him to help.

Jesus used as an example a hen that gathers her chicks. The Jewish nation, unlike little chicks that would naturally run to their mother hen in a time of harm, deliberately refused, scripture says, (ye would not) meaning they would not turn to the yoke-destroying and burden-removing power of God's ability to set them free.

Just as this Jewish nation was faced with making the decision to allow Jesus to help, you will be faced with the same decision. Will you allow other people to help you? If not, you will have the same consequences as the audience that Jesus was speaking to; they received ultimate ruin because they refused good help.

Jesus desired to heal, deliver and set them free of all cares that this world would bring; however, Jesus could do nothing for these people unless they accepted what He had to offer. The Lord himself had to get permission to rule and reign in people lives. Note this scripture; *"Behold, I stand at the door and knock: if any man hears my voice and opens the door, I will come in to him, and will sup (ultimate fellowship) with him, and he with me." (Revelation 3:20)*

Now there are two things that Jesus cannot do: 1) He cannot fail, because there is no failure in him. 2) He cannot help a person who refuses to be helped. *"He came unto his own, and his own received him not. But as many as received him, to them gave he power to become the sons of God, even to them that believe on his name." (John 1:11-12)* Those who believed on Jesus' name gave Him permission to rule in their lives, thus receiving the yoke-destroying and burden-removing power of God in their lives.

KEY THOUGHT: A closed hand receives nothing, but an open hand receives what is coming into it.

A good example of allowing people to help is about **the man who was out in the sea and his boat began to sink.** He immediately called on the name of the Lord. A small boat arrived. The people in the boat asked the man whose boat was sinking to get in their boat. He replied, "No, the Lord is going to save me." Then, another boat arrived. This one was very large. They asked the man to get in their boat, for he was about to sink. He replied, "No, the Lord is going to save me." Then a helicopter came by dropping a rope; the man closed his hand, and refused just like at other times.

When the man drowned and went to heaven, he asked the Lord why He had not saved him. The Lord replied, "I tried. I tried. I sent the boats and the helicopter but you refused to be helped." This is one of the major setbacks to overcoming bad habits; we do not allow God to use others to help us. When this occurs, we then tie the hands of God and He can do nothing. A closed hand receives nothing, but an open hand receives what is coming to it. Will you be open enough to allow people to help?

Be Good to Yourself

In order for you to be good to yourself, you must know that you have goodness in you and that God desires to bring out the goodness in you. The Bible says, *"And God saw every thing that he had made, and, behold, it was very good. And the evening and the morning were the sixth day." (Genesis 1:31)* The very goodness that God made includes you; God made you in His own Image. (Genesis 1:26-28) Therefore, you have goodness in you because God made you, and God does not make junk.

Many times, people are not good to themselves because of the shame and guilt that is associated with the negative things from their past. Because of shame and guilt going unchecked, people have negative thoughts that constantly bombard and harass their minds to where their lives in the present are affected.

Pastor Don Shorter, in his book, *Casting Down Imaginations,* says,

> *Satan desires to bombard your mind through every means possible: radio, television, newspaper, anyway he can. However, without the incubation process of negative imaginations and thoughts, he cannot effectively cause your life to be changed by these bombardments. Satan can't put you in a neck hold, pull you down to a bar, and get you drunk. He first suggests the idea. He may use anyone, perhaps someone you believe is a friend. Remember, the thought must always be planted first. Many Christians silently deal with areas of temptation and bombardment in their minds, while trying to cover them up from people around them. (P.33)*

The thing to know is that God loves you, and He cares for you, regardless of what you have done. You cannot go so low to where God cannot pick you back up; you cannot do so badly, to where God cannot make things better in your life.

"For God so loved the world that he gave his only begotten Son, that whosoever believeth in him should not perish, but have everlasting life." (John 3:16) God so loving the world includes you; God's love for you is not contingent upon you, but it is solely based upon who God is and what God has chosen to do for you. Whether or not people love God, He still loves them and desires to bring the very best out of them.

Many people put limitations on God's ability by looking at their weaknesses, failures and shortcomings an by thinking that God is angry. God is not angry with you: *"For I know the thoughts that I think toward you, saith the Lord, thoughts of peace, and not of evil, to give you an expected end." (Jeremiah 29:11)*

Scripture says that God does not think evil toward us, so, where does evil thinking come from? Evil thinking comes from within the mind. Thoughts of negative behavior that torment you are not of God. God's desire is for you to be good to yourself and that you enjoy life and live well.

Pastor Joyce Meyer, in her book, *Straight Talk on Discouragement*, says,

> *"So often people lose their joy because they had something in the past that made them joyful but which is now gone. Many are pining away for the move of God that was but is not any more. It is too bad it no longer exists, but it doesn't and there is nothing you and I can do about it. Instead, we must learn to live in the present. God is moving now—let's enjoy now!"*
> *(P. 66)*

God desires to give you an expected end, with a hope and a future with great participation in God's unlimited supply of available resources. Therefore, God expects you to be good to yourself and to feel good about yourself. God expects you to enjoy the good life. God desires the best for you. Scripture says, *"Fear not, little flock; for it is your Father's good pleasure to give you the kingdom." (Luke 12:32)*

Dr. I.V. Hilliard, in his book, *Ten Mistakes Most Failures Make*, says,

> *"If you look to Jesus, the starting place of your faith, He will finish it in you. You are not the only one who has ever made a mistake or fallen. You may not have the resources you thought you were going to have.*

You may not be able to do everything you thought you were going to do, but do not compound the problem by "dumping" on yourself." (P. 32)

In order to enjoy the goodness of God you must not be too hard on yourself. You will need to be patient and not torment yourself. Stop beating yourself up! Understand that all men fall; the great ones will get back up and keep moving forward.

Notice what the Bible says, *"Rejoice not against me, O mine enemy: When I fall, I shall arise; when I sit in darkness, the LORD shall be a light unto me." (Micah 7:8)* Do not let the fear of past and present mistakes discourage you. God loves you. He will keep you safe. He will not allow you to suffer harm, injury or evil. It is God who will allow you to arise again when you fall.

Scriptural Promises for Safety

1. "Then Nebuchadnezzar the King was astonished, and rose up in haste, and spake, and said unto his counsellors, Did not we cast three men bound into the midst of the fire? They answered and said, unto the king. True, O king. He answered and said, Lo I see four men loose, walking in the midst of the fire, **and they have no hurt;** and the form of the fourth is like the Son of God." (Daniel 3:24-25)

2. "Behold! I give you authority and power to trample upon serpents and scorpions, and [physical and mental strength and ability] over all the power that the enemy [possesses]; and **nothing shall in any way harm you."** (Luke 10:19 AMP)

3. **"No evil will conquer you;** no plague will come near your dwelling. For **he orders his angels to protect you**

wherever you go. The Lord says, I will rescue those who love me. I will protect those who trust in my name. When they call on me, I will answer; I will be with them in trouble, I will rescue them and honor them. I will satisfy them with a long life and give them my salvation." (Psalms 91:10-11, 14-16, NLT)

4. "We know [absolutely] that anyone born of God does not [deliberately and knowingly] practice committing sin, but the One who was begotten of **God carefully watches over and protects** him [Christ's divine presence within him preserves him against the evil], and the wicked one does not lay hold (get a grip) on him or touch [him]." (I John 5:18, AMP)

5. "**No weapon** that is formed against you shall prosper." (Isaiah 54:17)

6. **The LORD protects me from danger—so why should I tremble?** When evil people come to destroy me, when my enemies and foes attack me, they will stumble and fall. Though a mighty army surrounds me, my heart will know no fear. **I remain confident**...For he will conceal me there when trouble comes; he will hide me in his sanctuary. He will place me out of reach on a high rock. Then I will hold my head high, above my enemies who surround me. At his Tabernacle I will offer sacrifices with shouts of joy, singing and praising the LORD with music. (Psalms 27:1-3, 5-6 NLT)

Understanding that God will not allow anything to hurt you is one of the key connectors to being good to yourself. Many people are afraid of stepping out and entering into their dreams and desires because they feel that they are unworthy. Some feel that they might mess up again, or they feel their past mistakes disqualify or exempt them from future happiness and good living. You have a right to enjoy your life.

Jesus said,

> *"The thief comes only in order to steal and to kill and destroy. I came that they may have and enjoy life, and have it in abundance (to the full, till it overflows)."* (John 10:10, AMP)

That abundant life is the goodness of God; it is experiencing God's unlimited access and maximum results in your life. To be good to yourself is taking care of you; you will not beat yourself up, you will not be down on yourself, but you will love yourself. When you are good to yourself, you will do things that will make you happy and do you good.

The Bible says, *"...and see the Lord is good; blessed is the man that trusts in him."* It goes on to say that God delights (*take pleasure in*) the prosperity of His people. The word **delight** means, *"To be caught up with excitement."* It carries with it the connotation of **being raptured.** When we do good things, God literally gets taken away with joy and happiness.

Like a marriage ceremony when the groom walks over and picks up the bride, there is a feeling of excitement, and joy as the bride is swept off her feet, so, it is with the God that we serve. He is enthralled or taken away by the goodness of his people. This fact is why you need to start confessing that you are good.

You have goodness in you and you can be good even to the point of becoming great. You must confess this over yourself, over your families, business or marriage. God is for you and not against you. God has placed many people in positions where there is much evil and deception. When you can bring some goodness and honesty into the situation that is evil and deceptive, God receives glory because of the goodness in your life.

Ways to feel good about yourself

Find a place where you can get alone and relax – It is important for you to take some time out for you. You should get alone and take a warm bath, listen to relaxing music, look at very nice scenery. The main thing about finding a place to get alone and relax is that you will do everything that you like to enjoy. By doing the things that are enjoyable, you will soothe and calm your nervousness and relax your mind and body; they will bring peace and joy to your life.

Waiting to exhale – When you feel angry, panicky, stressed or over-worked, try breathing. When you are consciously aware of your breathing, it will slow your pulse and decrease your heart rate sufficiently; this technique will help you not to become agitated, or over reactive when things are not really all that bad. When you breathe in slowly and exhale, this will send a message to your mind that you are deliberately slowing your thought process down; your mind will, in turn, send a signal to your body that you are now calm and are in a safe mode.

Lay off the sugars – things such as hot coffee, caffeine drinks, soda and candy have a tendency to give you a considerable amount of energy at the moment, but later will leave you emotionally drained, unable to focus, causing you to lose concentration. Moreover, a large amount of sugars will destroy your white blood cells, prohibiting your body to fight off germs and infections. In addition, large amounts of sugars will increase your possibility of hypoglycemia, which can lead to diabetes. Drink plenty of water; it is the best drink for you.

Exercise daily – On a minimum, you should exercise at least 20 to 30 minutes a day. Some trainers will even suggest that you exercise 45 minutes to one hour a minimum of three times a week. The important thing to remember about exercising is that you need to do something. Many people make the mistake of doing nothing. Exercise makes you feel better emotionally; it makes your muscles and bones strong, and will make you sleep well and live longer.

Eat healthy – Eating healthy is important because it will improve and maintain your well being. Eating healthy will contribute sufficiently to your academic success allowing you to be mentally and physically sharp and alert. Eating healthy will lower the possibilities of heart disease, cancer, stroke and other diseases that are some of the leading causes of death in the United States of America. Eating healthy is associated with decreased incidents of obesity, dental care, and iron deficiency anemia.

Become better organized – When you arrange things in their proper place, such as cleaning a messy room, this action will have the tendency to create a sense of cleanliness and a relaxing atmosphere to where you feel good about yourself. One of the things about being organized is that it will produce the mindset of order that will bring about structure so that you can move about smoothly. Let's face it; no one really loves to look at a messy room. When things are congested, chaotic and disorganized you don't feel well, but when things are clean and in order, you want to move around.

Talk about your problems – Out the window are the days when counseling is just for "the mentally ill." One of the healthiest ways to overcome hurt, frustration, and overwhelming problems is to talk to someone about them. When you talk about your problems, not just complaining, allows the listener to comfort, support and direct you. Talking about your problems will allow what is negative in you to come out so that you can feel good about yourself.

Arrest Your Bad Habit

It is time to arrest your bad habit. It is time to put your bad habit behind bars and throw away the key. We are putting the cuffs on your bad habit and we are putting it on lock-down right now. That is right—we are putting the cuff on every addiction, every bad habit, every negative behavior, anything that is causing chaos, confusion, destruction, set backs or hard times in your life. We declare that it stops right now and the struggle is over—that is right—the struggle is over.

I declare that you are healed, forgiven, delivered, set free and restored from every pain, hurt, disappointment and wrong. I declare that no weapon that is formed against you will prosper; I declare that this is the best day of your life. You will go over and not under, you will excel and not propel, you will achieve what you believe, no more fear and no more failure, only true success in abundance to the full and running over in your life.

It is time to tell your bad habit that you are under arrest. You have the right to remain silent. Anything you say and do will be brought directly into contact with my Lord and Savior Jesus Christ. Every negative thought, word and behavior are covered, wiped out, totally forgiven and washed away by the blood of Jesus.

I declare that you are vindicated, restored, illuminated, and transformed into all that God has called you to be. You are the best, the greatest, and sharpest at everything that you do. May you experience the God that is exceedingly beyond. *"Now to*

Him who is able to do above and beyond all that we ask or think –
according to the power that works in you." (Ephesians 3:20, HCSB)
You have to know that God's desire is to make every day better
than the day before.

There are some final points that I would like to make concerning arresting your bad habits. **First,** you have been forgiven
by God. Scripture says, *"Who forgives all my sins and heals all my*
diseases." (Psalms 103:3 NLT) God has already forgiven us; the
only thing we have to do is accept God's forgiveness.

When a person is arrested and charged for a crime that
requires prison time, the only way the person convicted of the
crime can be forgiven of the crime committed is that he or she is
pardoned. In Psalms 103:3, the word **forgive** is translated according to the New Strong Exhaustive Concordance of the Bible as
"calach, saw-lakh, it means *to pardon or spare."* In addition, the
word forgives means to *remove or take away an offense.*

The Bible says, *"Let the wicked forsake his way, And the unrigh-*
teous man his thoughts: And let him return unto the LORD, and he
will have mercy upon him; And to our God, for he will abundantly
pardon" (Isaiah 55:7)

When you have been forgiven or pardoned that means that
you do not owe anyone anything. You have been totally released
to go free with no strings attached. You do not owe any debt to
society; you have the forgiveness of the crime and the penalty
associated with it. To be pardoned is a gift from the Higher
Power, Jesus Christ our Lord and Savior.

Jesus Christ has forgiven you of all wrong doings, which is
great because you do not have to live another day in the prison
of your mind, body or spirit. You do not have to live another
day feeling guilty, confused or not knowing what to do. You
can do all things through Christ. Your help is in the name of

Jesus; He has released you of all wrong which gives you the right to be free.

Therefore, be steady and firm in what you know to be true and what God has done for you. Do not hamper, exhaust, confuse, or frustrate yourself over the wrongs that you have done. Only believe that you have received everything that is necessary to make you whole, healed, delivered and free.

Finally, may you walk in the fullest of every promise of increase, promotion and total restoration from all that has been stolen or taken away from you. May you experience the God of too much wealth, health, promotion, increase, joy and goodness. Therefore, be steady and firm in what you know to be true and what God has done for you.

Again, do not hamper, exhaust, confuse, or frustrate yourself over the wrongs that you have done. Only believe that you have received everything that is necessary to make you healed, delivered and free. You can, shall, will and have overcome bad habits.

Finally, I say unto you, get up child of God, go and possess what God has given you. There shall be no man to stand before you. (Joshua 1:5) God will not allow anyone or anything to destroy you. Just as the wall of Jericho fell (Joshua 6:20), God will bring down the strongholds and the high places that are standing before you. Only believe that you can, and you will achieve God's best for your life. Congratulations on overcoming your bad habits and breaking the cycle of chronic addictions.

Works Cited

Alcoholics Anonymous World Services, Inc. *Living Sober.* New York, NY. A.A. General Services. 2004. P. 52.

Barna George and Mark Hatch. *BOILING POINT: MONITORING CULTURAL SHIFTS IN THE 21ST CENTURY.* Ventura, CA. Regal A Division from Gospel Light. 2001. P. 173.

Black, Barry C. *FROM THE HOOD TO THE HILL. A Story of Overcoming.* Nashville, TN. Thomas Nelson, Inc. 2006. P. 22.

Brinkley, Douglass. *Rosa Parks: A Life.* New York, NY. Penguin Group (USA) Inc. 2000. P.2.

Bronner, Dale. *GUARD YOUR GATES.* East Point, GA. Carnegie Books. 2002. P. 17-18.

_____. *PASS THE BATON. The Miracle of Mentoring.* Austell, GA. Carnegie Books. 2006. P. 31.

_____. *TREASURE YOUR SILENT YEARS.* East Point, GA. Carnegie Books. 2004. P. 45.

Buttrick, A. George. *The Interpreters Dictionary of the Bible: An Illustrated Encyclopedia.* Nashville, TN. Abingdon Press. 1962, 2000. P. 547-548.

Cherry, Reginald. *The DOCTOR and the WORD: Discover God's Pathway to Healing for You and Your Family.* Orlando, FL. Creation House. 1997. P.51

Clinton, Hillary. *LIVING HISTORY. Hillary Rodham Clinton.* New York, NY. Simon and Schuster. P.478

Clinton, William. J. *My Life Bill Clinton.* New York, NY. Vintage Books, a division of Random House, Inc. 2004, 2005. P. 845.

Colbert, Don. *DEADLY EMOTIONS: UNDERSTANDING THE MIND – BODY – SPIRIT CONNECTION THAT CAN HEAL OR DESTROY YOU.* Nashville, TN. Thomas Nelson, Inc. 2003. P. 169.

_____. *STRESS LESS.* Lake Mary, FL. Siloam, A Strange Company. 2005. P. 119-120.

_____. *WHAT YOU DON'T KNOW MAY BE KILLING YOU!* Lake Mary, FL. Siloam, A Strange Company. 2004. P. 82-84, 87, 89, 91-92.

Copeland, Kenneth. *How to Discipline Your Flesh.* Forth Worth, TX. Kenneth Copeland Publications. 1894. P. 51, 52, 53.

_____. *KNOW YOUR ENEMY.* Forth Worth, TX. Kenneth Copeland Publications. 2002. P. 81.

_____. *PRAYER YOUR FOUNDATION FOR SUCCESS.* Forth Worth, TX. Kenneth Copeland Publications. 1983. P.82

_____. *The Winning Attitude.* Tulsa, OK. Harrison House, Inc. 1981. P. 4-5

Copeland, Gloria. *God's Will for Your Healing.* Fort Worth, TX. Kenneth Copeland Publications. 1972. P. 61-62.

_____. *SHINE ON: OVERCOMING PERSECUTION.* Forth Worth, TX. Kenneth Copeland Publications. 1998. P. 7-8.

Dickow, Gregory. *HOW TO NEVER BE HURT AGAIN.* Chicago, IL. Gregory Dickow Ministries. 2003. P14.

_____. *Taking Charge of your Emotions!* Chicago, IL. Gregory Dickow Ministries. 2003, P.13.

_____. *The Power to CHANGE ANYTHING: The Ten Commandments of change.* Chicago, IL. Gregory Dickow Ministries. 2003, P. 25-27.

Dollar, Creflo. A. *BREAKING OUT OF TROUBLE: God's Failsafe System for Overcoming Adversity.* College Parks, Ga. United States of America. 2004. P162.

_____. *Confidence: The Missing Substance of Faith,* College Park, Ga, World Changers Ministries. 1993. P. 2.

_____. *CLAIM YOUR VICTORY TODAY: 10 Steps That Will Revolutionize Your Life.* New York, NY. Warner Faith. 1993, 2006. P. 19.

_____. *HOW TO TROUBLE YOUR TROUBLE.* College Park, Ga. Creflo Dollar Ministries. 1998. P. 195.

_____. *LIVE WITHOUT FEAR: Learn to Walk in God's Power and Peace.* New York, NY. Time Warner Book Group. 2006. P. 61

_____. *Not Guilty: Experience God's Gifts of Acceptance and freedom.* Tulsa, OK. Harrison House, Inc. 2002. P. 128.

_____. *Overcoming Bad Habits: When "No" Isn't Enough.* College Park, Ga. Creflo Dollar Ministries. 2006. DVD part 1.

_____. *SOS! Help My flesh Needs Discipline.* College Parks, Ga. United States of America. 1998. P.55.

_____. *The Anointing to Live: Accessing the Power, Avoiding the pitfalls.* College Park, Ga. Creflo Dollar Ministries. 1999. P. 5.

_____. *THE COLOR OF LOVE: Understanding God's Answer to Racism, Separation and Division.* Tulsa, Oklahoma. Harrison House, Inc. 1997. P. 8.

_____. *The Hand of God,* (part 2) Teaching on DVD, 10/16/05 at 11:00 am. College Park, Ga, United States of America. 2005.

_____. *Walking in the CONFIDENCE of GOD in Troubled Times.* New York, NY. Time Warner Book Group. 2006. P. 100.

Dollar, Taffi. L. *The Portrait of a Virtuous Woman: Finding Your Freedom in God's Perfect Plan for You.* Nashville, Tennessee. Thomas Nelson, Inc. 2000. P. 80-81.

Four Square Church fellowship Website. www.foursquare.org/landing_pages/8,3.html

Friedman, H. Edwin. *GENERATION TO GENERATION: FAMILY PROCESS IN CHURCH AND SYNAGOGUE.* New York, NY. The Guilford Press. 1985. P. 71.

Green Bay Packers Official Website. www.packers.com/team/players/gado_samkon.

Hagin, Kenneth. E. *Casting Your Cares Upon The Lord.* Tulsa, OK. Kenneth Hagin Ministries. 2001. P. 49-50.

_____. *How You Can Be Led by The Spirit of God.* Tulsa, OK. Kenneth Hagin Ministries. 1986. P. 39.

Hilliard, Bridget. E. *HOW TO DREAM BEYOND YOUR MEANS.* Houston, TX. Light Publications. 2003. P. 25.

_____. *THE WILL TO WIN: Principles for Disciplined Living.* Houston, TX. Light Publications. 2003. P. 9.

Hilliard, I.V. *CONTENTMENT: Your Passport to Fulfillment.* Houston, TX. The Light Christian Center Church. 1999. P. 17.

_____. *LIVING THE MAXIMIZED LIFE: How to win No Matter where you're starting from.* Nashville, TN. W Publishing group, a Division of Thomas Nelson, Inc. 2006. P. 146.

_____. *MENTAL TOUGHNESS FOR SUCCESS: Proven Biblical Principles for Successful Living*, Huston, TX. Light Publications. 2004. P. 25.

_____. *Ten Mistakes Most failures make. How To avoid the Pitfall to success*. Tulsa, OK, Vincom Publishing Co. 2002. P 32.

Jakes, T. D. *HELP ME: I've Fallen and I can't get up*, Dallas, TX. Pneuma Life Publishing. 1995. P. 48.

_____. *Loose That Man & Let Him Go!* Bloomington, MN. Bethany House Publishers. 1995. P. 22.

_____. *SAINTS WITH SINNER'S PROBLEMS*. Dallas, TX. International Communications Center. 2000. P. 20-21.

_____. *SO YOU CALL YOURSELF A MAN?* Bloomington, MN. Bethany House Publishers. 1997. P. 62, 96.

_____. *WOMAN THOU ART LOOSED: Healing the Wounds of the Past*. Shippensburg, PA. Destiny Image Publishers, Inc. 2001. P. 48, 49.

Kelsey, T. Morton. *Healing and Christianity: A Classic Study*. Minneapolis, MN. Augsburg Fortress. 1973, 1988, 1995. P. 191-192.

King, Martin Luther. Jr. *THE WORDS OF MARTIN LUTHER KING, JR*. New York, NY. Newmarket Press. 1987. P23.

Krauss, Barry and Moore, Joe. M. *AIN'T NOTHIN' BUT A WINNER: Bear Bryant, The Goal Line Stand, and A chance of a Lifetime*. Tuscaloosa, Al. The University of Alabama Press. 2006. P. 22.

Lacado, Max. *Facing Your Giants*. Nashville, TN. W Publishing Group, a Division of Thomas Nelson, Inc. 2006. P.107-108.

Liardon, Roberts. *KATHRYN KUUHLMAN: A Spiritual Biography of God's Miracle Worker*. New Kensington, PA. Whitaker House. 1990, 2005. P. 14.

Mandela, Nelson. *LONG WALK TO FREEDOM*. New York, NY. Back Bay Books/Little, Brown and Company, Time Warner Book Group. 1994, 1995. P. 149, 240-241.

Mathew, Thomson K. *Sprint-Led Ministry in the 21ˢᵗ Century*. Tulsa, OK. School of Theology and Mission. 2004. P. 92

McCutcheon, Marc. *ROGET'S SUPER THESAURUS*. Cincinnati, Ohio. Writer's Digest Books. 2003. P 433.

McGee, J. Vernon. *THRU THE BIBLE*. Nashville, TN. Thomas Nelson, Inc. 1982. P.328.

Meyer, Joyce. *APPROVAL ADDICTION: Overcoming the need to please everyone,* New York, NY. Time Warner Book Group Inc. 2005. P. 116, 117.

_____. *Battlefield of the Mind: Winning the Battle in your Mind,* Fenton, MO. Time Warner Book Group. 2002. P. 186.

_____. *EIGHT WAYS TO KEEP THE DEVIL UNDER YOUR FEET,* Fenton, MO. Life in The Word, Inc. 2003, P. 10.

_____. *MANAGING YOUR EMOTIONS: Instead of Your emotions Managing You.* New York, NY. Time Warner Books, Inc. 1997. (P.55-56)

_____. *Me and My Big Mouth! Your Answer Is right Under Your noise,* Fenton, MO. Life in The Word Inc. 2002, P. 173.

_____. *Reduce Me To Love.* New York, NY. Time Warner Books, Inc. 2000. P122.

_____. *STRAIGHT TALK ON DISCOURAGEMENT: Overcoming Emotional Battles with the Power of God's Word!* New York, NY. Warner Books, Inc. 1998, P. 66.

Mooney, AL, Eisenberg, Arlene, Howard Eisenberg. *The Recovery Book:* New York, NY. Workman Publishing Company, Inc. 1992. P 543.

Murdock, Mike. *The Making Of A Champion: 31 Power Keys To Understanding Your Personal Greatness.* Denton, TX. The Wisdom Center. 2002. P.16.

_____. *WISDOM FOR CRISIS TIMES.* Denton, TX. The Wisdom Center. 1992. P. 19.

_____. *101 Wisdom Keys,* Ft Worth, TX. The Wisdom Center. 1994, P.2, 6.

Parks, Rosa L. and Reed, Gregory. L. *Quiet Strength: The Faith, the Hope, and the Heart of a Women who Changed a Nation.* Grand Rapids, MI. Zondervan Publishing House. 1994. P. 46-47.

Powe, Greg. *SUCCESS HABITS: Eleven Steps to Becoming an Uncommon Achiever!* Tampa, FL. Revealing Truth Ministries. 2002. P.134, 137.

_____. *Soaring Above Average: Developing The Power of True Leadership.* Tampa, FL. Revealing Truth Ministries. 2004. P. 161.

Price, Fredrick K.C. *Faith, Foolishness, or Presumption?* Los Angels, CA. Faith One Publishing. 1997. P. 97, 99.

_____. *INTEGRITY: The Guarantee for Success.* Los Angles, CA. Faith One Publishing. 2000. P. 102

_____. *Race, religion, and Racism, Volume One: A Bold Encounter With Division in the Church*. Los Angeles, Ca. Faith One Publishing. 1999. P. 164.

_____. *Three Keys to Positive Confession*, Los Angeles, CA. Faith One Publishing. 1994, P. 17, 39, 46.

Roberts, Oral. *EXPECT A MIRACLE: My Life and Ministry*. Nashville, TN. Thomas Nelson, Inc. 1995. P. 166.

_____. *If You Need HEALING Do These Things*. Tulsa, OK. Oral Roberts Ministries. 2002. P. 45.

_____. *JESUS SAT WHERE YOU SIT*. Tulsa, OK. Oral Roberts Ministries. 1972. P. 11.

Robertson, Archibald T. *Word Pictures in the New Testament*. Grand Rapids, MI. Baker Book House. 1930. P. 220.

Savelle, Jerry. *FREE AT LAST from Old Habits*: Crowley, TX. Jerry Savelle Publications, 2003. P. 27.

_____.*THOUGHT-The Battle Between Your Ears*. Crowley, TX. Jerry Savelle Ministries International. 2002. P. 100, 101.

Shorter, Don. *Casting Down Imaginations*. Tulsa, Ok. Harrison House, Inc. 1991. P. 33.

The Atlanta Journal – Constitution. *Oxycontin: Executives plead guilty to lying about drug*. Atlanta, Georgia. 2007. (P. A1, A6)

Thompson, Leroy. *I'LL NEVER BE BROKE ANOTHER DAY IN MY LIFE: Real Answers to Financial Hardship*. Darrow, Louisiana. Ever Increasing Word Ministries. 2001. P. 168.

_____.*What To Do When Your Faith Is Challenged*. Darrow, Louisiana. Ever Increasing Word Ministries. 1998. P. 103.

Trudeau, Kevin. *More Natural "Cures" Revealed*. Elk Grove Village, IL. Alliance Publishing Group, Inc. 2006. P. 79.

Turk, Ruth. *Ray Charles: Soul Man*. Minneapolis, MO. Lerner Publication Company. 1996. P. 87-88.

Universals Studios. *RAY*. Universal City, CA. Universals Studios, 2005. Disc 1.

Vine, W.E. *THE EXPANDED VINE'S: EXPOSITORY DICTIONARY of NEW TESTAMENT WORDS*. Minneapolis, MN. Bethany House Publishers. 1984. P. 359.

Wikipedia, The Free Encyclopedia. http://en.wikipedia.org/wiki/Samkon_Gado

Wilkinson, Bruce. *THE 7 LAWS OF THE LEARNER*. Sister, Oregon. Multnomah Publishers, Inc. 1992. P. 342.

White, Thomas. B. *The Believer's Guide to Spiritual Warfare*. Ann Arbor, MI. Servant Publications. 1990. P.90.

Woog, Adam. *Ray Charles and the Birth of Soul*. Farmington, MI. Lucent Books, an imprint of Thomson Gale, a part of the Thomson Corporation. 2006. P. 68.

Ziglar, Zig. *OVER THE TOP*. Nashville, TN. Thomas Nelson, Inc. 1994. P. 217.

About the Author

Loy B. Sweezy, Jr was born and raised in Shelby, North Carolina. As a child, he attended church on a consistent basis and while there, gained a personal intimacy with God. At age 21, he received the Baptism of the Holy Spirit.

He is a graduate of East Coast Bible College in Charlotte, North Carolina, with a Bachelor of Science Degree. While at East Coast Bible College, he did missionary work in India, Germany and Jamaica. He is a graduate of the School of Theology in Cleveland, Tennessee, with a Master's Degree.

After receiving his Master's Degree, he moved back to Charlotte, North Carolina, where he worked as a Chaplain in pastoral care and counseling for Carolina Medical Center. Later he moved to Birmingham, Alabama, to work at Princeton and Montclair Hospital in pastoral care and counseling. There he met a lovely lady named Nyouka, D who later became his wife. He is currently working on a doctoral degree at Oral Roberts University in Tulsa, Oklahoma.

God has called Loy B. Sweezy, to teach the Word of Faith and to encourage and inspire people who are sick, afflicted, hurting, and seem to be in a hopeless situation. He has been called to change their thinking and circumstances by the knowledge and practice of the Word of God enabling them through the working of the Holy Spirit to be all they can be in God and experience a life full of victorious living. *"For with God nothing is ever impossible and no word from God shall be without power or impossible of fulfillment." (Luke 1:37, AMP)*

Contact Information

To contact the author write:

Loy Sweezy Ministries
P.O. Box 131
Austell, Georgia 30168

You can order this book and other material
by calling toll-free 1-866-873-6330

Internet Address: www.loysweezy.com

Please provide your personal testimony or how this book
has helped you when you write. Your prayer requests are
welcome.

BOOKS BY LOY B. SWEEZY, JR

Breaking Free

Notes

Notes

Notes

www.ingramcontent.com/pod-product-compliance
Lightning Source LLC
Chambersburg PA
CBHW051726260326
41914CB00031B/1760/J